The Odyssey of a
U-Boat Commander

The Odyssey of a
U-Boat Commander

Recollections of Erich Topp

ERICH TOPP

Translated by Eric C. Rust

PRAEGER

Westport, Connecticut
London

Library of Congress Cataloging-in-Publication Data

Topp, Erich.
   [Fackeln über dem Atlantik. English]
   The odyssey of a U-boat commander : recollections of Erich Topp /
Erich Topp ; translated by Eric C. Rust.
     p. cm.
   Translation of: Fackeln über dem Atlantik.
   Includes index.
   ISBN 0-275-93898-0 (alk. paper)
   1. Topp, Erich. 2. World War, 1939-1945—Naval operations—
Submarine. 3. World War, 1939-1945—Naval operations, German.
4. World War, 1939-1945—Personal narratives, German. 5. Germany.
Kriegsmarine—Biography. 6. Seamen—Germany—Biography. I. Title.
D781.T6713 1992
940.54'51—dc20   91-47593

British Library Cataloguing in Publication Data is available.

Library of Congress Catalog Card Number: 91-47593
ISBN: 0-275-93898-0

First published in English in 1992

Praeger Publishers, 88 Post Road West, Westport, CT 06881
An imprint of Greenwood Publishing Group, Inc.

Printed in the United States of America

The paper used in this book complies with the Permanent
Paper Standard issued by the National Information Standards
Organization (Z39.48-1984).

10 9 8 7 6 5 4 3 2

Originally published in German under the title
Fackeln über dem Atlantik by Verlag E. S. Mittler
& Sohn GmbH. Copyright © 1990.

To my grandchildren

Philip, Dirck, Erik, Matthias, Christoph,
Johannes, Clemens,
Charlotte, Benjamin, Gabriel, David

Contents

Preface

I did not write this book of memories to escape from them, for what would my life be without them?

I let my diaries speak for me, without modification, unedited. By doing so I may run the danger of leaving the sphere of the real. After all, these journals, written decades ago, seem to come from a different world. But they are genuine. They bring back youthful dreams, the years of deadly games, the times of terror and grief. I will try to interpret my diaries based on everything I know today, well aware that such judgments can never be entirely sure-footed and that no memory is perfect.

This book is meant as a commentary on the ambivalence of the human condition. It seeks an answer to the question why we followed the siren songs of a totalitarian regime whose deeds even today hover over us like dark shadows. My journal stands for all the faith and hopes, the errors and transformations of a human life.

Hegel saw human history as a unitary process, forever moving toward higher levels of freedom according to God's plan, a design he called the *Weltgeist*. Marx and Engels appropriated from Hegel this belief in the procedural unity of history; however, they viewed the process as being purely of this world and materialistic. Thus, for both Hegel and Marx, past human actions were of mere preliminary character and were interpreted accordingly from a preplanned and desired future condition. In other words, our understanding of the world depended on the light cast upon the past by the present and the future, not on the illumination of the present and the future by the light of experiences past. Tocqueville, in contrast, wrote in the 1830s, "Since the past has ceased casting its light upon the future, the human spirit wanders in darkness."

Who is right?

We have experienced in our century at least two attempts to provide history with a narrow teleological meaning and to transform it into an instrument for political purposes. Under Lenin's Bolshevism all history became a struggle between classes. From this notion Stalin later deduced the right to spread world revolution, even if it meant mass destruction for those who dissented. Hitler justified his genocide by reducing history to a struggle between races. Both believed they fulfilled the purpose of history after having carefully defined for their own ends what such purpose should be. Consequently, history and the past lost their function as teachers and enlighteners and instead became mere servants in efforts to create a perfect world.

I do believe history is a *magistra vitae,* and therefore we must ask again and again what lessons the past offers to guide us. I am also convinced that human history is open-ended and not predestined. It is from this personal insight that I draw the authority to present this book.

Erich Topp
Remagen, September 1990

1

The Sinking of the
Reuben James

I would like to begin my otherwise chronological narrative with a war-time experience that placed me in a political borderline situation and that has determined how I look back on my life from a moral perspective. An excerpt from the war diary of the U-Boat High Command:

> In the morning hours of October 31, 1941, *U 552* sighted the British convoy HX 156 in the central Atlantic. Its screen consisted of five destroyers. At 0834 the commanding officer, Lieutenant Commander Topp, sank one of the escorts, U.S.S. *Reuben James*, in position lat. 51° 59′ N, long. 27° 05′ W. The U.S. destroyer belonged to the escort of the British convoy even before the United States entered the war on December 11, 1941.

THE POLITICAL DIMENSION

Adolf Hitler had hinted at his expansionist intentions as early as in *Mein Kampf*. Later, according to the so-called Hossbach Protocol in 1937, he provided details about his designs. This does not mean that Hitler acted according to a carefully prepared plan. His determination to expand Germany's borders, however, made war inevitable. The war was prepared and carried out in such a way that it took a coalition of world powers six years to bring Germany down militarily.

After the *Blitzkriege* against Poland and the West, Hitler's territorial acquisitions remained unrecognized under international law. For this reason Hitler felt driven to keep up the momentum of conquest, to add expansion to expansion, just as others had done before him: Alexander the Great, Julius Caesar, Napoleon. In addition, there was racial hubris and the notion of a "people without space." I compare Hitler to Alexander, Caesar, Napoleon, and other empire-builders only in terms of their determination to conquer territory, certainly not with regard to their overall personality or historical stature.

Historians disagree whether a politically consolidated continental Europe, based on a generous peace with France and a confederation of states, would have been feasible. Sebastian Haffner, for one, seems to think so. Others, like Joachim Fest, point out that England, backed by the United States, would not have accepted such a concept of Europe. In reality Hitler did not achieve any such political solution. Prodded on by the Allied demand for unconditional surrender, he felt condemned to extend—indeed, to overextend—his expansionist drive. This was a strategic mistake, considering the fatal gulf between Germany's means and objectives. Hitler's dilemma was rendered worse by countless political miscalculations and senseless crimes, not to mention his pathological determination to carry them out regardless of consequences. In the Napoleonic era world power status hinged on hegemony over the continent, including Russia, and on the defeat of England. By the twentieth century it also meant the destruction of American power.

For a while Hitler was careful enough not to provoke the United States. To the contrary, he deliberately put up with provocations from the other side, as these examples bear out:

September 1940: Delivery of fifty destroyers to England.

March 1941: Lend-Lease Act, enabling England to buy U.S. weapons without paying cash.

April 1941: Extension of the already unusual, 300-mile-wide "Pan-American Security Zone" into the central Atlantic (to 30° West longitude). Inside this zone U.S. forces shadowed and reported German ships until they could be seized by the British. This behavior was difficult to reconcile with a policy of neutrality.

Since April 1941: U.S. forces escort British convoys in the western hemisphere.

April 10, 1941: The U.S. destroyer *Niblack* attacks a German U-boat.

July 7, 1941: U.S. forces occupy Iceland as a military base.

September 4, 1941: A British aircraft sights a German U-boat, drops depth charges, and reports its position to the U.S. destroyer *Greer*. The latter pursues the U-boat. The submarine in turn fires two torpedoes against the *Greer* under the assumption that she is a British warship. The *Greer* responds with eleven depth charges. Even though the U.S. President was informed that the German U-boat did not know the destroyer's nationality, Navy Secretary Frank Knox issued orders to use all available means to seize and destroy German surface and underwater "pirates."

Compared to President Roosevelt's "short of war" policy, the German Naval High Command exercised extreme restraint in its actions toward the United States.

Then, in the dawn hours of October 31, 1941, I attacked and sank an escort vessel out of a British convoy. A short while later we learned by monitoring radio broadcasts that the destroyer belonged to a country with which we were not at war: the *Reuben James* of the United States.

I immediately remembered Germany's resumption of unrestricted submarine warfare as the occasion for the U.S. entry into World War I and was thus aware how politically explosive the sinking of the destroyer might become. Until we reached our base I was alone with my thoughts. As far as international law was concerned, I felt no qualms whatsoever. After all, I had attacked a British convoy screened by warships. Nevertheless, I felt bewildered. The tension a man endures when he thinks he is making history, however unintentional, is indeed enormous.

Only much later did I learn that the political course had already been laid out, that history would merely shrug its shoulder over an incident such as the sinking of the *Reuben James*. Of course, I was ordered to Paris where I had to describe in every detail the attack and the sinking to Admiral Karl Dönitz of the U-Boat High Command. I also began to realize that Germany's declaration of war against the United States after Japan's actions of December 7, 1941, was not merely the result of irrational expectations one encounters in the course of all great territorial expansions, but that political forces were likewise at work. To this one must add the underestimation of U.S. resources in terms of manpower and economic potential. I can still hear today the snide comments Hitler made in his table talks at the Führer Headquarters. He made fun, for example, of Roosevelt's physical paralysis and of "Liberty" and "Victory" ships being allegedly so poorly designed that they could not withstand Atlantic storms.

From time to time, moral arguments have entered the debate over the origins of Hitler's hubris. His racial mania and its consequences, his genocide of the Jews, and the enslavement of the Slavic peoples are said to have pushed the world into a total war against Germany. However terrible and incomprehensible this genocide based on racism will remain, one must understand that it was not the moral reason behind the U.S. entry into the war on the Allied side. Today we know that neither the Americans nor the British helped the Jews when it would have been possible; indeed, they refused to do so in specific cases. In the end it was Germany's (and also Japan's) territorial aspirations, and the Allied refusal to give in to such expansionist drives, that made the war both total and global.

The political dimension of the sinking of the *Reuben James* is not without ambivalence. The U.S. media used the incident deliberately to incite the public mood in favor of entering the war against Germany. They did so, not by analyzing the legitimacy of the attack under international law following a political and military provocation on part of the United States, but by emphasizing the national challenge posed by those "Hitler pirates." Even Woody Guthrie, as early as November 1941, wrote a song about the sinking of the *Reuben James* that was sung everywhere: "Did you have a friend on the good *Reuben James?*" According to the second and third verses, the destroyer "watched for the U-boats, and waited for the fight," and "now our mighty battleships will steam the mighty main." I will not equate poetic license with political will, but it seems easy to prove that already in this critical phase of the war the media and the politicians worked closely together on all sides.

On November 14, just two weeks after the *Reuben James* had gone down as the first U.S. warship lost in World War II, Roosevelt asked Congress to pass legislation that would allow the arming of U.S. merchant vessels. Reflecting the country's mood, Congress agreed to the request by a vote of 212 to 194. With this measure the Neutrality Acts became history and the U.S. entry into the war occurred *de facto*.

When Hitler declared war on the United States on December 11, 1941, four days after the Japanese raid against Pearl Harbor, he did so not as a result of American public opinion but under political pressure. I believe his need to extend his territorial conquests played a vital role.

What mattered for me was the nagging notion of being caught up in the making of world events, the need to work out what the sinking of the *Reuben James* meant in political terms. I had the feeling of being somehow involved in weighty political decisions, which, given the experience of World War I, seemed most ominous to me.

THE HUMAN DIMENSION

The hit, as observed from the boat's conning tower in the dawn's gathering light, appeared to us as follows: "An explosion some 1,000 yards away. The rear part of the ship sank first, its unsecured depth charges detonating in a huge secondary explosion and throwing tall columns of water skyward. A nearby destroyer picked up survivors. We left the scene."

Many years later I read details about the end of the *Reuben James* and her men in Patrick Abbazia's book, *Mr. Roosevelt's Navy:*

> The explosion broke the spine of the *Reuben James,* and she cleaved in two.
> . . . Quartermaster Bill Appleton was blown from the helm through the
> top of the wheelhouse . . . into the sea. Everyone else in the forward sec-

tion of the ship . . . was killed almost immediately by the blast, fire, and onrushing sea. . . .

The men aft had more chance. Seaman Dan del Grosso was asleep in his bunk when the force of the explosion flung him to the deck; bent lockers were on their sides, and bunks and mattresses were crisscrossed in a tangled shambles in the narrow passageway. . . . Topside, flames burned across metal surfaces, feeding on paint; ruptured fuel tanks spewed thick, black oil into the water. The stern was settling. Del Grosso did not have to dive overboard; he merely stepped off the deck into the sea. . . . Last to go were the wounded and burned, who knew that they had little hope in the water; finally, as the heat grew too intense, they gamely helped each other off the black and slippery deck into the sea. . . .

The sailors were black with oil and shivering from the cold; some were choking and gagging, vomiting oil and salt water. . . . Some . . . suffocated in the oil, or died of their wounds and burns, and a few drowned. The bodies of the dead bobbed inertly on the black swells.

It was quiet on the water. . . . Then from inside the destroyer came the screams of badly wounded or dazed men who had not been noticed amid the tangle of wreckage below and were now drowning as the stern sank. Soon it was quiet again.

As the stern went under . . . several of the destroyer's ready depth charges exploded, and the sea erupted in a huge, shuddering blast. . . . [It] flipped rafts into the air and ripped and crushed the bodies of swimmers; jagged slivers of steel and debris whirred through the chill air, splashing in the water. . . . About one hundred men died on and in the water around the old *Reuben James* on that bitter Halloween morning.

This formative impression stood at the very beginning of my wartime experiences, and it changed my life. Since then I have often had occasion to contemplate a famous quotation from Jacob Burckhardt's *Reflections on History:* "You cannot draw lessons from history for the next time around, but you can become wise for all times!" I have never attained this high level of insight. To the contrary, I have learned that the passing of decades does not cushion anything. As years go by they may eat up the words of the past, but they cannot stop the onslaught of the images. These images continue to haunt me; they take away my sleep.

Long after the war, when I was visiting San Diego in 1962, the commanding officer of an LSD (Landing Ship, Dock) invited me for lunch. He sent a boat and received me with the usual ritual at the gangplank. It turned out he had been a watch officer aboard the destroyer *Niblack*, the vessel entrusted with the task of picking up the survivors of the *Reuben James.* His best friend had been a watch officer on the *Reuben James.* In vain he had looked for him among the men in the water. I will never forget my conversation with him as he told me about the search for survivors and for his friend in the twilight of the breaking day, about the slowly heaving swell covered with a thick layer of oil from which debris and human beings were tossed up and pulled down as if in a scene from Dante's inferno.

In the course of our talk I received the impression that we all had lost a very special person in that officer on the *Reuben James*. He must have been an individual endowed with great talents, a creative man who never sat in the shade and who, like a flower, always and instinctively turned toward the light. He was a gift for his friends, his comrades. He radiated cheerfulness. Whatever he did, however he treated his men, whether he spoke, wrote, or clowned around: he appeared complete, perfect. That is how the commanding officer of the LSD portrayed him.

What would have become of his best friend had he lived? Perhaps he would have been a successful destroyer captain, a charismatic leader of his men; perhaps a squadron commander later on. Or he may have reawakened the chorus of the Eumenides, filled out old pictures with new meaning and new colors, or used his words to create a new world atop foundations a thousand years old. Perhaps he would have opened new dimensions in the ways we express ourselves so that our creative genius may better spread its wings and take the human soul on a lofty ride, if only for a while. Who will ever know? These were the thoughts that went through my mind.

I thought of my wife's brother who had always wanted to become a stage director. He had studied acting, was a superb painter, and played the piano as few others could. Totally opposed to National Socialism, he studied theology instead and joined the Confessing Church, only to be relieved of his duties after his inaugural sermon and sent to the front. There he stayed for the balance of the war until he was felled by a partisan's bullet on January 9, 1945, on the eastern front in Courland.

He was full of temperament and good cheer, just like that officer on the *Reuben James*. Everyone would wait for him; only after he had arrived could the party begin. On the piano, using only a handful of notes, he created the most fantastic improvisations. For him everything became music. Once, coming back from an evening at the opera where he had just seen and heard Weill's *The Threepenny Opera* for the first time, with its picaresque-romantic plot and its entirely novel, revolutionary music, he sat down at the piano and played whole passages from the opera as he had memorized them, as though he had the sheet music in front of him. During the day he studied philosophy, theology, and art history. In the evenings his genius came alive: Beethoven, Schubert, and whole cascades of compositions of his own.

There are not many individuals whose creative powers are strong enough to lend mankind on its miserable journey an occasional moment of bliss. The watch officer on the *Reuben James* appears to have been such a man. And so does my brother-in-law. As shepherd of his flock he would have commanded far greater reservoirs of healing strength than many pastors in today's church with all their political involvement.

The name of the officer of the *Reuben James,* along with those of the other dead, can be found printed below the lyrics of Woody Guthrie's song, a song meant to shake up the American nation and to prepare it for war. My brother-in-law's name is gone with the wind.

Approximately 26,000 names are engraved on bronze tablets at the U-Boat Memorial in Möltenort on Kiel Bay. These men thought they knew what they were dying for—their fatherland. Much later, Americans sought to ensure that some 58,000 of their war dead would never be forgotten. Their names are engraved on America's "wailing wall," the Vietnam War Memorial in Washington. They, too, thought they knew what they were dying for—the freedom of others.

Man's fascination with might and power has always been a guiding theme in works of art. Indeed, it has illuminated the history of western civilization on many occasions: just think of the heroes of the *Iliad;* Marathon and Salamis; the battles of Alexander; the sagas of the Nibelungen and of Roland; El Cid, the Campeador; the legend of Joan of Arc; Shakespeare's dramas; Albrecht von Wallenstein; Heinrich von Kleist's *The Prince of Homburg;* Heinrich Heine's *The Three Grenadiers;* or Rainer Rilke's *The Cornet.* The Naval Memorial at Laboe at the entrance to Kiel Bay, too, is a work of art, as is the wedge-shaped, 244-foot long wall of polished black granite bearing the names of American soldiers killed in Vietnam.

Behind all these monuments, legends, dramas, tragedies, and poems stand men who dedicated themselves to a single idea: the pursuit and exercise of power. This holds true even if their actions did not conform to existing laws or moral codes, or if they displayed vanity and selfishness in the process. And power often knew no bounds. At other times it was barely reined in by religious restraints or humility. Only the unimaginably destructive potential of nuclear weapons has brought a transformation in the application of force because the logic of survival requires clear standards and moderation.

We have been forced to abandon the ever so resplendent myth of force and power and with it the glorification of heroes. As Balzac once wrote, "Glory does not soar on white wings." Inquiries into the complexity of human nature did not begin with modern psychology. No, we already encounter them in the works of Euripides, as we do more recently in the plays of George Bernard Shaw. Today it has become fashionable to glorify the underdog and, far worse, to celebrate what is mediocre in our world.

This we may regret. The tragic ties that link those who act to those who suffer, the connections between glory and guilt, have grown more complicated. But they will not disappear.

Glory finds a proper place only beyond victory and defeat. Moderation, self-limitation, and self-discipline today define the bounds within which man proves himself and creates examples for others. This is not new. None other than Aristotle coined the phrase, "To act reasonably means to avoid extremes." Measured moderation is all the more vital in our days as the criteria for the application of force have changed and those in power have little choice but to seek arrangements and compromises where confrontations and war were once the rule.

My generation tottered blindly into the madness and drama of the war and became entangled in the crimes of the regime without personal guilt. For we never were given a chance or choice to influence decisions. We were like extras in a drama. Many were not even that, because they failed to recognize the development of the plot. They somehow did their "duty"—an oscillating word, for it covers the entire spectrum between honorable and unscrupulous deeds, between what men did deliberately and what they failed to do.

We learned that one cannot allow oneself to be carried along by the tidal wave of mass hysteria, be it to drown oneself in it or to try to reach the Island of the Blessed. One must steer one's own course, must remain one's own navigator. Above all, one must stay inside the markers of the channel that 3,000 years of history have laid out for us and that is brightened by the shining beacons of our western civilization.

On the conning towers of my three boats—*U 57, U 552,* and *U 2513*—we painted as our distinguishing emblem two dancing red devils, one holding up the torch of life, the other the torch of death and destruction. One torch, the one representing the forces of destruction, has now been lowered, with all its implications for remembering and forgetting, fate and actions, certitude and opacity. The torch of life, however, still burns. Once it was a glimmer of hope; today it has become a signpost and a beacon—beginning and end.

2

Before the War

CHILDHOOD AND ADOLESCENCE

My earliest recollections reach me as if through a veil. The images have become pale, detached from real time. Some occurrences from my youth have entered my life's kaleidoscope, indivisibly woven into an ornament. Without this benefit of a rearview mirror many events in my adult life would be difficult to untangle.

My ancestors were carpenters and peasant farmers in Lower Saxony. It may well be that the memory of those carpenters, especially as journeymen, left in me an interest for the construction industry, would later determine my choice to study architecture and encourage me to see the world. My peasant forebears, by contrast, had their feet rooted firmly in the soil.

The Topps have always worked hard, trying doggedly and steadily to improve their situation. By the time of my father's generation they had made good headway; his brothers became architects and merchants, he himself became an engineer.

We lived in the countryside until I was eight. At that point my father was transferred to the city of Hanover where he became the director of a maintenance plant for the Imperial Railways. For our family this meant moving into rented quarters with less space than we had enjoyed before.

As a member of the *völkisch* youth movement (*Bündische Jugend*), I realized for the first time that there was a way out of the labyrinth of given social conditions, family obligations, and similar limitations. We searched for, and tried to define, the true values of our world, away from conventional institutions and organizations. Nature in particular appeared genuine and unadulterated; in the company of like-minded companions drawn from all social classes I undertook short and even extended hiking tours through the countryside. We searched history for meaningful guideposts and found them in literature and in music. Madrigals and Passions by composers like Schütz and Bach underwent a renaissance. The youth movement took on both romantic and elitist characteristics. We removed ourselves from the bourgeois world around us as much as we could. The impulses I received from the movement were of lasting influence. I have always tried to live my life according to the values inherent in our western culture while rejecting what mere civilization might offer as a substitute.

By the time I was fifteen and we had moved to Celle, I found these ideals embodied in the musicians' guild. We sang the Mass in B minor as well as the Passions of St. John and St. Matthew by Bach. We also enjoyed good times together in the guild's rural retreat. I spent more time with this circle of friends than at home with my parents. For here I discovered not merely a forum for music but a fascinating center for broader artistic interests and activities. I began to believe that art, and culture in a broader sense, was the best preparation for meeting the imponderables of the future. Only much later did I realize that imagination and reality are creative in wholly separate ways, leaving behind quite different traces. At first I noticed hardly more than a sense of dissatisfaction that my emotional escapism provided no answer for the pressing problems of the day.

What were the problems that confronted us? Nearly 7 million workers were unemployed. The political parties fought one another without mercy. Every day brought public demonstrations and paramilitary parades in the streets, often involving violence, gunshots, death. The political and economic chaos was complete, a consequence of the Versailles *Schanddiktat*, as we called the treaty in those days. The victors of the war appeared to have honored the dictum of the Roman senator Porcius Cato: "*Ceterum censeo Carthaginem esse delendam.*" The treaty hinged on the theory of Germany's exclusive war guilt, which in turn justified all other measures: the demilitarization of the Rhineland; the limitations imposed on Germany's armed forces; the reparations whose burden defied all economic sense; and the territorial amputations.

Books, newspapers, and our history lessons in school reflected antirepublican sentiments. Responsibility for Germany's decline, we learned, rested on the shoulders of *Erfüllungspolitiker*—those leaders of the Weimar Republic who seemed to do the enemy's work by honoring the terms of the Versailles treaty. As a result the entire republican system came under fire.

The National Socialist German Workers' Party presented itself as the best hope to solve Germany's problems. We defined "workers," as Ferdinand Lasalle had done earlier, as those who somehow dedicated themselves to the benefit and progress of human society, as serving the *bonum commune*. At the same time we understood "socialism" to mean a system of government that allowed for the development of the individual while fostering a climate of equal opportunity and reducing economic hardships. Naturally, we also harbored reservations toward the image of this party with its brown columns, the violence it created in the streets, and its Führer cult. But for us such reservations did not outweigh the promise of the party's national and social program. I, as most people, became part of an irresistible, almost mechanical movement. We joined this movement voluntarily and tried to justify our decision as best we could.

For half a year I served in the Voluntary Labor Service. Then, after having taken up the study of medicine, I decided to pledge one of Germany's old student fraternities. I joined the Navy on April 8, 1934.

During the first year in the *Reichsmarine* we had to keep an "official diary," its daily entries to be written in ink and in a legible script. Criticism concerning "official matters" was taboo. For this reason the journal is like a meal without spices, like sailing without a breeze. Nevertheless, it is a mirror of that year—a year that imposed harsh discipline on me; indeed, more discipline than I was prepared to bear given my natural predisposition and questioning mind. Many measures were sheer chicanery, and we put up with them only because everyone had to suffer from them, some more, some less.

From today's perspective the education and training we received in the *Reichsmarine* was one-sided. Instead of learning and appreciating discipline dictated by the tasks we would have to master, we encountered unconditional obedience and inflexible harshness. The theory seemed to be that anyone who could survive that kind of treatment without giving up had been recast in the Navy's image and thus acquired the leadership qualities it desired. The cadet training program, at least in our Crew 34 (those men who took up officer training in 1934), remained stuck in superficial military drill. It was not designed to make us a part of the currents flowing from the reservoirs and fundamental values of our western culture. I am making these observations not merely from the viewpoint of a *Bundesmarine* officer and with the knowledge of improvements that have since been introduced. Even in those days, among comrades, I recall heated debates about this subject—debates that confirm the critical distance we kept from the Navy's methods of indoctrination.

The diaries are revealing in other respects as well. They show how little we knew about critical and comparative historiography, how deeply we believed in the positive forces at work in the German people, and how profound our ignorance remained with regard to the techniques and effects of mass psychology. After all, who among us had read the works of the Frenchman Gustave le Bon, or those of the Spaniard Ortega y Gasset? Instead, we heard about the racial utopias of men like Alfred Rosenberg and Hans Günther, that the Nordic race had been the global and universal carrier of culture and civilization throughout the millennia. Then there was Nietzsche. We completely misunderstood that he had meant his superman to be a philosophical rather than a political creature. We also did not know what genuine science had to say about genetics and anthropology. We had faith in ourselves and in our role in the rejuvenation of the German people as it was advanced in National Socialist propaganda.

Above all, it was service to the state that concerned us. Whoever did his proper duty toward the state could do no wrong, no matter what he did. There were many things we did not like, but any doubts and hesitations we might have had were wiped away through discipline and asceticism. We were taught to be decent to our fellow men, but fulfilling one's duties toward the state always ranked first. This philosophy appealed to us all the more since the state itself seemed based on social principles; it did something for its citizens. Service to the community came before pursuit of personal gain; the very idea of a people's community appeared to make sense. The state itself seemed to be off to new and exciting shores. Politically and morally we believed Germany stood poised on the threshold of a thousand-year Reich. Who really cared if there were a few minor blemishes in the beginning?

Only much later did we see the limitations and dangers inherent in the substitute state religion to which we all had pledged our loyalty. When we realized its base perversions at last, complete emptiness and resignation took their place. To fill this vacuum again with hope and faith in the *bonum commune* will take generations.

What was the composition and self-image of our Crew 34? We were born in the Second Reich under Emperor William II and later experienced the collapse of the Weimar Republic. Every year the *Reichsmarine* took in a limited number of cadets, about one hundred. Our Crew 34, reflecting Germany's restored military sovereignty, contained 318 cadets. Later classes in the 1930s and during the war were larger still. Crew 34 was selected from a much larger pool of applicants, and for this reason we may be forgiven for considering ourselves an elite. Our average age at induction was about nineteen. Some of us were a little older than the rest because we had studied at universities for a while or had transferred from the merchant marine.

Most of my Crew comrades came from northern Germany. Socially we were drawn from the upper middle class, from educated, respected circles. Very few were nobles, some were sons of admirals; but they received no special treatment as a result of their background. The Navy gave us respectability and responsibilities at an early age, something we cherished greatly. In the broader context of Germany's national renewal the position of an officer as the "nation's warrior" was an elevated, privileged one.

At home and at school we had been raised in the belief that the Treaty of Versailles had inflicted damage on the fatherland. We became convinced that the treaty needed to be revised by diplomatic and political means backed by strong armed forces. Our sense of patriotism reflected Prussian values like order, discipline, and thrift, all seen in the interest of serving the *bonum commune*.

Soldiers submitted to the primacy of politics—in this case, National Socialist leadership—much too long, until some rebelled and joined the resistance instead. Franz Werfel once wrote: "The primacy of politics destroys the spirit by reversing the roles of master and slave."

BASIC INFANTRY TRAINING

Diary:

The most important event of the week came on April 12, 1934, when we received our arms. In a festive ceremony the company commander spoke at length about a dictum by the Führer: "The soldier is the nation's weapons carrier." He added: "This implies that a soldier must hallow his weapon and be ready for the highest commitment." Our platoon leader, representing the state, handed the weapons to us. With a solemn handshake we vowed to honor our weapons, to become good warriors. Spontaneously I was reminded of a poem that had been popular in the *Deutsche Freischar,* an organization of the youth movement:

> The plough points downward toward the earth,
> Breaks up the hard and heavy soil;
> The spear points upward, to God and the skies:
> Both bound together for work and defense.

May 31, 1934, turned out to be a special day for the city of Stralsund [where we underwent our basic training]. The German Navy commemorated simultaneously the great Battle of Jutland; the death of the young poet Gorch Fock, who fell on that occasion; and the 125th anniversary of the death of the Prussian freedom fighter Ferdinand von Schill, who gave his life in this city.

The ceremonies began Wednesday evening when two platoons of No. 6 Company performed the Great Retreat. Today all citizens of Stralsund gather in the old market square, surrounded by its historic buildings such as the magnificent gothic-style city hall, the houses of the patrician families, and the mighty steeple of St. Nicholas Church. Delegations from the various military units in town take up their positions. As dusk falls the contours of the square disappear into the growing darkness until they suddenly return in the light of countless candles, placed one each in the windows of every building that surrounds the square. The steeple of the church rises sharply into the cold night sky, while the city hall offers but a dark silhouette. Floodlights whisk across the facades of the houses until they come to rest on the square in front of the officers' casino where the commandant, the officers, and the invited guests are waiting. As the military band approaches, the beating of the drums begins to drown out the humming of the crowd until the marching music itself can be heard. The people stop talking. Our company, in field-gray uniforms and steel helmets, moves in. The adjutant on horseback makes his report to the commandant. The Great Retreat begins. On two ledges of the city hall first green and later red fireworks are lit, burning like incense. The drums roll, trumpets blare. Then we enter the church for the service.

Afterwards the guards present arms, the officers leave the church, the companies take up their formations. The commandant, the major, and a few veteran officers inspect the assembled troops. Then the commandant steps up to the decorated rostrum. He reminds everyone of the significance of this day and stresses the obligation we assume in memory of the dead, of their commitment, and of the sacrifice they made for our nation. We shout a triple "Hurrah" for the Führer and for our patron, the venerable Field Marshal von Hindenburg. The ceremonies conclude with the singing of the national anthem and the Horst-Wessel Song.

NAUTICAL TRAINING ON THE *GORCH FOCK*

Diary:

June 14 to September 26, 1934

I am once again in Kiel. We march around the bend of the inner harbor. On the left we are greeted by the castle, and a few steps later we behold for a brief moment the mast tops of the *Gorch Fock*. We respond with a sudden motion in our ranks, as everyone wants to be the first to get a glimpse of the Navy's most beautiful vessel. We pass my alma mater where I had been a student for a short while and go along the Düsternbrookerweg, the latter unexpectedly splendid in the foliage of early summer. Next comes the building of the Naval High Command, as massive and mysterious as always, followed by my fraternity house, once the scene of a merry student life but today stripped and empty. Then we turn left onto the shoreline drive of the Hindenburg-Ufer where on Sundays I had taken many a walk. At last we reach the pier of the Blücherbrücke and the *Gorch Fock*, whose snow-white hull rises up from the grayish water, her masts pointing straight into the blue afternoon sky.

Once on board, we are divided up into groups and assigned to our corporals without regard to the bonds that have grown among comrades during basic training. And then the circus starts in earnest. We receive our hammocks and try to sling them. How in the world are we to know what a *Schlippsteg* is (sailor's knot), or that a hammock has two ends instead of one? We have no idea where to get gear to clean ship (in the *Rumpelkammer*, of course), what a *Versaufloch* is (a spillway allowing water to run off from the upper deck), or where to find the various *Hellegats* (storage areas below deck). We have to ask the old hands what the

Barring might be, a *Kuttenlecker* (cleaning brush), or a *Schlagpütz* (bucket made from canvas). Several times we simply run into each other or trip over all kinds of unexpected obstacles. With awe we glance up into the maze of masts and yards, already imagining ourselves climbing all over. Certainly we won't have to wait much longer.

There are no bunks on board. Sleeping in a hammock requires some practice. One side may be too loose, so that the whole thing hangs through and you have to wriggle like a worm to find a comfortable position. Despite all these challenges we slept perfectly that first night. The next morning we were not a little astonished when the chief boatswain's mate announced that the ship was in terrible shape and a thorough cleaning was called for to erase all vestiges of our past as landlubbers.

Cleaning ship is different from the corresponding procedure ashore. First you take off your shoes and socks. Then the deck is inundated until the water reaches your ankles. You hold your broom in a very special grip and turn it around 180 degrees when you hear the command, *"Achtung Null."* We save a lot of soap by using sand to scrub the deck. The superstructure is to be cleaned with fresh water only, and never, ever, smear paint around when you are polishing brass!

At this point I must add a comment. A comrade of mine hated cleaning ship so much that he allowed his frustration to inform the entries in his official diary:

Easter Sunday: Clean ship, two eggs.

Easter Monday: Clean ship, one egg.

Easter Tuesday: Clean ship, not even one egg.

For this he was punished by having to climb several times all over the ship's masts, yards, and rigging.

At noon our commanding officer, Captain Raul Mewis, spoke to us. This is the gist of his remarks: Our posting to the *Gorch Fock* means the beginning of our nautical training and thus of our chosen profession. The transition may not be easy, but we will get used to it. Often times will be tough, but we must give our best and endure. Certainly we know other men who have suffered through it all before and can guide us in doing the right thing. German history is full of magnificent deeds from which we can draw the necessary enthusiasm, inspiration, and strength for our task. Above all, we should remember the man for whom our ship is named. He did not rest until he had fulfilled his dearest dream, namely, to join the Navy. He later paid with his life for his undying desire to serve his people and his fatherland. Our motto for the weeks ahead will be: Eyes open, mouth shut, and hard work. Eyes open to get to know our job; mouth shut to learn how to obey and to work. Our true motto was: "One hand for the ship, one hand for yourself," in order to survive.

June 17, 1934

This afternoon [the former Free Corps leader and governor of Bavaria] General Ritter von Epp visits the ship. His picture had decorated the walls of my room when I was a boy. After a brief tour of the vessel the governor addressed the crew with these appropriate remarks: At least 50 percent of all young men in Germany yearn to go to sea. We are privileged to serve aboard a sailing vessel that represents in itself the basis of a mariner's profession and extends highest challenges to each and every one of us. From his own personal and military background he urges us to work hard from the beginning, to take advantage of all opportunities to learn, because the acquisition of knowledge and skills is the key to future careers. A man can only get as far as his will is prepared to take him.

The same holds true for the nation: The greatness of a nation depends on its will to achieve. For fifteen years the German nation had forgotten this crucial maxim, had chosen to be small. That has now changed for good. But to raise the nation again to its former stature it is absolutely imperative that everyone subscribe to this principle. We, our generation, have taken up the challenge. Another irrefutable truth is that the fate of an individual is determined by his community. Our ship provides a particularly solid education on the basis of both those principles.

June 18, 1934

The sound of gunfire and a plume of smoke over the [ancient pre-dreadnought] *Schleswig-Holstein* make us look up from our chores. There is no time to think; more shots are fired, and we come to attention, face to starboard. Again and again guns are fired in salute. We learn that the Chief of the Naval Command is paying a visit to the [light cruiser] *Leipzig.* A short while later the [light cruiser] *Karlsruhe* hoists the flag of the Reich Minister of Defense and joins in the firing of salute.

Firing salute is an ancient custom among seafaring nations. It goes back to the times of the muzzle-loaders. In those days a man-of-war was allowed to enter a foreign port only after having fired all its guns to show it had no hostile intentions. Likewise, piping the side for a visiting officer and receiving him with the proper number of honor guards at the gangway has a long tradition. In the old days visitors were heaved aboard in large baskets. Since men tend to gain a little weight as they grow older, it was not uncommon that, say, an admiral required more attendants in that particular procedure than a young lieutenant. Thus, many seemingly nonsensical and ridiculous customs, today merely observed pro forma, are based on valid historical precedents. If one is familiar with such historical developments, one appreciates what for others remains unintelligible. Tradition acts as a firm link between us and our forebears.

June 26, 1934

An address by the commanding officer: Today everywhere in Germany flags are flying at half-mast and half-staff. Fifteen years ago the delegates Dr. Müller and Dr. Bell signed the Treaty of Versailles. This treaty did not issue from genuine negotiations for peace but was a diktat based on intransigence and hatred. At its core is Article 231, which assigns the war guilt to Germany. This lie about the war guilt is the legal basis for all other articles and is reflected in the incredible burdens Germany has to bear: the payment of reparations, the loss of our colonies, the restrictions on our military establishment, and last but not least the humiliation we all feel. [Comment: Germany was supposed to pay reparations until 1988, the very year I am writing this book.]

The great campaign against the diktat of Versailles began with the National Socialist movement. A first success was the discontinuation of the reparation payments. Next will come the enlargement of the military. Nothing demonstrates more firmly Germany's desire to restore her national honor than her withdrawal from the League of Nations, that guardian over Versailles, on November 12, 1933. But our moral rehabilitation is not yet complete. Nobody should rest until our honor and respectability are fully restored. We vow to make this our life's goal. To underline our determination we join in a triple hurrah for our fatherland.

June 30, 1934

At 2 o'clock in the afternoon, against all normal routine, both watches are instructed to stand by on the upper deck. The commanding officer announces an order by the Reich Minister of Defense: An increased state of alert because of domestic political difficulties.

After we are dismissed, our first reaction is that we will be deprived of liberty ashore today. We assemble in groups, some large, some small, and speculate wildly about what kind of political tensions might have arisen. One comrade suggests that the whole thing is just a smokescreen for a foreign crisis. Another mentions a possible rebellion by the SA [Stormtroopers] against the Army, while yet a third hints that the government may have run out of money. No one had any idea what had really happened. We were astounded to learn that the SA Chief of Staff, Ernst Röhm, along with several other SA leaders, had been arrested and shot because of rebellious and treasonable activities. Soon, news of the events reaches us more rapidly and in greater detail. The Führer himself had supervised the arrests after SA leader August Schneidhuber proclaimed that the Führer and the Army were out to get the SA. Police president Viktor Lutze has taken over as Chief of Staff. His appointment is part of far-reaching reforms inside the SA and a redefinition of its role, especially a return to Spartan simplicity of purpose, blind obedience, strictest discipline, and moral character. We all feel relieved because the SA had departed from the path that had made it great, had been led astray by less admirable elements in its leadership, either through neglect or deliberate lapses.

Comment:

In such and similar ways we experienced the situation on the *Gorch Fock*. The state-controlled media of the press and radio, but also the officer corps itself, silenced any criticism from the start.

The leadership of the German Army, itself implicated by supplying arms to the *Schutzstaffel* (SS) for its purge of the SA, welcomed the action as a strengthening of its own power base. It even accepted the fact that two recently retired and entirely uninvolved officers, Generals Kurt von Schleicher and Kurt von Bredow, were liquidated in the course of the affair. Their SS murderers were never brought to justice. When the Schlieffen Society issued a feeble "Declaration of Honor," all criticism among soldiers ceased. Inasmuch as we never learned all the facts about the Röhm Affair, we did not develop reservations about its legality. Besides, we held a strong conviction that the state was ultimately responsible for dealing with matters of law, of right and wrong.

In retrospect, today we are appalled that the *Reichswehr* leaders chose to do nothing even though they knew full well the details of this night of murder and that dozens of people had been killed in cold blood without the benefit of a trial. By taking no action, the officer corps violated the moral principles of its upbringing and its traditional dedication to a state based on law and order. Only a few realized that the Nazi regime had dropped its mask. But even they remained essentially silent until mid-1941 when Hitler's Commissar Order and restrictions regarding the Army's jurisdiction in the theater of operations revealed for everyone the regime's criminal character. At that point one member of the German resistance, Henning von Tresckow, wrote these prophetic words: "With these actions the German people assumes a measure of guilt that the world will not forgive us in a hundred years."

Diary:

July 13, 1934
As part of the second division of the starboard watch it is our responsibility to work the capstan. We sing the time-honored tune of *"Lampenputzer ist mein Vater"* as we slowly bring the anchor up. Each turn of the capstan is the equivalent of 40 centimeters of chain cable. One hundred meters of cable thus mean 250 turns altogether—hard work and lots of sweat indeed. The rhythm of the music helps. But even better is the incentive provided by several young ladies, all of them student sailors of the local yacht school, who circle our ship in their small boats and cast curious glances in our direction.

July 15, 1934
At noon we enjoy a well-earned hour of rest. Who cares about the sea and the weather? We know the boatswain's mate watches out for us. Today the 'tweendeck seems darker than usual, but we hardly pay any attention. Then, without warning, the alarm whistle chases us to the upper deck. The spars and masts creak under the pressure of a sudden storm gust. It begins to rain. "Furl all sails!" The Fehmarnbelt [a strait between Germany and Denmark where the bark *Niobe* went down under similar circumstances two years before with heavy loss of life] is not far away. We climb up the rat-lines as fast as we can. The storm drives raindrops straight into our faces. "Lay out!" It's not raining any more; it's pouring. We can barely make out the deck below. It seems the storm wants to push us right off the snatch-locks that we need for balance. With great difficulty we haul in the sails—heavy, wet, stiff, and hard to handle as they are. Finally they are properly secured, the ship is safely at anchor, and we stand rain-drenched on deck. Then the squall has passed, we weigh anchor, set sail again, and the sun laughs from the sky as if to make fun of us.

July 18, 1934

Not every day is a day of sunshine. Sometimes the sun seems to set on you, especially if nothing you try with best intentions wants to go right. This brings on despair and depression, as you contrast your restless life on board with that of others whose daily challenges appear trivial in comparison. You may even be tempted to ask: "What's the use of doing all this?"

Those are dangerous hours, but they can also be a blessing in disguise. They can teach you to regain your proper balance, to carry out your inner struggles like a man.

Comment:

The words of the diary hint at how terribly the petty officers treated us. This is something no longer comprehensible from today's perspective.

Because of my build I was slower than my comrades. I got stuck in the rat-lines and often reached my work station later than the others. As a consequence I became a virtually permanent member of the infamous "Climbing Club." After hours, usually in darkness, we had to assemble on deck and then were chased up the rat-lines, all the way to the top yard. We might have endured these procedures stoically had the petty officers not added extra chicaneries. Most notable was the obligation to carry along our hammock, almost the size of a grown man and quite heavy, draped over our left arm. We had to drag it along wherever we climbed as we carried out our acrobatic act on the top yards. The petty officers below, to keep track of us aloft, strapped oil lanterns to our backs. Our ordeal became particularly hairy when, handicapped by our hammocks, we reached platforms at the juncture of masts and yards that could be circumnavigated only by leaning dangerously backward. Needless to say, the whole exercise was life-threatening. To this day I cannot understand why the officers tolerated such actions.

Diary:

July 20, 1934

An excursion to the Marienburg [East Prussia]. Through a high gateway we step into the outer court of the castle once built by the Teutonic Knights. Everyone is silent. We sense the historical significance of the state the Teutonic Knights ran here so many centuries ago and its underlying ideas, now forever cast in stone. What an attitude that created this state and its gothic architecture!

We proceed to the *Westpreussenkreuz* [where the borders of Germany, Danzig, and Poland converged]. One has to have seen the inscription *"Traité de Versailles"* in order to realize the influence the former French government had in creating these borders. One has to have experienced with one's own eyes how unnatural the lines are: how everywhere they reflect military considerations; how they violate the right to self-determination; how they run straight through German farms and estates, rendering them economically difficult to operate; how, for instance, villages and towns are cut off from their train stations, their only way of reaching the outside world; how the borders discourage and depress the local population; and how, in the end, the seeds are planted here for a renewed confrontation in the future. We see the consequences of "solving" the question of access to the Vistula River: a narrow strip, 4 meters wide. No wonder the levees are in disrepair, the river is silting up.

Tannenberg—the stone embankments and towers of the memorial [where Hindenburg defeated two invading Russian armies in 1914] project into the July sky under the black clouds of a gathering thunderstorm.

August 2, 1934

Field Marshal von Hindenburg is dead. Whoever has not yet noticed that our flag flies at half-mast learns of the Reich President's death in a brief memorial address delivered by our commanding officer. His words: A life dedicated to duty, sacrifice, and faith in Germany has come to an end. But what Hindenburg will be remembered the most for, what will indeed make him immortal, is his contribution to the new Reich. The Reich President was well aware of the far-reaching significance of his decision to become the patron of the National Socialist movement. Aware of his responsibilities and concerned about the destiny of the Reich, he joined the best elements of the past with the political forces of a rejuvenated and future-oriented Germany. By doing so he laid the foundation for the reconstruction of the Reich.

Such was the diction used everywhere in those days. Captain Mewis's words were no different from what hundreds of Nazi officials from local representatives to the highest leadership had to say.

August 9, 1934

We enter the port of Helsingfors [Helsinki], Finland. This afternoon I met a man from Württemberg. He told me why he had left Germany: economic reasons, as usual. Deep down, however, he could never get away from Germany. He returned home at the beginning of the World War to experience life in his fatherland for five years, but eventually he decided to leave again because he felt restricted by the many limitations on his life, pulled away by the promise of more breathing space abroad.

He also told me about the plight of the local German colony here, a plight that is more emotional than economic. As everywhere abroad, he explained, the press is for the most part influenced by Jewish interests. After January 30, 1933 [the day of Hitler's installment as Reich Chancellor], the press disseminated atrocity stories of the wildest kind in order to direct the mood of the Finnish people against the handful of Germans here. He suggested that I exercise caution in my public remarks and not praise without reservations the ideas of the new Germany. He assured me, however, that the German colony stood behind the Führer and his ideology.

He talked much about the Finnish countryside, which he had come to love as if it were German soil. And yet, from his gestures and behavior and from looking into his eyes, you could tell how much he missed his native Württemberg. I tried to make him feel better by sharing with him my impressions about the new Germany.

August 10, 1934

Since Germany is in a state of mourning, the German colony has arranged an excursion to the old Swedish fortress Sveaborg in lieu of more festive ceremonies. As we march toward the southern end of the port, we pass the memorial for those Germans who fell while helping the Finns gain their independence from Russia, some 400 men altogether. To commemorate those times and to honor the dead, we form a circle around the memorial. Names like Admiral Alexander Meurer and General Komar von der Goltz remind us never to forget the 400 men whose actions and death helped bring freedom to the Finnish people.

August 12, 1934

A ceremony in Hammskär. On November 17, 1917, having successfully penetrated Russian minefields, the German U-boat *UC 57* reached the area of low-lying, rocky islands near Hammskär. It carried war materiel crucial to Finland's continued struggle for freedom. The boat also took along an eight-man Finnish scout unit whose task was to destroy bridges on the Karelian Isthmus and thus sever communications to Russia. The following morning *UC 57* left to return to safety and was never seen again.

Twenty-seven Germans went down with the boat. To express its gratitude the Finnish government built a granite memorial in the island district of Lovisa not far from Hammskär. While our commanding officer makes the six-hour trip on the coastal battleship *Vainämöinen,* and our executive and division officers do the same on a submarine, we reach the island aboard the gunboat *Turunmaa.* An old Russian boat, it is now being used to train cadets. We are welcomed most cordially, and before long we are engaged in a lively conversation in the course of which we get to appreciate and respect our Finnish counterparts more and more. Those six hours have given me a good insight into the conditions the Finns face, and also into their recent history. Not those Mongolian-looking faces in the port district have created the Finnish state, but rather a type of man like the ones we met aboard the *Turunmaa*—disciplined, ascetic, manly; with faces etched by determination; modest, reserved, taciturn, and always eager to make their guests as comfortable as possible. Their ideology reflects the same principle as ours—indeed, that of all young peoples. As Nietzsche once put it, "If you despise comfort and a soft bed, if you distance yourself from weaklings as much as you can: that is the true source of your virtue."

They tell us openly what is on their minds. Our conversation touches primarily on military matters.

Our itinerary takes us through a beautiful district of low, rocky islands off the coast. Only a few vessels can navigate the narrow channel. The strength of the Finnish fleet rests on its small craft, all of which have the capacity to lay mines. In fact, mines are Finland's principal weapon. In case of war it is easy enough to block the ship channel with mines. This strategy is even reflected in the wide bellies of the submarines that follow in our wake. They, too, are full of mines.

August 13, 1934

At 9 A.M. we leave Helsingfors. A sinister spirit seems to be haunting the ship. Physical exercises are being reintroduced, including entirely new ones. At first they take place below deck, apparently for practice purposes. In the afternoon, more exercises on a larger scale. Our starboard watch undergoes a thorough inspection of clothes and uniforms, followed by *"Flagge Luci"* [so named after the colors of the signal flag for the letter "L", i.e., blue-white-blue] in all its variations. The narrow confinement of our quarters under deck is worse than at Stralsund, but at least it is bearable. Things can get out of control, however, when you find your clothes strewn all over, with comrades dashing here and there at top speed. In their haste and excitement they tend to step on your possessions and make them dirty, and later it takes an hour to gather everything together again.

Comment:

Flagge Luci was a new form of chicanery. It went like this: "All hands to the upper deck!" Then the order: "Change into white uniforms in three minutes!" We had to dash down to our quarters, change from blue to white uniforms, and reappear on the upper deck within three minutes. Once reassembled, we were told to change into blue again and be back in three minutes; then it was white again, and so on. This game could go on for an eternity.

During one of these exercises I forgot to secure my locker properly. Immediately, our corporal emptied its entire contents onto the floor, including all my underwear. My comrades had little choice but to step on it while changing their clothes. Afterwards it took hours until everything was neatly cleaned and ironed.

To be assigned duty in the corporals' quarters, or *U-Raum*, was an especially hated task. We all had to do it at least once, and for everyone it was a hellish experience. There the corporals were among themselves and could mistreat us at will without fear of being disciplined. Some slept in bunks, others in hammocks. For reasons never quite clear to me, they preferred to sleep in their underwear. When you arrived early in the morning you would find the air indescribably poor and stifling. Half the men were still asleep, some were in the process of getting up, others were already eating breakfast amidst cigarette stubs and half-emptied beer glasses from the night before. The stench was so bad it took your breath away. The order to remove the cover from the parrot cage, so that the poor bird might breathe some fresh air, seemed to me the height of hypocrisy.

One day, when I was on duty down there, Maltus—"Tiger of the Baltic," as he was known—expressed his opinion of me and my comrades as follows: "The era of privileges for officer cadets is over. The only reason why you can wear regular shirts and ties with your uniforms [while all enlisted personnel had to run around in traditional sailors' outfits] is your parents' financial ability to send you to secondary schools. But times have changed, and we will show you how. Just wait."

Not long afterwards my comrade Waldecker was on duty in the corporals' quarters. In a seemingly jovial tone one of the men, Tom Schark, involved him in a conversation. Schark was known to be hot-tempered and vengeful toward those who slighted him. "Well, Waldecker, what will be your next command, cruiser *Emden* or cruiser *Karlsruhe?*" "Emden, Sir!" "Well, in that case you better be careful that the cannibals don't eat you." "Sir, if I can manage to survive in the petty officers' quarters, there should be absolutely nothing to fear from those cannibals." The next thing we heard was a horrible noise and outcry from the direction of the *U-Raum*, and moments later Waldecker came dashing up the companion hatch, pale but once again in control of his emotions. In the weeks that followed, until we left the *Gorch Fock*, he had to suffer terribly.

Diary:

August 26, 1934
The entire day, as everywhere in the Reich, is marked by the Rally for the Saarland. Hitler speaks at the Deutsche Eck [in Koblenz on the Rhine River]:

> The principles of the new Reich are clear in its foreign policy as well as domestically. We want peace, but there must be equal rights for all nations. We fight for our honor and freedom. At home we strive to improve the lot of the German worker and preserve the position of the German farmer. We are against unemployment! Against social divisions based on parties and classes! Only bigots and biased people can ignore and reject the immeasurable changes that have occurred. If alien elements criticize us and point out the problems our government has to face, we respond that such difficulties exist only because they are imposed on our people from the outside. Nothing will stop us in our efforts to remove and conquer these difficulties. Just as the German people have existed for thousands of years, so it will in the future. Any pessimism with regard to our economy is as unfounded as certain accusations with regard to religion. We believe in positive Christianity and defend religious and spiritual freedom. However, we will not tolerate any attempt to use religion as a pretext for political purposes.
>
> The Saarland has always been a model for us. While inside Germany political parties divided the population into innumerable camps, the actions of the Saarlanders have been imbued by one thought only, namely, "rejoin the Reich." On January 14 they will regain their place in the German fatherland. [On January 14, 1935, the Saarlanders voted overwhelmingly to rejoin Germany after 15 years of French occupation and exploitation sanctioned by the Treaty of Versailles.] Everyone will be accepted with open arms, no matter what his party affiliation, as long as he is ready to help in the reconstruction of Germany. At the same time, we hope that beyond our

borders more people are prepared to cooperate with the new Germany peacefully once we have rebuilt our country and take up greater challenges. It would be our greatest joy and satisfaction if, as bells are ringing out, we can not only welcome back many Germans into the Reich, but witness the arrival of a genuine peace.

In this way, and in the face of many press reports to the contrary, Hitler paints a clear picture for the Saarlanders of the Germany for or against which they will soon have to cast their vote.

August 29, 1934

Pressed together like sardines, we crowd the deck of a Swedish fishing vessel as it slowly takes us out into the misty world offshore. The storm envelops us with its drizzle and spray. We view the shoreline as if through a veil. Today the rocks seem softer and less jagged, the grass greener, the landscape more forlorn than in the sunshine of the day before. We reach Stensholm, a desolate, rocky island virtually unknown to anyone except those who know and care about Gorch Fock, Germany's poet of the sea. The island seems to swallow us as we hold a quiet ceremony and honor the contributions of the dead. United, we mourn on the tiny cemetery that is lovingly preserved by people in nearby Fjellbacka. Here, after the Battle of Jutland and in foreign soil, the poet and mariner Gorch Fock was laid to rest, not far from the sea that meant his life. Next to him are the gravesites of a few comrades and unknown British sailors, all joined together in death. Usually all is quiet here. The storm whistles between the rocks as if to accompany the eternal breaking of the waves upon the rocks.

August 31, 1934

The night is cold. Even oilskin clothing cannot entirely shelter us from the strong winds. But then one has to think good thoughts and cheer up, especially when things are getting a little rough and uncomfortable. Clouds chase one another across the sky; just above the horizon a few oscillating lights appear—fishermen, no doubt. Otherwise everything is dark. Immediately in front of the ship, illuminated by the riding light, the crests of the waves roll in and break up, turn into white foam, and surge along the hull. Lines and cables tense up and relax, depending on the movement of the ship. On our beam the sky lights up from distant lightning. The moon becomes visible for a few seconds, half veiled by the low clouds. Then it is gone and everything is dark again. From time to time it briefly reappears, leaving a bright spot on the bobbing water whose reflection rolls toward the ship like liquid silver. Gorch Fock used to hail the time between midnight and 4 A.M. as the "King's Watch"; we call it the graveyard watch.

September 9, 1934

Karlskrona. Swedish visitors came on board, some 2,500 in all. In the evening we gave a party for our hosts. There were tables and benches, as well as colorful decorations fashioned from signal flags. We received our visitors on the upper deck, matching every Swede with a German crew member. Given physical restraints and our general disposition, the meal was not opulent but still provided a fine opportunity to exchange ideas and experiences. Both sides enriched the occasion by singing songs representative of their respective countries. It became quite clear that we Germans did this with somewhat greater enthusiasm. We finally parted in the knowledge that we had forged links that went beyond superficial contacts.

With one of our visitors I kept up a correspondence for quite some time afterwards. It proves how important the work of the Navy is in showing the flag abroad and in helping the peoples of the world understand one another.

Epilogue:

The voyage on the *Gorch Fock* was our first true acquaintance with the sea. We got a feeling for the element that would eventually become home to us, an element whose characteristics and moods would become so familiar as to constitute a part of ourselves.

A voyage on a sailing vessel is the basis of all seafaring, for in its course you are forced to slug it out with the elements. After all, in a fight you get to know and appreciate an enemy the best. We did not have the reassurance of simply starting our engines if we got into trouble. We also experienced the romanticism of the sea as we had imagined it in our boyhood dreams. Anyone who has stood watch as a lookout on a clear July night knows what I mean. It, too, was the first time that we grew together as a Crew. Our basic attitude as a community of officers received its formative impulses on the *Gorch Fock*.

In Stralsund we lived together in squads and formed two companies. Now our midshipman cruise will tear the Crew apart into two halves. One half will embark on the cruiser *Karlsruhe*, which will take us to North and South America. Our comrades on the *Emden* call our itinerary the "salon and parquet" cruise, for their main destination is Africa, "to visit Negroes in the bush," as we label their endeavor with contempt.

MIDSHIPMAN ON THE *KARLSRUHE*

Diary:

August 27, 1934

We line up on the pier alongside the cruiser *Karlsruhe* and report to the officer on duty. This is an important day for us. As we later assemble on the quarter deck we wear our cadet uniforms for the first time, complete with "monkey jacket," shirt, tie, and sword knot [*Portépée*]. Our new uniform brings many new obligations, but we fulfill them gladly because this is, after all, our desired profession. There is the old Prussian saying: "Whoever dedicates himself to the Prussian flag retains nothing that is his own." My comrades think as I do, and it is not difficult to exercise tolerance. What I understand Prussian values to mean, the poet Stefan George has expressed in this poem:

> If you are searching for new nobility,
> do not look for men of ancient shield and crown.
> All so endowed exhibit mere corruption of the senses,
> their glances have grown raw and furtive.
> Rather, there rise up from the nameless masses
> rarer products of highest rank;
> you will recognize them, your fellow nobles,
> by the glowing fire in their eyes.

Comment:

I have always loved poetry. In those days it was Stefan George who fascinated me. In him I discovered a new feeling for poetic language, something both aristocratic and ascetic, to which I and many others felt strongly attracted. Many young people would show up when he read his works in public. Writers, philosophers, and the Stauffenberg brothers (the latter instrumental in carrying out the assassination plot against Hitler on July 20, 1944), among others, belonged to the circle around Stefan George. That he also spoke out against totalitarianism, I only realized later.

Our daily routine aboard, however, was far removed from any soaring flights of the soul. One day the petty officers held an inspection of our quarters. Count Pückler, a fellow cadet, had to open his locker. The petty officer saw a few books in it and grabbed one at random from the shelf: poetry by Rainer Maria Rilke. Question: "Are you telling me that you are reading poetry, Pückler, and on top of that poems by a woman?" No comment necessary.

Diary:

October 21, 1934
Telegram from Berlin: "I expect that the *Karlsruhe* will, in true devotion to her duties, represent the honor of Germany on her trip abroad. Bon voyage to the ship, its commanding officer and its crew, and a safe return. Adolf Hitler."

Central Atlantic, November 17, 1934
Sleeping in the warm, fresh air on the quarter deck is immeasurably more regenerating than sleeping in the stale air below. You even need less sleep to feel relaxed. When you wake up at night you see the sky above filled with twinkling stars; in the morning you can watch the pelicans go fishing.

Crossing the Line, November 26, 1934
Today is the day when we will wash off the dirt and dust of the northern hemisphere and receive the baptism required for a dignified entry into its southern counterpart.

We take up formation on the quarter deck. Neptune's banner flutters merrily from the top yard. Pleasing but loud music, played by his gentlemen companions, announces the arrival of the ruler of the oceans. In a festive procession the royal couple and its entourage are moving toward the quarter deck and inspect the assembled crew.

Wavy flaxen hair surrounds the mighty king's dignified face. Thetis, too, cannot complain about a sparse growth of hair. One of their companions constantly fans fresh air toward the couple to render them more comfortable. With a practiced eye the court physician spies those who suffer and provides professional relief. Meanwhile, the barber does not fail to make the unshaven among us worthy of the festive occasion.

The royal couple is now seated under a canopy, surrounded by its court, while the officials get ready for their next activities. His majesty welcomes us to his realm. He emphasizes the importance of seafaring, reminds us of the naval battles of Coronel and the Falklands [1914], and encourages us to continue our careers with pride. Then he introduces everyone in his entourage. Once the astronomer has taken the proper measurements to ensure that we have indeed reached the equator, and medals are being distributed with appropriate speeches, the real baptismal procedure gets under way. It is said that regular baptisms are more humane, but then they cannot quite match the festive character of our ceremony.

The court barber sharpens his long knife. The physician rolls up his sleeves. A large number of tubs and boxes contain "baptismal snacks." Like sea monsters, Neptune's helpers hover around the huge water basin, eager to grab their first victim.

Our chief artillery officer is the first to come up the steps, stoically resigned to his fate. Neptune's officials seem like wild beasts whose ferocity comes to the fore only after the first spilling of blood. One look at the staff surgeon makes clear that there will be no mercy this time, especially with regard to the prescribed immersions, beverages, and concoctions. The latter seem to be an awful mixture of mustard, torpedo oil, soap, seasonings, and grease. Those who do not swallow the stuff voluntarily are forcefully pacified until they no longer know whether it tastes better going down or coming up. Any resistance is useless. Half drowned and half numb from the stench and taste of the contents of this cesspool, and bereft of all hope of ever seeing the light of day again, we dive into a new dimension of uncertainty: the long wind sleeve. But fortunately it turns out to be a rather harmless affair, indeed a first step toward recovery, if you do not mind too much Neptune's helpers trying to beat you with short pieces of rope. At the far end of the sleeve, virtually out of breath, we receive a glass of brandy as encouragement to make peace with the world around us. The baptism is over; we have at last been accepted into the world of ancient mariners.

Rio de Janeiro, December 9, 1934

We have many visitors on board, most of them German-Brazilians from all over the country, but especially from the state of Santa Catarina. After a tour of the ship, the commanding officer addresses our visitors in a clear and matter-of-fact speech. He delivers greetings from the old country, which is presently undergoing a transformation, and emphasizes the desire of Germans to belong together no matter where on earth they may happen to live. Then it is the turn of the local party leader. The manner in which he speaks belongs to a different era. But there is no reason to doubt the sincerity of his remarks, to reject them as empty phrases. In the evening, under palm trees on the grounds of the German school, a party is organized, complete with a huge tent, benches, tables, and a small dance floor. Most of the German-Brazilians are already there when we arrive. By an odd coincidence I happen to be seated next to a woman born in Celle [near Hanover] whose fate had taken her to Brazil after the World War. But even she is unable to engage me in a longer conversation.

Again and again my eyes and thoughts wander off to the men and women who sit silently here and there in the midst of the bright festivities. Only their faces betray that they share a common fate. They are the real colonists, the frontiersmen. Not only do their hard and weathered faces tell the story of a harsh and cruel life, but their whole demeanor and behavior distinguish them from the others.

Broad-brimmed hats cover half of their faces. Their shirts and coats appear clean but worn; their narrow ties remind me of pieces of string. These people have lost all concern for their outer appearance, even if they have the means to dress up. I make my way from one to the next. Everywhere is the same fate. Where 130 people are crowded onto a square kilometer, carving out an existence is tough. In one case the grandfather had owned vineyards on Lake Balaton in Hungary. The father had still been able to derive a living from the farm, albeit with some assistance from the neighbors. The two cows were barely enough, but there was no way to support the three sons. The oldest son, already married, was ready to emigrate when the two younger ones, drawn by the illusion of prosperity abroad, decided that they would go instead. They saved money for the train trip to Bremerhaven; the voyage to Brazil itself was free.

Immediately upon their arrival the misery began. All they had was a piece of jungle and the realization that their neighbors were no better off. After clearing the land, they built a primitive hut to provide some shelter against the rain. Then they planted their first crop of corn. Things got worse. In those first weeks they buried at least one man every day. None of the survivors would have stayed if they had had money for the trip back home. Once the jungle has you in its iron grip, there is no escape.

Today, some forty years later, things are looking up. This particular man owns two oxen and two horses, along with pigs and chicken. Of eight children born, two sons are still alive. One of them will take over the farm; the other one will be forced to move on. Both sons, I am told, no longer have the courage and enthusiasm of their youth. They don't see the liberating difference between being a slave on a large estate and being a master on your own parcel of land. Those sons no longer are prepared to take risks, even though their father would help them get started, and even though a network of roads and pathways has made things much easier.

Such are the stories I am told. Not unlike rocks with runic inscriptions, their faces bear the marks of living a harsh life, just as their mood and expressions reflect bitterness. Bent and bony they sit there, seemingly untouched by all the merry-making around them. Their eyes have lost the radiance of the old days. They come alive only when I tell them of the new Germany where hard work is rewarded and men are judged by their achievements. I talked to many of these colonists, and every one of them was grateful for the opportunity. I can still see them before my eyes today, a unique type of human being, standing out in any crowd.

December 21, 1934

We enter the estuary of the River Plate. Montevideo. About six thousand Germans live here. They include many recent immigrants who divide the local colony into two factions: those for and those against the new Germany. Within the former group one encounters a further division. Many are prepared, without second thoughts or the least hesitation, to refashion things in Uruguay in the image of the Third Reich. Others, likewise enthusiastic for the Third Reich, are more cautious when it comes to drawing parallels and consequently less willing to depart from their traditional attitude as Germans abroad. The split begins in the youth organizations. On the one hand are the Hitler Youth, on the other the Boy Scouts. Their feuds do not stop short of the use of violence. This division continues with the adults, so much so that it is not easy to assess the situation properly. For the duration of our visit both sides appear to have buried their hatchets in order not to spoil parties and private invitations for us. But their animosity has deep roots. May the attitudes and behavior of our crew serve as a model of unity and reconciliation for them in the years ahead.

December 24, 1934

Today nobody goes ashore. We want to celebrate Christmas among ourselves. Local ivy and pine branches provide the traditional green. Flags and the soft red of our tablecloths transform our living quarters into a special place. Posters remind us of winter scenes in Germany. The people at home have not forgotten us and have sent precious tokens of their affection: a few real Christmas trees, which we will decorate and light tonight. It is hard to imagine that today is Christmas Eve. There have been none of the ordinary reminders: no secretive preparations or the usual Christmas activities; no cold or snow; no hot stoves to warm up red-frozen faces or the delicious smell of hot baked apples; no fur hats or coats to shield against the winter weather; in fact, no long celebration of advent at all where you gradually increase the number of candles burning and sense the growing feeling of expectation and joy as Christmas approaches. Busily we decorated the Christmas tree, and when we saw those silver and golden ornaments gleaming against the green, we indeed caught some of the Christmas spirit.

Later, we made our way to the quarter deck where an altar had been erected, framed by a Christmas tree on each side. We sang our old Christmas carols and the chaplain read the Christmas story. It was like home. Many of our German guests had tears in their eyes. Then the gifts were opened as a special mood of happiness spread. It is hard to describe the love and care that went into the wrapping of the packages and gifts, fastened with green ribbons and decorated with branches from fir trees, the latter all dry and yellowed after their long voyage. Underneath the tree in our deck, on long tables covered with white cloth, we displayed our presents as the mess attendants served tea punch. That was our Christmas. The commanding officer joined us for a short while, then a special Christmas newspaper was read and distributed:

Born to live—ready to laugh;
To annoy the fools—to see the world;
To honor our homeland—to die for our people:
May that be our motto, freely chosen.

December 31, 1934

At 3 P.M. we stand down from our watch. Quickly we decorate our decks with
signal flags. At 6 P.M. the celebrations begin with the opening of beer bottles—
just as in Germany all kinds of fireworks fill the nightly skies and bells ring in the
New Year. We drink a toast to the people back home.

Then we resume our voyage into the New Year. The sea is celebrating with us.
A storm is blowing, force 8 to 9. Heavy breakers cover the forecastle and the
quarter deck, their spray drenching those on duty on the bridge.

January 1, 1935

About noon we enter the Strait of Magellan. At Punta Arenas we take on our
pilot. Mr. Pagels, who had been [the German cruiser] *Dresden*'s pilot after the
Battle of the Falklands, does not join us as scheduled, but he waves to us from
the pilot boat.

The passage through the Strait of Magellan was one of the most memorable
parts of our voyage because the weather remained unexpectedly pleasant
throughout. The country somehow resembles Norway's fjords, but it impresses
more through its ever-changing vistas. On both shores steep rocks rise high
above us, barren except where patches of stunted bushes grow halfway to the
top. Small areas of snow suggest a long, harsh winter. Farther inland, on the
higher ranges, the snow never melts. Glaciers reach down deep into the valleys.
In a few places they actually touch the water's edge. Some inlets are entirely covered by chunks of ice. The water is emerald in color and as smooth as a mirror.
The seemingly soundless ship cuts through it, our bow waves moving away
smoothly toward the shores. Disturbed by our presence, some ducks paddle
around. Here and there seals break through the surface and disappear again;
otherwise everything is quiet. To both sides wrecks of ships remind us constantly
how deadly this place can be. Shortly before nightfall we drop anchor in 28 fath-
oms of water.

January 3, 1935

We proceed through the Chilean channels, most notably the Smith Channel.
The mountain ranges around us are even more majestic, the navigable channel
even more restricted than before. Half an hour before we enter the English Narrows the order is given, "Close all watertight doors!" On the forecastle our anchor is readied to be dropped at a second's notice in case something goes wrong.
Like a wedge the shores of the narrows, flanked by mountains of medium altitude, close in on the ship from both sides. We are the longest vessel ever to try to
pass through this strait, challenging the record of the *Emden*. A British cruiser
once ran aground when trying what we are about to undertake.

The commanding officer himself takes control of the ship. Just where the channel is narrowest we have to make a 90-degree turn around the rocks. Those of us

on the quarter deck are unusually quiet. Some of us fix our eyes on the stern, others on the bow. Will we be able to clear the narrows? To enhance maneuverability the commanding officer orders an increase in the ship's speed. The *Karlsruhe* is literally bending over. At 21 knots we negotiate the last remaining turn. Whoever did not take a look around at that point missed one of the most beautiful sights of our entire voyage as the dark silhouette of the ship glided by the huge snowfields of a massive mountain ridge. Toward evening we leave the narrows behind and regain open waters. From the distance we marvel at the mighty coastal range with its uncounted snow-covered peaks.

Valparaiso, January 16, 1935

We start the day with special morning colors while the band plays the Saarland Song [Saarlanders had just voted by a huge margin to rejoin the Reich]. At 11:30 A.M. Captain Lütjens calls the crew together for a brief celebration in the presence of several representatives of the local German colony. Just as the victorious [Prussian] forces after the Battle of Leuthen [Seven Years' War] gave vent to their overwhelming sense of gratitude by singing "Now God Be Thanked," so we let the hymn echo across this great Chilean port. Millions of Germans share our joy in the Saarland's return. In the evening we are invited to a grand ball at the German Club.

Peru, January 31, 1935

We take a trip from Lima to Rio Blanco. Some people have compared this segment of railway line to the stretch between Garmisch and Innsbruck. As far as wildly romantic landscape is concerned, the comparison seems entirely apt. Bridges, tunnels, and steep slopes offer magnificent vistas. Runoff from the glaciers has created canyons of incredible depth and with impressive waterfalls. A road, snaking its way alongside the tracks, is at several places covered by fallen rocks. Farther on, the train seems to cling to the steep rocky sides of the mountain as it winds its way ever so slowly upward, loop after loop. By now we encounter no more vegetation.

High up on the slope the remains of Inca terrace agriculture come into view. Once they gave the land its richness; today they are without use, without life. It is rare to run into people at these altitudes.

At 11,000 feet we reach our destination. There is little time for a look around. Massive but half-collapsed walls give a hint that this place has enjoyed better times. A house carries the designation "Hotel" in huge letters, but it certainly has not functioned as such for ages. We discover a small settlement of native Indians almost obscured by a hill. Their huts are most primitive, the walls made from a coarse fabric covered with clay. They offer little protection against the wind. The enclosed room, perhaps 10 feet square, has no floor. In one of the huts we notice a loom that must have been used by these Indians for centuries. Behind the loom sits an old man, like a mummy. As if he were an animal, his eyes betray the fear he feels upon our arrival. His face is leathery and waxen, man and loom forever joined together. When we offer him a few cigarettes he reaches out hesitatingly, drawn between alarm and desire. His wife occupies a seat next to him, her eyes cast down, all the time spinning thread from a bundle of wool.

Other Indians sit in their huts spinning, surrounded by a large group of un-washed children. Dogs in a state of utter neglect bark constantly, their noise not abating until we return to the tracks in response to the engineer's whistle.

Comment:

That was my impression of South America as I experienced it, however briefly and superficially, as a midshipman on the cruiser *Karlsruhe*. I was supposed to be an ambassador of Germany and was proud of it. I viewed the countries, ports, and people we encountered in the light of the official "information sheets" that had been distributed to us. But what real story lay behind the misery we saw up there in the Andes? What should we have known in order to understand this continent, its people, and its culture properly?

On his voyage to the New World, Christopher Columbus carried along a work by Marco Polo in which he could read, among other things, "The inhabitants of Cipango [Japan] own gold in immense quantities, and their mines are inexhaustible." Columbus, whose intended destination was this fabled island, believed he was headed for a place blessed with all the treasures of creation. Spain's royal couple decided to support this adventurous search for the sources of the Orient's wealth to free itself from the chain of middlemen and to monopolize all trade with the East. Thus the thirst for precious metals, the latter needed as exchange for the goods of the Orient, served as a prime incentive to cross the oceans with all the risks such ventures involved.

All of Europe felt a need for gold and silver. The deposits in Bohemia, Saxony, and the Tyrol were virtually depleted. Gold and silver were the keys for the men of the Renaissance to open the gates of the heavenly kingdom and to launch the mercantilistic system here on earth. Before Francisco Pizarro slit Atahualpa's throat and then had the last Inca leader beheaded, he extorted from him a ransom composed of "litters made from pure gold and silver worth more than 1.326 million thalers of purest gold." Next he turned to Cuzco and plundered its Temple of the Sun. Pizarro's soldiers smashed the precious objects of worship and hammered them flat to carry them off more easily. Finally they threw the entire treasure into a furnace to recast the precious metal into bars.

If you visit the Museo de Oro in Lima, or if you have marvelled at what little can still be seen of the ancient gold treasures in the Banco Central in Quito and Bogotá, you learn to appreciate the loss all mankind suffered with the destruction of those precious objects of art and culture. The importance of the Inca hoard was soon overshadowed by the avalanche of silver that followed. By the middle of the seventeenth century, silver alone accounted for 99 percent of all metal exports from Spanish Amer-ica. The silver Spain extracted from the New World in the first 150 years after Columbus was worth more than three times the value of all of Europe's metal reserves combined.

In the sixteenth and seventeenth centuries the "Cerro Rico" of Potosí (Bolivia) became the center of colonial commercial activity in South America. Over the course of 300 years Potosí was to devour 8 million human lives. Along with their wives and children, the Indians were uprooted from their villages and driven to the "Mountain of Silver." Of every ten natives deported to the icy heights of Potosí (16,000 feet), seven never made it back. For hundreds of miles around, the Spaniards combed the countryside in their quest for forced labor. Working conditions on the Cerro were utterly inhumane. Outside temperatures fell well below freezing, while inside the mountain the heat raged like an inferno. At night some 6,500 fires lighted the slopes of the mountain as workers took advantage of the updraft to purify the silver.

Within 6 miles of the mountain all vegetation ceased to grow because of poisonous gases in the air, deadly for fauna and flora alike. Suffering was worst inside the mines. Here the use of mercury to extract silver more efficiently produced toxic fumes that could not be vented properly and gradually poisoned the human body. Loss of hair and teeth along with uncontrollable nervous shaking were common symptoms. "Mercuried" victims dragged themselves through the streets begging for handouts.

Today Potosí (literally, "the mountain that quakes") is deserted. Burrowed into and gnawed up, as if attacked by a colony of termites, it stands as a silent memorial for other, similar events in South American history. The "Conquista" broke apart a civilization based on collectivism by destroying its leadership. But far worse than the excesses of war and conquest was the introduction of mining. It displaced populations on a massive scale and tore apart the old village communities. What remained were rootless remnants of a once coherent people, as unskilled workers little more than cheap fuel for the colonial economy.

Today I look upon these developments in a broader historical, economic, and social context. When the Spaniards arrived in South America they found themselves confronted by the mighty theocratic empire of the Incas, an empire stretching from Colombia to Chile and Argentina. Despite prolonged destruction, the magnificent culture and civilization of this people has left behind impressive testimony to its greatness. Among the evidence that has reached us one must emphasize architectural structures whose dimensions and attention to detail attest to a high level of sophistication; achievements in technology and engineering, such as irrigation systems and terrace agriculture, the remains of which we saw ourselves; transcontinental highways; and, not least, art objects of high value. In Lima's museum one can still look at hundreds of skulls that show signs of trepanning by Inca surgeons and implantations of silver and gold plates. The Incas, like the Mayas, were great astronomers, able to measure time and space with remarkable precision.

No one can deny South America's wealth in terms of raw materials: oil in Venezuela and Ecuador; natural gas in Bolivia, in the Gulf of Guayaquil, and farther down the coast; copper in Chile; tin in Bolivia; rich fishing grounds off Peru and Ecuador. There have been many attempts to unite the continent politically to enhance its economic strength. The first such effort under the Incas miscarried. Indeed, the struggle between North and South, between Huascar and Atahualpa, made the region ripe for the Spanish invasion. Simon Bolivar's grand vision of a unified and centrally ruled continent could not be realized either. Greater Colombia disintegrated into five separate countries. The great liberator died a vanquished man, confiding to General Urdenata, "We shall never be happy, never!" Urdenata's great-granddaughter passed these words on to me. Bolivar enlarged on this comment in an address to the Venezuelan Congress:

> Señores, we are neither North Americans nor Europeans. Already the Spaniards, to whom we trace our ancestry, carried in their veins a good measure of African, Arab blood. Our population has absorbed Indian elements. All of this is crucial. We respect the equality of all before the law; however, we should also be realistic enough to accept that mental and physical inequalities in our population force us in a brutal way to reflect on our situation.

Diary:

North America, February 26, 1935
We approach San Pedro, California. "All hands on deck!" A chilly breeze greets us above. Through the morning mist we hear distinctly the fog horn of the nearby lighthouse. Soon we can make out the contours of several battleships, vaguely at first, later more clearly. The flagship of the Pacific Fleet, along with several battleships, cruisers, and transports, has just returned from spring exercises. We are impressed by her massive superstructure and the odd masts that look like huge oil-drilling platforms. As we pass the entrance to the base we fire salute. Seaplanes take off and land around us. One of them is trailing a practice target. Then out of the fog emerge the shapes of torpedo-boats, and a little later the *Pennsylvania*, broad and plump in her design, from certain angles looking almost as wide as she is long.

We moor alongside a narrow pier, ahead and behind us the comfortable shuttle boats of the battleships anchoring offshore. Noisy loudspeakers direct the flow of boats and sailors. Ashore we see immense parking lots for the cars of the officers and enlisted personnel. Here every sailor who does not waste his money on drink has his own car.

What can you do in San Pedro? Not much. So we hop on the streetcar for Los Angeles, about an hour's ride. Along the way we pass the extensive oil fields of

Long Beach. From a distance they look like a scorched forest with burnt-out tree stumps everywhere. Hundreds of drilling platforms testify to the vast oil deposits below the surface. Storage tanks and refineries hug the train tracks.

We reach the suburbs of Los Angeles with its ethnic mix of Chinese, Indians, Japanese, Negroes, and whites. Without a sense of direction we stroll about downtown. Every once in a while someone will stop and talk to us, ask a question, or take us along to some site of interest. This way we begin to learn more about the huge city. What we often refer to as the "Yellow Peril" finds a different explanation in this place. The Chinese are industrious and frugal. As cheap labor they are an important factor in America's social structure.

An elevator takes us 465 feet up to the top of the tower above City Hall. Now we see the entire city in all its magnitude. Suburbs stretch all the way to the foothills of the Rocky Mountains. Hollywood with its expensive mansions stands out like a green oasis. Toward the south, toward San Pedro, likewise a bewildering sea of houses as far as the eye can see, neatly cut up by streets that run parallel to each other and create a checkerboard pattern.

In the meantime dusk is settling over the city. The skyscrapers with their illuminated facades stand out against the dark sky. Wild neon lights are everywhere along the streets of downtown. Red and green letters chase one another on commercial buildings. Floodlights play their games and brighten Los Angeles's main street, Broadway. We did not see a single bicyclist. Instead there are long lines of cars wherever you look. At intersections they grow into veritable traffic monsters. The city seems tyrannized by this traffic, only signs like "Stop" and "Go" allow for some sense of order.

There are many German clubs and associations in Los Angeles. Someone is kind enough to invite us to the German Club. Its walls are decorated with pictures of German landscapes and the words of German toasts and drinking songs. But we are struck by the fact that the receptionist does not speak German any longer, and the waitresses, even though they wear Bavarian dresses, do not understand the German language. It's the same old song: Their grandparents had come from Germany, their parents grew up bilingual. The young ones do not even know what part of Germany their grandparents lived in. During the war many were forced by public pressure to anglicize their names. Thus the United States shows a great capacity to absorb Germans in a short time. The picture is different in South America, where immigrants from northern Europe differ from the Mediterranean race and retain their unique way of life.

February 28, 1935

On my trip to Los Angeles today I became involved in a conversation with an American. First came the usual questions about Hitler and the economy of the Third Reich. He pointed out that Germany's educated circles would never recognize Hitler because of his lowly social origins. This kind of attitude had always been around throughout history, and America was no exception. For instance, Roosevelt enjoyed the confidence of the masses but not that of nation's leaders, especially in the economic sector. I replied by emphasizing Roosevelt's election successes and added that Hitler had almost 100 percent of the German people behind him. I tried to explain to him what Germany's real situation was like and that direct comparisons to the United States made little sense. Germany is searching today for her own identity and proper place among the nations of the world. Since nobody wanted to help her, she was forced to take matters into her own hands. Not surprisingly, this has provoked reactions from those who either envy or hate the Germans. These elements are very busy besmearing Germany's reputation. Sadly, they are also quite successful because they control the means to do so.

Then I told him about Germany's Voluntary Labor Service. In Germany one's career is not dependent on personal wealth but on one's character and accomplishments. My acquaintance then suggested that America, too, had labor camps where every worker was paid a dollar a day. It might not be much but certainly was better than being unemployed. At that point I decided not to pursue our conversation further, for it would have been impossible to tell this American who can think in only two dimensions—namely, comfort and business—about our ideals.

March 2, 1935

San Francisco. This is our official reception in America. A delegation of female students from the local medical school delivers a first welcome from the city in the form of a huge flower bouquet. The young women move about graciously in their blue capes, every once in a while lifting them to reveal the bright red lining underneath. An American band on the pier competes with ours for attention.

A motorcade is standing by to take us to the official reception at City Hall. Group after group is stowed away in the cars. The latter carry signs, "Visit of Cruiser *Karlsruhe*," and most fly flags on their hoods—the American one, the black-white-red [the colors of the Reich], and the swastika flag. Convertibles are decorated with bunting in the national colors. Incidentally, the signs were soon removed, even though it was planned to retain them throughout the occasion. About halfway to City Hall, on Market Street, we are suddenly passed by our commanding officer. Escorted by two police motorcycles with their sirens howling, and at high speed, his car is moving unbothered through dense traffic straight across town. That was something new for us.

While waiting for the light to change at intersections we have to listen to many spiteful comments, but most faces are friendly. Our motorcade, too, is being escorted by policemen to forestall unpleasant incidents. On all newsstands you could read the banner headlines, "3 Beaten in German Cruiser Row." Immediately upon our arrival an unfortunate incident had occurred. A U.S. naval officer, who had been mistaken for someone of our crew, was attacked by two men with anti-German attitudes before the latter could be restrained by police. This was the kind of affair the press was likely to blow out of proportion.

Several hundred yards before reaching City Hall we leave the cars. Accompanied by our band, we march in parade formation the rest of the way while large crowds of people look on. A tiny group of female honor guards awaits us outside, apparently not unaware of how comical the whole situation really is. Under shouts of "Heil!" and "Long live Germany!" we move into the spacious, domed interior of the City Hall. Up on a platform the city leaders are assembled, also delegations from the U.S. Army and Navy. Various leading citizens extend their welcome to us and express their hope that our stay will be enjoyable, especially since so many preparations went into it. Many other Germans, placed in the galleries as well as next to us, also attend the ceremony.

March 12, 1935
We sail early in the morning. Only a few friends are there to see us off. The reason for our spectacular reception in San Francisco was that the mayor needs the votes of the 60,000 Germans here in the next election. The visit of our cruiser gave him a fine opportunity to buy their support. This interpretation seems borne out by the fact that not a single newspaper wrote about the official festivities given in honor of the *Karlsruhe*. Under similar circumstances, coverage of the visit of a French cruiser filled column after column in the papers. Nevertheless, we had a jolly good time, and many people were eager to make our stay as pleasant and exciting as possible.

March 15, 1935
Vancouver. The pier is filled with waiting people, but they do not wave. The city gives us a peculiar welcome. On its way to Moose Hall, where the German colony has organized a reception, our delegation meets angry crowds and vociferous protest. The police are barely able to escort us safely to the place. It reminds me of the situation in Germany just a few years ago.

We see faces tired out by life's hardships and distorted by deep hatred. This burning fury and hatred is the product of local press reports that characterize us as representatives of the Nazi regime, a political system allegedly responsible for the degradation of workers, for the brutal execution of innocent women, for the suppression of any form of humanitarian principles. This is how the press dictates public opinion here as it does everywhere, easily manipulating the unemployed laborers from the countryside who are being swept into Vancouver during the winter months.

March 17, 1935
I am on duty. The pier is crowded with people eager to come aboard and see the ship. All alongside the cruiser policemen have erected barricades to keep the people at a distance and to allow for an orderly flow of visitors. Through some misunderstanding the gates are opened and the crowd surges forward all the way to the ship. The guard on duty at the gangway is overwhelmed by the onslaught. Six more men are sent to assist him. Linking arms, we form a semicircle around the gangway and use all our strength to keep the crowd from surging ahead. The people keep up the pressure. Women faint, children cry and are passed forward, half crushed and with mortal fear on their faces. Our shoes and trousers are wet and soiled from the dirt. Canadian police try to help out, but with little effect. Finally the gangway is pulled back onto the ship, a section of the pier is cleared, and we try again to put down the gangway. But the crowd simply will not behave in a reasonable manner. People push and shove even worse than before, all trying to be the first on board. When the supports of the gangway threaten to collapse, orders are given to call off the visitation hours. Nobody is being allowed to come aboard.

April 1, 1935
We approach the Mexican coast. Acapulco Bay swallows us with its stifling heat. One more turn and the fishing village lies directly ahead. It is small, insignificant, boring.

Today's luxury resort—in 1935 we experienced it as a collection of pitiful huts.

April 2, 1935

Reveille at 4 A.M. We are to wear our special blue uniforms and take along a bag of provisions for the twelve-hour bus trip on seats without backrests.

The vistas are quite impressive. The driver, however, seems to have gone berserk. He takes the turns in the road in the wildest manner; it's up and down, up and down. Within minutes we cover differences in altitude of several hundred yards.

The country is empty and dead except for huge cacti and eucalyptus trees. Here and there we encounter primitive human settlements. They consist of huts thatched with reeds or straw to provide some protection against the cool nights. Young children play everywhere. The road is not paved, merely covered with gravel. We have eight cars in front of us as we speed along, like a worm enveloped by a thick cloud of dust. At times the dust is so impenetrable that we cannot see anything on either side. It descends like a veil upon our special uniforms, the latter now reduced to trousers and shirts with sleeves rolled up. The heat is unbearable. Opening the windows does not seem to bring relief at all. Having passed Iguala, we are off to Taxco. The mountains become more rugged. The engines of the camións howl to meet the challenge. In front of the church in Taxco a lively market fair is under way. Hand-woven fabrics stand out with their brilliant colors. In no time we are surrounded by the local population and drawn into the milling crowd. Then a funeral procession passes by, the coffin carried by four men. Behind it is an entourage of black-veiled figures along with several guitar players. For a moment the people fall silent to honor the dead before the hustle and bustle of the market resumes as if nothing has happened.

At last, after some 280 miles on the bus, we reach Mexico City. What comes next sounds almost like a fairy tale. That same evening I can finally take a bath, followed by a long-prepared, excellent dinner, and then it's off to bed in my own guest house in the backyard. The Germans here seem to compete with one another to render our impressions as pleasant as possible. I am staying with the von Kügelgen family, a name that is certainly not unfamiliar in Germany. He is a physician, she is from Hamburg, née Countess Holk.

On April 4, on our way to the pyramids, we drive along an old dam once built by the Aztecs on a lake that is now dried up. Years ago the government advertised this project as a means to gain fertile land for agriculture. In reality they were after the treasure of the Aztecs, which according to tradition had been dumped in the lake. They never found the treasure, nor did they ever bring the land under cultivation because of an alleged lack of chemical fertilizers. The city still suffers terribly from the saltpeter dust the winds carry off from the dry lakebed.

The old sacrificial grounds of the Aztecs lie on a high plateau completely surrounded by a mountain range and guarded by the snowy summits of the Pococatepetl and the Ixtacihuatl. The ceremony conjures up images both magnificent and terrifying. It must have been an impressive sight when the various tribes in their colorful costumes took their place on the designated areas around the perimeter of the courtyard, awaiting the procession of the thousands of victims in their white gowns marked by the symbols of death, and as the latter were then dispatched, facing the winged dragon, by the familiar triangular cut. The hearts were pulled from the bodies and collected in a wide sacrificial bowl, while the dead were pushed down from the heights of the pyramid. Only a select few were awarded the status of a deity for the duration of one year. They had access to every dwelling in the city, and women considered themselves fortunate to be impregnated by these gods. Herr von Kügelgen suggests that in those days notions of racial purity may have played a role.

April 22, 1935

Along with three other cadets I am invited to eat dinner with our commanding officer in Captain Lütjens's cabin. He tells us about his experiences in the World War, especially about the fight for the jetties that protected the approaches to Zeebrugge in Belgium, an engagement whose eighteenth anniversary will be tomorrow. Zeebrugge was a U-boat base of immense strategic importance. Farther inland, in Bruges, the Germans maintained submarine repair facilities. Two canals connected Bruges with the sea, one leading to Zeebrugge, the other to Ostend. The British attack was directed against the locks at both those places. According to the plan, a cruiser was supposed to keep the German batteries on the jetties occupied while two other vessels endeavored to neutralize the locks and the port by scuttling themselves in the channel. The attack was carried out with much courage, but in the end it accomplished little.

April 26, 1935

We enter the port of Houston. A long ship channel connects Houston with the sea and its traditional port, Galveston. Ever since the channel has been deepened to accommodate ocean-going vessels, Galveston has lost much of its former business to Houston.

It is raining cats and dogs. Our commanding officer, the executive officer, and the pilot on the bridge have donned oilskin clothing. On the pier we see only a few umbrellas. In my capacity as Captain Lütjens's personal aide it is my responsibility to handle the onslaught of the press representatives, all of whom would like to interview the commanding officer personally. The captain's cabin is soon filled to capacity. The others will have to wait their turn. But we underestimate the tenacity of these seasoned reporters. Disregarding our arrangements, they enter the captain's quarters from the outer deck and through his personal study. It is not easy to get rid of them. The floor is covered with cigarette butts.

April 28, 1935

We get to know Houston a little better. Thanks to the oil business it is a growing city, but it seems to lack character. The only exception are the mansions of the oil barons in their park-like surroundings.

May 1, 1935

Today our thoughts reach out to our *Heimat* as we celebrate Labor Day. For us it is a day of honor for all working men, a visible expression of our people's com-

munity where there is no room for class hatred, where everyone respects everyone else as either a worker of the fist or a worker of the mind, and where
everyone is convinced of the contributions that the others make to society.

May 2, 1935
We undertake a trip to Galveston. At high speed we pass through the countryside in military vehicles, for we are guests of the U.S. Navy. The enormous heat
reminds us of the conditions in Mexico just a few weeks ago.

Galveston, generously designed, impresses us with its many trees, bushes,
flowers, and lawns. A wide avenue hugs the waterfront along the beach. We
stop, leave our cars, and wade into the onrushing waves, some of them as tall as
we are. This we have missed for a long time. Our hosts go out of their way to
provide entertainment for us, and we spend a pleasant time well into the night
hours.

May 4, 1935
Many Houstonians have come to take leave of us under bright, sunny skies.
Once again we follow the ship channel out into the Gulf of Mexico.

We really felt at home in Houston. The people were most hospitable and understanding. For us sailors and cadets it was so much easier to establish contact
with the local population here than in San Pedro and San Francisco. What may
explain the difference? Was there still the memory of the Civil War and the suffering it brought? We met many soldiers who had fought in the World War against
Germany and had been assigned to the occupation forces. It is well known that
after all wars the soldiers of both sides will provide the first points of contact.
Was it their influence that allowed us to find so many friends in Houston? Or was
it simply curiosity, or perhaps sympathy for what has happened in the new Germany?

May 10, 1935
Through a wall of mist and rain we get our first glimpse of Charleston, South
Carolina. Our eyes catch the huge bridge, the many piers and landings for the
fishing boats, a few small shipyards, virtually all without business. As far as we
can make out the city's skyline, there are no skyscrapers; instead, its most outstanding feature is the very tall steeple of a church.

May 11, 1935
We go ashore for the first time. A friendly American offers to take us sightseeing for an hour in his car. One hour turns out to be too short, and before we
know it we have spent the entire evening with him. The city looks almost European with its many houses from the colonial period. It also boasts one of the oldest theaters in America. It is only natural that our host points out his hometown's
brightest features: Charleston has the third-largest bridge in the world, the oldest drugstore, and the oldest "society," not to mention the most beautiful girls.

We spend the evening in a mixed company of Americans, Englishmen, and a
Frenchman. Even though the possession and sale of alcohol is strictly forbidden
in this state, we are told there is hardly a family without it. Everyone is eager to

have the best whisky. The more bloodshed and criminal cunning is involved in its procurement, the better it tastes and the stronger its effects—as we can testify ourselves, for we could hardly conceal the latter as we made our way back on board.

May 12, 1935

A German-American from Charleston who is still in command of his mother tongue takes us on a tour of the countryside. We drive for many miles without encountering a human soul. After some 60 miles we reach a small town, Walterboro. The low population density goes back to the times when the land was divided up into large plantations with slaves as the principal work force. The Methodist church is the center of town, very modest in style and decoration. The pastor is dressed in ordinary civilian clothes, with a rose in his buttonhole, and during his sermon he keeps both hands in his pockets. Behind him on a platform a group of girls in white gowns takes up formation and delights us sailors with their angels' voices. During hymns the congregation rises, during prayers the people remain seated on the pews. The women use huge fans to keep comfortable in the tremendous heat. We are glad to leave the church and enjoy a natural breeze and bright skies once again.

For lunch we are invited to the local hotel. The food is great and we listen to many speeches, including one with a rather odd conclusion, namely, that America is really a German country, not only because of the many German immigrants over the years but because the British and the Dutch came originally from Germany as well.

In the afternoon we inspect a so-called SCC (State Conservation Camp) for the unemployed. For $30 per month every man must work six hours per day, not all that different from the way it is in Germany. The remaining hours are reserved for entertainment and education. The latter is the responsibility of special instructors.

On the way back we pass through Summerville, a very attractive country town, lush green and pretty with its clean white wooden houses. By the time dusk falls we are passing through a dense forest with fog slowly settling on nearby meadows. It reminds me of the country around Oldenburg back home.

May 14, 1935

This afternoon another German-American, a Verdun veteran, takes us on a tour of Fort Sumter, one of the two forts that used to guard the entrance to Charleston. In front of the casemates of the other fort are buried the remains of the Indian chief Oneola. We are told that he had been asked by the white men to show up for some negotiations. When he did, he was arrested and later died from his treatment in captivity.

May 16, 1935

This afternoon I befriended two West Point cadets. After showing them around our vessel, we exchanged the cockades of our caps as souvenirs. One of them was the grandson of Vice Admiral Charles Wilkes, the Antarctic explorer.

Later that evening we gave our farewell party on board. Besides a number of beautiful young ladies, many German-Americans were present. When the time came to take leave, an elderly man, who had entertained us earlier with many jokes, suddenly had tears in his eyes. As if in a hurry to leave the ship, he shook everyone's hand and disappeared into the night.

May 18, 1935

The signal flag "A" for America comes down; instead we set "E" for Europe. It is not easy to leave America behind, especially the personal friendships that have grown over the weeks that we spent here. But America and Germany are also very different in many ways. The Americans are a people with a brief history and few traditions. Their rugged individualism characterizes the entire population and determines the political system. Ethnically, America represents an almost incredible mix, but it has produced men that are handsome, strong and healthy, good-natured and hospitable.

How one-sided this judgment was, and to what extent I had to correct it, I learned when I spent a longer period of time in the United States from 1958 to 1961.

May 22, 1935

Our forecastle and quarter deck are awash from the heavy breakers of an angry sea. It is difficult to concentrate on our course of instruction, as benches and tables are constantly in motion. Not a ray of light penetrates into our living quarters, and the air is stale.

In the evening we listen to a Führer address, but because of poor radio conditions we pick up only fragments of his speech. These days of tremendous change in Germany's military posture are the backdrop before which the Führer reassures feverish world opinion in a speech before the Reichstag of his and Germany's unwavering commitment to peace. The speech is based on a simple premise: We will disarm to the last man as long as everyone else does likewise. Since nobody except us seems prepared for such a step, it was a matter of our honor and security, not to mention the danger of a power vacuum in central Europe, for us to rearm. We will not reduce our present strength by a single soldier. The Führer leaves open the question of offensive weapons, such as heavy tanks, bombers, and submarines, which should be limited by international agreement. The fleet will be restricted to 35 percent of that of the Royal Navy. Another naval race is out of the question. Germany recognizes England's hegemony at sea. Germany's interests are decidedly continental in scope.

May 31, 1935

Today we celebrate the anniversary of the Battle of Jutland. The old and our new service flags are hoisted together, symbolizing the common attitude and spirit that unite the former and the new Navy. The commanding officer in his address talks about the Battle of Jutland, the mightiest clash of battle fleets ever, and how the invincibility of the British fleet was reduced to a mere myth. Then he speaks about the Red Revolution—so painful and humiliating because it started in the Navy—before the deed of Scapa Flow, where Admiral Ludwig von

Reuter scuttled the German fleet just as it was to be handed over to the British, restored the honor of the German Navy.

June 10, 1935
At last we enter German territorial waters. The *Heimat* greets us with an impressive display of sheet-lightning over the horizon. For a long time we sit together on the forecastle, taking in the warm smell of hay and earth wafting toward us from the coast. We have missed it for so long. It reminds me of springtime in the Lüneburg Heath, where I grew up. Another cadet next to me thinks it may have been the soothing smell of fir trees in the Harz Mountains. Then, suddenly, the wind freshens up, the tide begins to roll in, and the sea stirs as rival currents vie for dominance. A heavy thunderstorm chases us below.

June 15, 1935
We enter the Holtenau locks at Kiel. The commanding admiral of the Baltic Station extends his official welcome. Then comes the moment everyone has been waiting for, as we leave the locks, enter Kiel Bay, and hoist our home pennant. Unfortunately, the latter comes loose and is carried off by the wind. Slowly, majestically, we swing around into the great naval base. Things look very different from last year. In the Wik we see the pocket battleship *Scheer* and also the *Gorch Fock*. I remember very well the morning a year ago when we had to climb up to the top yards and bring out three hurrahs when the *Karlsruhe* returned from an earlier cruise.

One after another we pass the cruisers *Leipzig* and *Königsberg*, the pocket battleship *Deutschland*, and the old *Schleswig-Holstein*, all moored to large buoys in the bay, and exchange hurrahs with all of them. Many small and even odd vessels, such as the replica of a Hanseatic cog, have come out to greet us. Flags are everywhere. Hundreds of yachts and smaller sailing boats enliven the waters around us. The Hindenburgdamm and the Blücherbrücke are packed with people as we finally moor across from the Fourth Torpedo-boat Squadron. Hurrahs and shouts of *"Sieg Heil"* echo back and forth. Our band strikes up and plays its most arousing pieces.

From the forward platform I enjoy a wonderful view over the whole affair. Everyone is trying to pick out familiar faces in the crowd. Waving arms and hands indicate successful contacts. Soon the gangway is in place and the reunions can begin. In our living quarters we practice a miniature *Flagge Luci*. We put on our blue uniforms, and then it's down the gangway straight into my mother's arms. Everyone tries to get away from the crowds and start talking about our adventures. There are enough stories to last for days, and we have many grateful listeners. Many of us believe that day in Kiel was the most exciting one of our voyage; certainly it was among the most memorable.

Comment:

The midshipman cruise had several purposes. It (1) familiarized us with the functions of a warship over a long period of time and under unusual climatic conditions far from home; (2) brought a class of cadets to-

gether, through strict discipline and service requirements as well as the
daily sharing of life in cramped quarters, as a genuine band of comrades,
Crew 34; (3) acquainted us with foreign peoples, customs, and cultures;
and (4) made us representatives and ambassadors of the new Germany.

The last-mentioned objectives were especially challenging, and we did
not always live up to them. We rarely established real contact with foreign nationals because of our obligations toward the local German colonies. San Francisco alone had seventy-five such organizations. For the
most part they consisted of simple people with limited horizons, hardly
equipped to further our education about the world abroad. We simply
lacked the basis—beyond the superficial data sheets handed to us in
every port—to learn about and assess the various economies, customs,
and cultures in a proper way.

The image of the Germany we thought we knew and wanted to represent seemed badly distorted through propaganda, especially in North
America. Our efforts to clarify the record had to remain limited. The successes of the National Socialist leadership—for instance, the reintroduc-
tion of conscription in the armed forces and the Anglo-German Naval
Agreement, both of which occurred during our midshipman cruise and
were positively commented upon by our superiors—rendered it difficult
for us to shed our own national bias. We soon realized how restricted our
contributions to rectify political imbalances had to remain. We therefore
chose to make the best impression possible by appearing well-mannered
and friendly. In addition we enjoyed the generosity of our hosts, sam-
pled life under faraway skies, and kept on dreaming of our exotic adventures even when the hard work at sea called us back to life's realities.

Other Commands:

After attending the Marineschule Mürwik, Germany's Naval Academy, in 1935 and 1936, I was posted once again to the cruiser *Karlsruhe*,
this time as aide-de-camp (ADC) and second torpedo officer. My new
commanding officer was Captain Leopold Siemens, our executive officer
Captain Hans-Georg von Friedeburg. The latter had just completed a
stint as naval ADC to Reich Defense Minister Werner von Blomberg and
thus enjoyed good connections to the leaders of the Wehrmacht as well
as the Party.

One day the Minister paid us a visit. There were the usual ceremonies,
and Friedeburg received Blomberg in a most cordial way. As ADC I was
allowed to attend the subsequent dinner in the officers' wardroom, sitting at the far end of the table. Under the table electric buttons had been
installed. It was my responsibility to signal to the band outside what
kind of music would be appropriate at any given moment, such as light
and entertaining tunes, marching music, or the national anthem. Blom-

berg and Friedeburg were engaged in very intense conversation. I could not hear what it was all about. Even our commanding officer was allowed to make only an occasional comment.

For a while the *Karlsruhe* functioned as a target vessel for our submarines. To observe and judge the progress of the boats properly, the commander-in-chief of Germany's U-boat forces, Captain Karl Dönitz, embarked on our vessel. I even had to vacate my cabin so he could use it instead. As a watch officer on the bridge I had many opportunities to talk to Dönitz about U-boat technology and tactics. From my interest in the matter he could gather that I was eager, as were so many of my comrades, to serve on submarines.

One year later I received my orders to transfer to the U-boat branch.

PARTICIPATION IN THE SPANISH CIVIL WAR

On December 27, 1936, the *Karlsruhe* raised steam and sailed for Spanish waters.

The turmoil in Spain was felt far and wide. For a long time, and for many different reasons, Europe's diplomats had striven to contain the conflagration to the source of the fire. All seafaring nations had dispatched parts of their fleets to Iberian waters. So we became part of a broader effort as we went south to rescue from the relentless civil war between Whites and Reds the lives and property of German nationals trapped in Spain and to safeguard German trade interests. These tasks meant being constantly alert and watchful, besides requiring much hard work.

Diary:

It is January, and the heavy swell of a forever stormy Bay of Biscay threatens to wear us out, as for days—sometimes weeks—we patrol the coast of northern Spain. Only rarely do we get a break and anchor on the roadsteads of La Coruña or Zarauz. On those occasions we tend to be beleaguered by smaller Spanish vessels whose crews demonstrate their unlimited sympathy for Germany by displaying the swastika flag or by hailing us with shouts of *"Viva Alemania."*

As we see it, Spain stands in the forefront of a struggle for all of Europe. The main protagonist in this drama is the Army. It has taken over the functions of the government until law and order can be restored to the country. In the new Spain the Army will continue to act as the state's main source of support. As General Emilio Mola has put it, the Army is the model for the whole nation as the guarantor of honor, tradition, and love for the fatherland. The Army collaborates closely with the *Falange Española*, founded in 1933 by Antonio Primo de Rivera and akin to the fascist movement in Italy. It is estimated that some 100,000 Falangists have joined the fight at the front. Their supporters come primarily from

Spain's working class. For a long time these Falangists have attracted the special hatred of the Reds. Thousands of them were held as hostages in prisons throughout the country. Only few escaped. Most, among them their leaders, perished in the bloody terror. Since those days the leadership of the *Falange* has vowed to support the military dictatorship unconditionally while retaining their desire to reshape the new Spain in the image of their movement once hostilities cease.

A second strong group are the Carlists, easily identified by their blue jackets and red caps. They consider themselves the guardians of Spain's Catholic traditions and insist on straight legitimacy in dynastic matters. They trace their origins to the year 1833, when King Ferdinand VII refused his brother the succession to the throne and instead picked his daughter Isabella. Today the Carlists make common cause with the Nationalists mainly because they resent the destruction of churches and monasteries by the Reds. Their main strength is in Navarre, home to the Basques, an old tribe of independence-loving freedom fighters. Navarre was once the base from which the Moors were driven south, and neither Charlemagne nor Napoleon could ever control it completely. Now some 70,000 of these Carlists have placed themselves at the disposal of General Mola. They demand an absolutist monarchy and Catholicism as the state religion. The rest of the Nationalists are sympathizers drawn from a variety of camps, such as the *Renovación Española*, the aristocracy, conservatives, the liberal bourgeoisie, and the clergy.

Spain is beginning a new and most promising chapter in her rich and varied history. But in between the machine guns and snooping patrols armed with rifles and bayonets, Spain lives out, seemingly unbothered, her ancient cultural life with its traditional manners and customs.

Off Gibraltar

We finally leave northern Spain behind and proceed southward. It is a hot and sunny day, like most we have experienced in these latitudes. Far to port we can make out the coastline of Portugal. As we pass Cape St. Vincent and Cape Trafalgar we must think of the great British naval heroes John Jervis and Horatio Nelson, whose fame is forever linked to these places.

At dawn we find ourselves off Gibraltar. On our starboard quarter the sharp contours of Monkey Mountain stand out against the morning sky. Gibraltar: This has indeed been a crucial crossroads of history. In my imagination I see the ancient Phoenicians arrive here, cast a knowing glance around, and then take possession of this geostrategically vital place. Later, Carthaginians and Romans fight bitterly for its possession. Germanic tribes are next and then the Moors, drawing one another back and forth across the straits. Eventually the British come in and with a decisive hand take control of the rock, perfect its fortifications, and make it the center of their worldwide network of strongpoints.

Such historical contemplations can easily distract from the sheer natural attractiveness of this massive mountain fortress. Looking at Gibraltar across mirror-like waters barely stirred by the early tide, and only faintly illuminated as it is under the light-embroidered clouds of the breaking day, one marvels at the beauty of the place and forgets entirely its military mission. I am also reminded of the year 1782 when troops from my native Hanover were instrumental in helping defend Gibraltar against French and Spanish attackers. At the time, Britain and Hanover shared a common ruling dynasty. When a mutiny in the Royal Navy broke out, Britain's enemies saw their chance to retake the rock. Hanoverian troops thwarted such designs, and their British commander, General George Eliot, paid them the ultimate tribute: "They fought so bravely that you might have mistaken them for British soldiers."

Comment:

I already mentioned that besides Germany other nations, such as France, England, and Italy, dispatched naval units to Spain to protect their respective interests. In early May 1937 the pocket battleship *Deutschland* paid Gibraltar a visit. In her honor the entire British Mediterranean Fleet put on a parade off Algeciras, involving some 30,000 officers and sailors altogether. Among others, Admiral Dudley Pound, in overall command of the British Fleet, and Rear Admiral Bruce Fraser, whose task force would later in 1943 sink the *Scharnhorst* in the Arctic Ocean, paid their respect to the commander of the German pocket battleships, Rear Admiral Max von Fischel. A squad of Scottish Guards and Royal Marines joined a detachment from the *Deutschland* to commemorate the Hanoverians who had given their lives in 1782. After a roll of the drum, a horn player intoned the British signal honoring the dead. Then a band played both the German and British national anthems, as well as the *Lied vom guten Kameraden* (a popular German dirge). This happened two years before the outbreak of World War II.

Diary:

The entire Spanish people endures many sacrifices for its soldiers. Nationalist Spain is marked by its commitment to the war. Everyone places himself at the service of the nation, well aware of the seriousness of the situation and the historic significance of the hour.

Jewelry and other items made from precious metals have long since been collected, golden wedding bands traded in for iron ones. Women and girls work hard in their communities for the men at the front. But even more essential than the material support is their solidarity with the fighting troops. The man in the trenches knows the loved ones back home feel just the way he does. He knows there is no rejoicing, no dancing at home as long as he is away.

The people shows itself worthy of its warriors. Young people, even if invited, refuse to visit the theater or the movies with the simple explanation that they have agreed to take upon themselves a *sacrificio*, a vow not to enjoy themselves until Madrid has fallen. Men and women voluntarily absorb these burdens; they watch out and pray for those at the front. Young women in the hospitals serve as nurses for wounded Spaniards and Moroccans. The soldier at the front knows he is respected, cared for, and loved by those back home. That gives him the strength to go on.

Victoria de Málaga

Long delayed by rainy weather, the major land, sea, and air offensive against Málaga got under way at last and led within days to a decisive victory for the Nationalist troops.

In El Ferrol we witness the immense release of joy and relief this victory brought to the entire country. The national colors, red-yellow-red, decorate the facade of every house. Detachments of the regular *Falange* and its youth organization, the *Flechas*, carry out a parade down the city's main street. After nightfall, uncounted lighted arches illuminate the Calle de General Franco. Until now, such celebrations had been out of the question for fear of aerial attacks, but today all caution is thrown to the wind. The narrow lanes are filled with joyous celebrants. Everyone is waiting for the great *manifestación*. The first formations arrive with bands playing and flags flying. Hours pass before all the units have marched past the commander in chief of the Nationalist Spanish Navy and El Ferrol's city commandant. The people get carried away, run into the streets, and hug the soldiers. There is laughing, crying, and dancing everywhere as the crowds march alongside the troops. The night is turned into day; the jubilation goes on for days.

I also came into contact with the men who have been out there winning these battles for Spain, men who will take their place where the fighting is fiercest and who have yet to lose a single battle. They are the *legiónarios*, the members of the Spanish Legion: daredevils all of them, haggard, deeply tanned by the sun and weather, men whose faces betray no emotion as they march down the streets and past the frenzied masses around them.

Never will I forget the look on these exhausted, weather-worn faces. There was much you could read in their facial expressions: contempt, hatred, fanaticism. The men had acquired these traits through years of harsh, unrelenting discipline in Morocco's desert sands, in the sun-baked rocky wilderness of North Africa. Their eyes betrayed the unscrupulousness and horror that only those encounter who are part of an everlasting struggle.

Some officers of the Legion are scions of the old Moorish aristocracy, their profiles almost classical in their lines. Not one of them has been wounded fewer than three times. They talk about their bloody duels with bayonets and knives in a manner so matter-of-fact and detached that it strikes the listener as almost eerie. Struggle is their life, and nobody dares resist when they attack singing their feared battle song, the *Canción de la Legión*. Never once did I hear one of the legionnaires join in the cheers all around them, to shout *"Arriba España,"* or something similar. All the more harsh and fanatical sounds their triple battle cry: *"Arriba la Legión! Arriba la guerra! Arriba la muerte!"*

War is their life. One day Spain will be deeply grateful and indebted to her last band of mercenaries.

Comment:

This is how we experienced the Spain whose side we had taken. Today we know the other side as well, its ordeal made manifest in Ernest Hemingway's book, *For Whom the Bell Tolls*. The split between the two

Spains, straight through country and people, continued throughout Franco's regime.

What the diary fails to mention is that the *Karlsruhe* searched and seized the freighter *Aragon*, bound for a Red port. We towed her into El Ferrol. That was our only and utterly unbloody action in the war.

To add a different voice to this commentary on the Spanish Civil War, I would like to reprint an excerpt from a letter my Crew comrade Hermann Rasch wrote to me on June 13, 1937. He was then serving on the pocket battleship *Scheer*, which had just bombarded the city of Almería in southern Spain in retaliation for a Republican air attack against the *Deutschland*:

Do you want an eye-witness report of our attack on Almería? The newspapers state there were 19 casualties. Ridiculous! I personally saw how multi-storied buildings collapsed in smoke and dust, among them fully occupied military barracks. Nothing but bare walls were left, and that after only half a salvo! The effect of the 11-inch shells with contact detonators turned out to be more amazing than I had imagined. As assistant artillery officer I could observe everything at close range through a telescope. We fired almost 200 rounds. Only four salvoes fell short into the water, all the others were hits. There was nothing heroic about the whole affair even though the enemy returned our fire sporadically. But then we only had to think of the *Deutschland* to feel good about every house we blew up. I shall never forget the peaceful picture this city offered before we opened fire. Despite the distance you got the feeling that everyone was still asleep and in for a terrible awakening. The sun had barely risen so that towers and walls cast long shadows. Beyond Almería rose the quiet, snow-covered peaks of the Sierra Nevada, on the other side the outline of our torpedo-boats black against the bright red eastern sky. Later the entire bay was engulfed in a gray-brown cloud.

The bombardment proceeded without incident, very professional and with a sure hand. We were almost certain that enemy aircraft would attack us, but all remained calm. Hannes Perl [also of our Crew 34] chased off two enemy patrol boats with our 8.8-cm guns, sinking one and forcing the other to run aground.

Since then we have been practicing general quarters almost ad nauseam, except for three days' rest at Tangier. Tangier is a dirty provincial place, but since I encounter oriental enchantment here for the first time, I should not complain. If you have visited here you are probably familiar with the "Chat Noir" and other abominations. It is almost amazing to realize how many varieties of such nasty things these Southerners are capable of. Conditions on board are terrible since the commander in chief of the pocket battleships and his staff have embarked. As I had feared for some time, I now have to share my quarters with three other lieutenants. We are expected to return home around June 25 for twelve days of refit. After that we will engage in gunnery practice and joint exercises with other units (I hear the *Karlsruhe*

will be one of them) before we sail once again for the Mediterranean on
August 1.

Today we read this eyewitness account of the bombardment of Almería
with quite different sensibilities. We know how many civilians, among
them women and children, perished in the attack. This act of revenge
was an act of terror, for it was primarily directed against helpless civilians
rather than military targets.

At the same time it seems appropriate in this context to correct the
myth of Guernica—immortalized in Pablo Picasso's famous painting as
the ultimate symbol of human suffering and genocide. The aircraft of the
Condor Legion attacked the main military targets—the bridge, the
streets, and a suburb that had become a part of the battlefield. But then,
he who has seen the truth knows how many lies are spread in its name.

The excerpts from my journal—are they mere ciphers from a world
now forever gone? The reflections they offer of the drama of life in those
days are full of color and yet seem dreamlike when measured against political preoccupations of our times. But one cannot judge the past by the
standards of the present lest the laws of history lose all meaning. Franz
Kafka commented on this problem in December 1911: "Diaries are proof
positive that in the past we lived under conditions which seem intolera-
ble to us today, indeed, that we analyzed and recorded them."

In 1974 I visited my friend Thomas de Liniers in Madrid. We had first
met in San Diego at the Senior Officers' Course for Amphibious Warfare.
At the time Thomas was about to take command of all Spanish forces in
Ceuta.

He took me to El Valle de los Caidos, the memorial erected to honor
the victims of the Civil War. Located in a park in the breathtaking mountain scenery of the Guadarrama, the compound consists of a huge basil-
ica hewn into the rock. An immense cross, some 500 feet high, is
perched on top of a promontory. At its base stand statues of the four
apostles sculpted from blackish limestone. Inside the dome, which itself
has a height of 142 feet and is decorated with mosaics, there is another
tall cross. It is made from unfinished tree trunks that Franco personally
selected for this purpose. The cross and my conversation with Thomas
brought home to me how closely kitsch and true emotion come together
in this place. Thomas is the scion of an old family—in fact, a destroyer in
the Spanish Navy is named the *Liniers*—and served as a young officer in
the Civil War. Captured by the Reds, he was cruelly mistreated, somehow managed to survive the war, and eventually became a monarchist
and democrat. But he made it very clear to me that "Spain will turn Red
again only over my dead body."

He had taken up arms, not to fight against the Republic but because the Republicans wanted to stop being Catholic, as their leader Manuel Azaña put it. I am sure Thomas did not imply in this statement that the Republic had been destroying the cultural values of the Christian West, which Spain has always cherished as much as any country. Rather, he saw these values in danger when the Marxist-anarchist left lashed out brutally against priests and monasteries. He himself, having become commanding general of the Spanish Army, paid a visit to the tomb of the Apostle James in the cathedral of Santiago de Compostela to put forth the nation's concerns in a prayer—as was prescribed by the Army regulations.

Many people refer to Franco's regime as having been fascist. That is incorrect, for fascism is marked by the following: (1) a dictator, recognized as the nation's leader; (2) a one-party system; (3) a totalitarian regime that controls all public and political activities; (4) no division of powers into different branches of government; and (5) the successful attempt by the all-powerful party to bring about a national consensus through persuasion and force.

Not one of these characteristics, in my view, applies to Franco's regime. Franco had no "totalitarian" party totally committed to his goals. Neither the Falangists nor the Carlists were led by him. Only the *Falange* met the criteria outlined above. But for them Franco was merely the *"Generalissimo."* They accepted his temporary dictatorship as a measure necessitated by the war. For them he did not represent the leader of a people's movement, nor was the union of the Falangists and the Carlists more than a marriage of convenience. What we experienced as national enthusiasm was false and superficial. It was not typical of the situation, certainly not during the Civil War. Franco never "mobilized" the people in any real sense of the word. In fact, the conscripts deserted in droves, as the example of the Battle of Guadalajara demonstrates clearly.

After the Civil War Franco presided over a conservative system built on a hierarchical order in which the military and the Church, along with syndicalist organizations, played dominant roles. For this regime to have been fascist, all power would have had to rest in one totalitarian party. Franco further developed middle-class enterprise, encouraged innovation and modernization in Spain's economy, and thus created the preconditions under which his country first moved toward and later joined the European Community.

But one must not forget the other side. Many great minds, among them the representatives of Spain's second "Golden Age" after the halcyon days of Cervantes and Lope de Vega, either emigrated or were murdered. I am thinking of men like Garcia Lorca, Machado, Jiménez, Alberti, Diego, and Guillén. Lorca, the great lyricist, once wrote a poem entitled *El Grito* (The Cry). It stands for the age-old suffering and the echo of all the cries forever silenced for which Spain's past has provided so many terrible occasions: from the history of the Iberian Celts to the Romans, the Goths, the Moors, the exodus of Spain's Jews, the auto-da-fés, the Conquistadors, and, not least, the Civil War.

Even today the memory of the Civil War divides the Spanish people, although both sides have reached a symbolic reconciliation as they honor all its victims in El Valle de los Caidos. The armed forces followed Franco's successor, King Juan Carlos, as their new Captain-General. Juan Carlos in turn moved away from Franco's authoritarian regime to a western-style democracy. For my friend Liniers, Spain's membership in the North Atlantic Treaty Organization (NATO) was the logical consequence of her traditional mission, namely, to defend Christian and western values.

Part of the self-image of Spain's armed forces holds that they prevented, through their victory in the Civil War, a political takeover by a victorious Stalin and French-supported Spanish Communists after World War II. Proud self-consciousness and long traditions characterize Spain's armed forces to this day, not to mention popular support. To become an officer in the Spanish Army is not easy. There are many more applicants than vacancies.

EARLY U-BOAT DAYS

On October 5, 1937, I reported to the U-boat School in Neustadt on the Baltic Sea. Dönitz had arranged for my transfer, and for me it was a dream come true. The dream soon turned into hard reality.

When I embarked on a submarine for the first time I felt as though I had stepped into a different world. I remembered having read in some book on Navy regulations that "living together aboard a vessel under cramped conditions requires the highest consideration for the needs of superiors and comrades." Not that life aboard a surface ship could be compared with a stay at a fancy hotel, but by comparison it was difficult to suppress a sense of claustrophobia when confronted with the confined space of a U-boat. In addition, you were forever exposed to terrible, penetrating diesel fumes and stale, humid air, to say nothing of the odors that came from the boat's galley and the perspiration of sweaty human bodies. This is what the U-boat of my imagination looked like in reality. The dream burst like a bubble. Otherwise we became quite aware that the submarine was an effective weapon system, quantitatively as yet only a small and insignificant part of the fleet, but in our eyes a well-sharpened sword when compared to other units in our naval arsenal. We got used to the more unpleasant sides of life aboard a U-boat more quickly than we had first feared. Indeed, eventually the atmosphere became so familiar to us that we could hardly wait, for example after a longer refit in a shipyard, to get back on board.

One of the participants in the submarine officers' course was Engelbert Endrass. He became my best friend until his death in December 1941, and the memory of our friendship has enriched my life ever since.

The course lasted until June 1, 1938. Since at that point no boat was available on which I could serve as a watch officer, the Navy posted me from June 2 until September 25 as an instructor and platoon leader to the teaching division for petty officers at Kiel-Friedrichsort. My commanding officer was First Lieutenant Harro Kloth von Heydenfeldt, a fine man all around and a model in terms of attitudes and professional ability. He, too, joined the submarine branch and was one of the first submarine commanders lost in World War II when his boat went down in the English Channel.

Another platoon leader besides me was my Crew comrade Werner Weinlig, a native of Cape Town in South Africa. He managed to invest our small officers' mess with a semblance of the generous lifestyle he had known in his homeland. Both of these officers embodied an inner independence that enabled them to be critical of existing conditions in a constructive way. They exhibited self-discipline on the one hand, and civil courage on the other. To work with them was a privilege and marked an important phase in my life.

On September 26, 1938, I at last embarked as a watch officer on *U 46* of the 7th U-Boat Squadron based in Kiel. My commanding officer was Lieutenant Commander Herbert Sohler, our squadron leader Commander Ernst Sobe. Our group eventually produced a number of well-known names, including Günter Prien, Herbert Schultze, Engelbert Endrass, and Reinhard Suhren. In that last year of peace we underwent a hard and demanding training schedule. We were under way literally day and night, exercising alone or with other units, testing our weapons, and perfecting our tactics. When the Sudetenland crisis broke, we were ready to sail on a moment's notice.

All the while we also found time for fun and games. At one point I assumed responsibility for organizing a party for the whole squadron ashore. There would be speeches and poems that made fun of our superiors in good humor, along with music and dancing. Everything had to be arranged and tried out during the few hours of liberty we enjoyed after the boats arrived from their daily exercises. The party turned out to be a full success. After the official program we congregated around the bar, totally exhausted. Certainly our alcohol consumption contributed to our condition. All I remember is that I woke up from a deep sleep at 5 A.M. the next morning in a small room not far from the bar. I immediately called a taxi and barely made it back to our boat in time for that day's activities. My good friend Ohm Krüger was not so fortunate. We could see him desperately running down the pier, his cape blowing in the wind, just moments after the boats had gotten under way. He spent the day aboard our tender, or mother ship, the *Hamburg*. This episode cost him a six-month delay in promotion.

Apropos the *Hamburg*. "Mother ship" is hardly the proper term to characterize that vessel. "Casemate" or "prison" seems more appropriate. Our quarters, each six feet by six feet, stretched out along a miserable corridor. A porthole provided but little natural light. The walls were made from sheet metal so thin that you could hear your neighbors all the time, no matter how quiet they tried to be. In the wintertime a central heating system based on hot steam was supposed to keep us comfortable, but the quarters were either hot as hell, or, if you were gone for any length of time on one of the submarines and looked forward to some rest and warmth, you could find your room completely iced up. When you turned on the system, the superheated air moved quickly through the pipes, sounding like the rattling of a machine gun. The noise awakened those who were asleep without mercy, and since there was a constant coming and going of men, you virtually never got any rest.

3

War

Between 1983 and 1986, I along with other members of my Crew corresponded with Eric C. Rust, the son of a former German naval officer, who was then collecting material for his doctoral dissertation, "Crew 34: German Naval Officers under and after Hitler." His questions and my replies to them have helped me gain a sounder perspective and understanding of those years.

Question: How would you describe the political, intellectual, and private atmosphere in which you grew up in the 1920s?

Answer: The political atmosphere, as far as we experienced it at school, was in line with the ideology of the German National People's Party (or DNVP). Our history teacher, who influenced us considerably, belonged to the *Stahlhelm* (the veterans' organization of the DNVP). Our history textbook, the *Plötz*, dealt almost entirely with wars. We had to learn everything about victories, army tactics and grand strategy, armistices, coalitions. In our imagination we marched all over the continent, became prisoners of war, blockaded enemy shores, and so on. The state reigned absolute. The age of German idealism had endowed war and warfare with mythological qualities. Our entire school solemnly commemorated the anniversaries of Prussia's victory over France at Sedan in 1870 and of the Battle of the Nations at Leipzig in 1813. We knew the details of every single battle Frederick the Great fought in his life. We learned virtually nothing about his philosophical contemplations, his book *Anti-Machiavel,* or his contributions to the organization of the Prussian state.

Our intellectual interests revolved around twentieth-century philosophy, notably Nietzsche who had destroyed all values of old: philosophy,
religion, theology. What was left was a nihilistic world, a void, which for
us young people was soon being filled with pseudo-values such as race
and nationalism.

My parents rejected political commitments and stressed humanitarian
ideas and toleration instead. My father was a Free Mason and thus was
open to all kinds of political currents without taking definite stands or
imposing a particular ideology upon me.

Question: Did you welcome Hitler's seizure of power in early 1933?
Answer: Yes. We hoped Hitler's takeover would annul the Treaty of
Versailles and initiate a time of national renewal.

Question: To what extent did you feel attracted and/or repulsed by the
ideology and practice of National Socialism?
Answer: The answer to this question depends on the time period under
consideration. In 1934, when I joined the Navy, I could only see how
Germany was moving forward economically, in domestic matters, and in
foreign affairs as well. Criticism set in later.

Question: At what point did you become convinced that Germany
would be involved in a war before long?
Answer: We had always believed Hitler would live up to his promises of
peaceful intentions. This implied he would do everything to restore our
national honor while avoiding war at all costs.

Question: How do you recall September 1, 1939, and how did you respond to the news that the western powers had entered the war?
Answer: September 1, 1939, was no day of jubilation for us, in contrast
to the outbreak of World War I. We were aware of our weaknesses from
the beginning, notably in the Navy. Everyone knew it would be a long
war.

Question: Did it happen frequently that you as an officer found yourself in a conflict between duty and conscience?
Answer: The conflict between duty and conscience arose for me in 1943
when Germany continued the U-boat war despite immense losses and
without the slightest prospects of success.

Question: Did you at any time believe the Navy should have openly opposed the excesses of National Socialism?
Answer: During the war our only concern was to win it. We accepted
restrictions of our personal freedoms to reach this goal, just as other na-

tions have in the past. Only after the war did I learn of the excesses and crimes of the National Socialism.

Question: How would you describe your personal and family life before and during the war?
Answer: We lived according to the motto, "He who dedicates himself to the Prussian flag retains nothing that is his own."

Question: What do (did) you think of officers and civilians who participated in the resistance movement against Hitler?
Answer: We fought at sea. During the first part of the war I did not see Germany at all. We operated out of St. Nazaire in France. Whatever information we received was restricted to the media of radio and newspapers—all, of course, censored. For that reason we knew nothing about a resistance movement. Consequently, on July 20, 1944, we were not only surprised but considered the plot a stab in the back of us fighting soldiers.

Question: How do (did) you judge German naval planning in the prewar era, and what is your opinion about the strategy and tactics Germany adopted during the war?
Answer: German naval planning was in line with the Anglo-German Naval Agreement of 1935 and based on the political assurance that no war with Britain would break out. When war came, the Reich was so unprepared for a war at sea that it could only needle the enemy but never critically hurt him.

To exercise sea power you need a fleet and a favorable geostrategic location. Germany had neither. Not until the occupation of France and Norway did we gain brighter prospects of success for the limited forces at our disposal. Given these improved preconditions, our units tried to do maximum damage to the enemy and in some cases achieved that objective.

Naval construction for a long time went down the wrong track by concentrating on large surface vessels. The so-called Z-Plan, which was never realized, shows how gigantic but unrealistic such planning was. Only when Dönitz succeeded Raeder as supreme naval commander did U-boat construction gain priority status, but by then it was much too late.

Question: How did you react to the attack against the Soviet Union and the subsequent entry of the United States into the war?
Answer: The attack against the Soviet Union hit me like a shock. Everything that history had exposed as disastrous, for instance in Napoleon's times, now came together: a two-front war and the overextension of our

limited resources. The Russian campaign was the beginning of the end, not to mention the entry of the United States into the war, which gave the Allies a material superiority of catastrophic consequences for the German side.

Question: From what point on did you consider a German victory illusory?

Answer: From the point when the Allies produced more merchant vessels than the German Navy was able to sink, that is, when Allied new construction exceeded losses at sea.

Question: What accomplishment during the war makes you particularly proud?

Answer: The fact that I led a crew who, despite constantly walking that thin line between life and death, never showed the slightest sign of disloyalty.

Question: In your view, what contributed the most to Germany's defeat?

Answer: The hubris of her leaders.

Question: Under what circumstances could Germany have triumphed at sea?

Answer: Under no circumstances. Naval supremacy rested unquestionably with the Allies.

Question: Do you think Germany should have surrendered earlier to the Allies instead of fighting on to the bitter end?

Answer: The Allied demand for unconditional surrender made an answer to this question at the time very difficult, if not impossible.

Question: How would you describe your political views since the war?

Answer: I am not bound to a particular political party. I am open to the challenges posed by new developments in science and technology without losing sight of the values we have rescued from the past into the present. In this sense I consider myself conservative.

Question: Did you reproach yourself after the war for having served the National Socialist regime?

Answer: This question makes little sense to me. In retrospect I cannot reproach myself for having served the National Socialist regime without knowledge of its crimes and considering that it had assumed power legally.

Question: Do you think German and international historiography since 1945 has come close to capturing your personal experiences and feelings as an officer in the *Kriegsmarine?*

Answer: This is a broad question. I am presently a military consultant to Bavarian State Radio for a program entitled "The Second World War." In this program I discuss various aspects of the war with journalists like Sebastian Haffner and historians such as Gerhard Weinberg of the University of North Carolina at Chapel Hill, Claus von Schubert, Andreas Hillgruber, Eberhard Jäckel, Manfred Messerschmidt, and others. I have also read very carefully the publications about the war at sea by Professor Michael Salewski, as well as more general works about German history by Professors Hellmut Diwald, Andreas Hillgruber, and Michael Stürmer. In discussing and reading about modern history I have noticed again and again how closely my own views coincide with the opinions of these experts.

Question: Which German naval traditions seem antiquated to you and perhaps even harmful? Which ones should be continued under all circumstances?

Answer: For me, tradition means the continuation of crucial intellectual and spiritual currents. Tradition should not be reduced to the practice of naming, say, destroyers or military barracks after certain historical personalities. Such superficial links are of little significance.

EXECUTIVE OFFICER, *U 46*

Diary:

March 1940

It is bitingly cold and the ice several feet thick. An icebreaker has us in tow. We watch anxiously as the floes come together again in its wake, crash against our reinforced bows, and move along the hull, all the while creating an infernal noise throughout the boat.

There are three of us as we transfer from the shipyard to the naval base. First comes Günter Prien's *U 47* of Scapa Flow fame, proudly sporting the symbol of a bull on its conning tower. Next is Curt von Gossler's *U 49*, off to her second patrol after the first time out she almost succumbed to a British U-boat trap and had to spend a long time refitting. And finally comes our *U 46*, by now the veteran of three patrols and so far nothing but bad luck. As if reborn, we leave the caring hands of the dockyard for new adventures.

As we approach the pier several men are awaiting us despite the bitterly cold March storm: our squadron commander, our staff surgeon, and "Daddy" Schultze's watch officers. Herbert Schultze ranks as our "tonnage king," having yesterday returned from his fourth patrol with 46,000 tons of enemy shipping destroyed. One of his victims carried a cargo of frozen beef that could have met England's needs for two days. For Endrass, my old friend, today is his last day as a watch officer aboard U 47. To show his appreciation, Prien allows him to direct the boat's docking maneuver. Endrass will take over command of a boat of his own now, just as I am scheduled to do after we return from our next patrol.

An old custom among submariners holds that whenever one of us goes out on a mission everyone joins him over a bottle of champagne, perhaps for the last time. Our toasts include the memory of comrades who have not come back. Today we repeat the time-honored ritual and are pleased to notice that neither the early hour nor the cold have prevented our friends from seeing us off with proper encouragements. We all belong together.

The horn sounds the familiar signal—one long, one short. Let go the lines! Soon the metallic thumping of the diesel exhausts echoes from the walls of the locks. We bring out a triple hurrah, wave to our friends for the last time, and then turn around with determination, our faces braving the icy wind. We leave behind what we love but also the things that have made us soft.

A gigantic icebreaker is waiting to guide us through the Kiel Canal. Two thick steel hawsers are passed to us; slowly the colossus takes up speed. Half of its propeller is above the water line, hurling water against our bows. Our boats are swinging back and forth. Suddenly one of the hawsers parts. It is no use. The icebreaker rides too high. We contact the leader of a patrol boat squadron that is also anxious to transfer to the North Sea. Again we try two hawsers. Now things go more smoothly even though the icebreaker's stern yaws like a duck's tail. We shout our greetings across to our new companion. As it turns out, the squadron commander once served on U 46 himself.

At first we make good headway. But the closer we get to Brunsbüttel [the Canal's western, or North Sea, terminal], the thicker the ice becomes. The floes crash noisily against our hull. All along the banks people watch and wave to us. We U-boat men mean something special to them after all. Guards in field-gray uniforms escort us from afar along the strategic road that runs from sea to sea. Here and there we see an anti-aircraft battery; otherwise everything looks cold and bare. When we return it will be springtime.

We reach Brunsbüttel late in the day. Word spreads that there will be an informal meeting in the "Kanalmündung" tavern. The officers of the air defense command, a few naval surgeons, and officials of the canal administration want to give us their farewell. Lots of smoke, beer, and noise. As soon as the people recognize Prien, nothing can hold them back. He remains busy all night, signing autographs and shaking hands. Just as we enter the tavern, Jürgen Oesten's U 61 returns from her latest patrol: 12,000 tons destroyed, many close encounters with enemy depth charges, and in recognition the Iron Cross, first class. Congratulations!

The next morning we are off to Heligoland. After breaking through the ice barrier and making a small course adjustment we reach the open sea, alone by ourselves at last. I fill my lungs with a deep breath of invigorating North Sea air. At last, after two months of refitting, we are ready to go again. Before long Heligoland's contours of ragged red rock emerge out of the afternoon haze. The closer we get the better we can see the island's outline and the greater becomes my appreciation of what has been created here since my last visit four years ago. Once again Heligoland has become a major naval base, the guardian of the German Bight. Like spider legs, long breakwaters stretch in different directions from the island's lower plateau. Through narrow channels we reach the U-boat base, well protected against stormy weather and home to us for the next few days. When we arrive, the U-boat tender "Mother" *Saar* is already surrounded by many of her children.

We enjoy life on Heligoland as if we want to make up for the deprivations we are certain to suffer on our forthcoming mission. We thoroughly explore the fortress installations with their underground shelters, passageways, and elevators. It is a veritable subterranean town and arsenal. We also discover there is no more whisky on the island, and you can enjoy a glass of grog only if you bring your own rum. At night everyone congregates at *"Tante Lotte's."* She is a true original. For many years now, thanks to her personality and business sense, she has exercised a virtual monopoly over Heligoland's entertainment sector. Tante Lotte also has a special book for U-boat men to sign.

There are not many females on this island, but they are very pleasant and friendly. Already on our first night ashore we all sit together in a happy circle. As daughters of the sea they know us and remember that sailors love some fun and action. The second night we celebrated into the morning hours and then everyone went to comb Katja's grocery store for any hidden treasures there. And indeed we discovered such delicacies as lobsters and whisky. Any protest on the part of Katja's mother was soon silenced: "Mom, I would like you to meet Mr. Prien." The poor mother had little choice but to go along with our little game; after all, how could she remain pedantic in the presence of such a great name?

During the day we exercised at sea: keeping a steady level, depth, and course under water; interminable practice dives; testing our radio gear, and the like. On the second evening the wind freshened. All shore leave was cancelled. The sea stood straight into our little harbor. Our boats were pitching restlessly in the swell, and where the protective fenders had been pushed aside the ships' bodies pushed badly into one another. Soon the order came: "All boats leave base and rest on the bottom of the sea until tomorrow morning. If weather does not improve, proceed to Wilhelmshaven." We cast off our lines and the dancing boats are tamed by the power of their engines. One after another we gain the open sea through the narrow estuary and disappear into the night.

Once we are beyond the shelter of the island, all hell breaks loose. The northwest storm with its heavy seas inundates the conning tower and the men on watch. Buoys are all but invisible in the darkness, and lights ashore have been extinguished for fear of attracting enemy aircraft. Thus we have to use intuition and experience instead. A small boat had sailed earlier in the afternoon and now had a very tough time making headway against the storm. We may suffer the same fate tomorrow. Even 150 feet below the surface on the bottom of the sea our boat would not come to rest entirely despite an extra three tons of seawater in our tanks. When I took over as officer of the watch, the boat swung and heeled considerably. After surfacing the next morning, the same grim picture as on the day before. So we head for Wilhelmshaven. Those "last" lobsters of Heligoland, which took us so much ingenuity and so many intrigues to obtain, are waiting for us to this very day.

Wilhelmshaven turns out to be as bleak and boring as ever. First we are on alert to sail on 24-hour notice. Soon this is moved up to two-hour readiness. Then one day at noon we receive the order: "Depart immediately." Mysterious briefcases full of charts are brought on board. Our commanding officer hints that "it will be a cold affair." This gives us a pretty good idea of where we are headed. At the last moment our radio telegraphy equipment goes on the blink. Hamberger, the petty officer in charge, uses a combination of terrible oaths and troubleshooting advice by landline to fix the transmitter in the nick of time.

As we are about to leave Wilhelmshaven, "Päckchen" Wohlfarth returns with his boat from his latest patrol. Four pennants with death heads painted on them fly from his periscope: four merchantmen sunk. Then the gates of the locks swing open and we are off. Course north.

Comment:

Today history books tell the story of "Operation Weserübung." I will restrict most of my comments here to my diary entries at the time.

In order to occupy Norway, and to forestall a similar design by the Allied powers, the German Navy employed all available fighting units—including U-boats, which are not very useful for such purposes. A submarine is designed to be a commerce raider and requires vast areas of sea space to be effective. Every once in a while a U-boat, operating singly, can be successful in coastal waters, provided it enjoys a measure of surprise against the enemy. Deploying U-boats in Norway's narrow fjords, however, went against all experience and common sense. Nights were short and days quite long, giving the boat little opportunity to recharge its batteries on the surface. Moreover, acoustic conditions favored the defenders; the ship channels were narrow and tricky to navigate; and we lacked reliable information about tides and what the seabed consisted of. To make matters worse, our torpedoes malfunctioned with terrifying regularity by failing to run at their preset depth and to respond to the intended victim's magnetic field. In short, the Norway operation turned out to be a bitter disappointment for German U-boats.

Diary:

For days now we are lying idle in one of the many Norwegian fjords to observe and report enemy ship movements. We are allowed to fire only on British warships, but so far we have not encountered a single one. Instead we are captivated by the beauty of the majestic landscape around us.

As dawn breaks, while the full moon to the southwest leaves behind but a faint glimmer of light, we can already distinguish the dark silhouettes of the mountain ranges against the red easterly sky. The sun climbs higher, the sky turns purplish. The mountain ridges take on clearer contours in shades of blue. Soon individual peaks stand out with jagged black edges and bluish-gray plateaus below which is hidden the eternal ice.

Every morning at about the same time we dive, because during the day we must stay submerged in order to remain undetected by the enemy. On occasion, as on Easter morning, the early hour enveloped us with sleet and snow flurries. In those cases we stayed above the surface a little longer, hands cold and feet uneasy on the icy planks, our bodies eagerly inhaling the clear, cool, salty air. Sometimes morning fog or snow-heavy clouds made the shoreline entirely invisible. But that happened only rarely. Most of the time cold, blue, bright northern skies prevailed. Then we could view the magnificent beauty of the fjord with its blue, clear waters, its snow-covered mountain ridges, and the glaciers reaching almost to the water's edge, only through our periscope. The untouched nature of the place casts a spell on us. Few things can compare with the changing vistas of the sharp-edged mountains, the bright snowfields of the higher elevations, or the gigantic, sun-lit glaciers that blinded us even as we looked at them from a distance through the periscope. Given these peaceful surroundings we had to remind ourselves that we were, after all, at war.

As the sun sent its last rays we surfaced, breathed hungrily the fresh air of which we had been deprived for so long, and once again stared in awe at the beauty of this unique natural wonder. The air so clear and cold, a brilliant starry sky above. Only the mountain ranges are decorated with a soft band of clouds. Before the daylight has completely faded away, the clouds to our south appear with gold-coated rims, announcing the rising moon. The sharp contours of the mountains seem to recede as a faint haze replaces the ebbing daylight. You can hear small waves breaking against our bows. At regular intervals the revolving beam of a distant lighthouse touches the horizon. Behind the protective armored cover of the bridge I see the men off-watch smoking their cigarettes. In fact, the bridge is crowded with men inhaling the fresh air and enjoying their cigarettes after the long, forced abstinence below.

Suddenly, the overture to a spectacle that pictures can but poorly recapture and words only imperfectly describe. A shaky beam of light appears behind the mountains, wanders off, brightens in intensity, then fades away. Soon there is another beam, hesitant at first, then more in short succession. The entire horizon is now lit up, a bright ring of heavenly fire right above us; indeed, it feels as if the tonal beauty of a fugue by Bach has been recast in brilliant lights. A veil of colors moves up and down like a woven fabric, then ebbs away only to reappear even more spectacularly to the southeast. Dark red to violet, the lights form huge Gothic arches in the sky, shoot up to the zenith in mighty columns. Such are the northern lights. Our eyes, ordinarily glued to the horizon where a potential enemy is likely to make his first appearance, lift up again and again to the skies lest we miss out on nature's dramatic entertainment. Almost every night we enjoyed this spectacle, never a repeat performance but always new, more beautiful and fantastic.

Today we mark the end of our third week out here, three exhausting weeks indeed. You have to have been with us to know what a seemingly endless waiting period can do to you. While on earlier patrols one surprise followed another in close succession, now we are practically devoured by the monotony of our daily routine. It is quite possible that we might be deprived of daylight for another three weeks. When we get home we will look like barn owls: pale and bloated, for our bodies lack motion and exercise. Every day we stay submerged for fifteen hours and during that time inhale stale, oxygen-poor air. Our oxygen supply is rationed to allow us to stay up to six weeks at our post. The same holds true for the number of so-called potassium cartridges that are designed to absorb toxic carbon dioxide. As a result every afternoon our heads swell, breathing becomes heavy, and every body movement is painful until we surface at dusk for the night. What makes things worse is the realization that nothing is likely to happen here. Nevertheless we have to be alert because the enemy is unpredictable. All we know is that for the past three weeks he has not shown up.

One night I am on duty on the bridge, the wind whistling around the conning tower. Suddenly out of the dark a formation of wild geese appears and is gone just as quickly. At that moment someone behind me recites in a low voice the famous lines by Walter Flex: *"Wildgänse rauschen durch die Nacht mit schrillem Schrei nach Norden."* [Wild geese are rushing through the night, northbound, the air filled with their shrill cries]. It was Steinweg, the radio operator, and we had a longer talk. He had read a lot and spoke about the poets Theodor Storm and Knut Hamsun, both of whom have given us a better understanding of the northern countries and the peculiar characteristics of their inhabitants. I became aware of Steinweg's literary interests and his efforts to broaden his education. And then he opened up and laid bare his frustrations: how the shipboard routine with its endless monotony had pushed him to the breaking point; how he had tried in vain to keep on reading while performing his other duties; and how the cramped living conditions on a U-boat, where people literally sleep on top of one another, rendered any such efforts impossible.

I tried to make clear to him that one cannot break out of the circle into which life has put us. Otherwise nothing would be accomplished. For instance, in our daily struggle with the sea we could not be content with partial solutions or compromises. Any mistakes on our part can have grave consequences. The sea educates those who have to live with it. But we can still enjoy the beauty of the Norwegian fjords and the colorful spectacle of the northern lights. This is Hamsun's homeland that we have come to know so closely now. I believe Steinweg agreed with me that the experience of true comradeship on our boat compensated him for much that he otherwise missed.

Those three weeks of sometimes paralyzing, sometimes invigorating vigilance and waiting, as recorded in such detail in my journal, came to a very sudden end and were replaced by a dramatic sequence of events that left me no time for contemplation. Only brief summaries could reflect the quick succession of incidents that followed:

Late on April 6 we receive code word *"Hartmut."* Emotions run high after the commanding officer explains its implications to us fellow officers. Now time passes so quickly that we hardly remember our days of boredom. We are completely absorbed by our task to help escort the ten German destroyers destined to carry out the occupation of Narvik. In the morning hours of April 8 we dive to evade a destroyer. It appeared without warning out of the haze and we have no clue as to its nationality. During the day strong southwesterly winds prevail. Will our destroyers make it?

Overnight we take up an intermediate patrol station further up the Narvik Fjord. The storm turns around to the northwest. Mist and fog reduce visibility. And still the anxious question: Will the destroyers be able to carry out their task? There are no navigational aids of any kind to help us find our way, and our charts are unreliable. We decide to dive to use our hydrophones to pick up information acoustically where visual data are unobtainable. We surface at 4 A.M. on April 9 and at last receive the long-awaited radio signal: "U-boats requested to enter Narvik." The city is in German hands. It is somewhat disconcerting that our destroyers managed to pass us undetected because of the poor visibility. The enemy might be able to do the same thing. Several hours later the German destroyer *Erich Giese* brings up the rear and passes Baröy—a remarkable navigational and nautical achievement considering the storm and fog.

We follow at high speed up the fjord after receiving the order "Assume final positions!" from U-Boat Command. Off Skraaom, suddenly alarm and general quarters. Ahead is the silhouette of a submarine, which disappears as we approach. Friend or foe? It is unlikely that one of our own boats has overtaken us since they were all stationed farther out to sea. We exercise caution. The periscope reveals nothing; the hydrophones pick up only faint noises. We must break through before the enemy can steal a march on us. Heavy snow flurries come to our aid. We surface and press ahead at full speed. We cannot even see the full length of our boat under the prevailing conditions. We have never been in these waters before, but so far we have been lucky and expect no troubles ahead. Off Tranöy the skies clear. We must have outdistanced the other submarine. Ahead we spot a steamer evidently bound for Narvik, so we follow in its wake. It turns out to be the Swedish vessel *Strassa*. When her crew recognizes us, panic breaks out. They lower their cutter and stand by in life vests. We decide to pass the *Strassa* because she is simply too slow. No one has time to admire the beauty of the fjord as we move on.

Again, general quarters. Out of the haze ahead emerge the contours of a destroyer pointed straight toward us. Because of the fog the periscope is of no use. We surface. Barely visible through the fog we make out the silhouette of a German destroyer. We exchange recognition signals. Soon the destroyer has disappeared again. When visibility improved shortly thereafter, we observed how the destroyer kept the Swedish vessel from escaping northward into the Tjeldsund.

We pass the island of Baröy. Snow flurries and sunshine alternate in quick succession. Off Ramnes we encounter two more destroyers. We close in and learn that they had been detached to silence two suspected coastal batteries at this point. We proceed and find ourselves soon at our prearranged position in the Ofotfjord. To both sides are snow-covered mountains, few houses. The fjord is so narrow here that one can distinguish individual skiers ashore. We are here to intercept the enemy in case he decides to interfere with the German occupation of Narvik. But things are destined to turn out differently.

On April 10, from midnight until 4 A.M., very heavy snowfall. You cannot see your own hand in front of your eyes. I take over as officer of the watch at 4 A.M. We can barely see the shoreline. Around 6 A.M. petty officer Scheunemann of the central control room reports knocking noises against the hull at irregular intervals. We have no idea what it might be. Suddenly, around 6:30 A.M., I hear distant gunfire from the direction of Narvik. Are the Norwegians offering resistance after all? The gunfire intensifies. Then, just off the coast, we spot a smaller vessel headed toward us. Our first thought is that this must be a Norwegian boat trying to escape out to sea. It does not respond to our recognition signal but stops dead in the water instead. Five rounds of our 2-cm gun persuade it to come closer. Then it is our turn to be surprised. The boat is full of German mountain troops under orders to occupy a Norwegian depot in the Ramsund. They, too, do not know what is going on in Narvik.

No sooner has the boat cast off than I see the silhouettes of three destroyers heading toward us from the direction of Narvik. Again, alarm and down to periscope depth. The commanding officer recognizes British destroyers at high speed on opposite courses. Under the circumstances there is no way for us to attack them. Instead we dive deeper. The knocking noises we heard earlier were from the duel between German and British destroyers at Narvik. We remain cautious and stay at periscope depth. The destroyers are now gone. Not long thereafter another comes in sight, likewise headed for the open sea under a heavy cloud of smoke. A few minutes later a heavy jolt grips our boat. The periscope reveals a high column of fire along with a gigantic plume of smoke as a burning vessel tries to beach itself before going down in deeper waters. The destroyer is nowhere to be seen. Later we learn that the departing British destroyer had encountered and attacked the German supply ship *Kattegat* (2,000 tons).

Many men aboard *U 46* are almost in a state of panic. Our radio operators manning the hydrophones identify the slightest sound as coming from a U-boat. Detonating depth charges in the distance further challenge our nerves. At nightfall we surface, close in on the dark shore for cover, and recharge our batteries. I had just retired for a short nap when the alarm was sounded again. This time the navigator panicked and wanted to take the boat down to our maximum diving depth. Our commanding officer issued countermanding orders just in time.

Two destroyers approach from the direction of Narvik. Our torpedo tubes are ready to fire, optical measurements being taken continuously as we track the targets. The silhouettes become wider. These are German destroyers that pass by at high speed. A few minutes later they return. At 11 P.M. we receive orders to go into Narvik for a conference with the commanding officer of the 4th Destroyer Squadron.

Narvik can be made out from a distance thanks to the illumination provided by a vessel set ablaze and driven onto the beach. It is an eerie scene: The snow looks as if it is covered with some red substance, and the flickering fires are reflected in the windows of Narvik's huddled houses. All navigational lights have been extinguished. We reach the port's entrance. The closer we get, the quieter we become. Shipwrecks everywhere. Here the bows of a vessel rise fantastically out of the water, there a stern, elsewhere only the masts still break the surface while the ship has settled on the bottom. Kindly, one of the destroyers sends its navigator over to help us steer safely through the wreckage. He fills us in on what has happened.

This is the Narvik story so far: The destroyers reach their target on schedule, each with 200 troops of the mountain division on board. Two Norwegian armored cruisers intend to resist our moves. The destroyer *Wilhelm Heidkamp* sends a representative of the task force commander over in a pinnace to one of them to inquire about Norwegian intentions. They insist on resistance. Thereupon the prearranged signal, a red flare. The destroyer loosens a spread of three torpedoes. After the explosions the cruiser is gone.

Bernd von Arnim is the first of our destroyers to enter the port and receives fire from the second Norwegian armored cruiser's 8-inch guns. Its first salvo falls short, the second hits the rocks, the third can no longer be observed because by then the enemy has been torpedoed and is out of action. Of seven German torpedoes fired, two score hits. The troops, all 2,000 of them, disembark as planned. Thereafter the destroyers go alongside the tanker *Jan Wellem* to replenish their fuel supplies. Four of them are then detached into nearby fjords under Captain Erich Bey. At that point five British destroyers manage to break through to Narvik undetected by our pickets. They exercise a turn at the port's entrance and fire their torpedoes against their unsuspecting victims. *Wilhelm Heidkamp* and *Anton Schmitt* go down, as do eight merchantmen. *Diether von Roeder* receives three serious hits. In the meantime Bey's division engages the enemy. The *Hunter* is damaged, rammed, and sunk; the *Hardy* is set afire and driven onto the beach. Three British destroyers escape.

We arrange with the commanding officer of the 4th Destroyer Squadron that we will stay for the day in Narvik and at night occupy a picket position down the fjord off Farnes. Toward daybreak we briefly get under way but soon return and dock alongside the destroyer *Georg Thiele*. On April 11 ten dead sailors are being carried ashore from the destroyer, all of them members of a gun crew killed in the engagement with the British force. *Bernd von Arnim* has docked on the opposite side. Both destroyers have sustained minor damage.

In the evening we take up our picket station. Nothing unusual occurs. The next day we decide to go alongside the destroyer *Hans Lüdemann* to top off provisions and fuel. Here I meet my Crew comrade Alexander von Zitzewitz. He shows me the papers of a captured British officer that contain the British attack plan and other information. When the *Lüdemann* gets under way we moor alongside the *Erich Giese*. This gives me an opportunity to talk to my Crew comrade Hannes Perl, who was destined to be shot to death the very next day while trying to reach shore after the *Giese* went down. The destroyer commanders Curt Rechel and Karl Smidt compare notes about their experiences. Both destroyers had lost several men en route to Narvik who were swept overboard by heavy seas. Even some of the motorbikes and guns of the mountain troops were lost. Rechel himself was almost swept away. There had been an artillery battle with a British destroyer off the Norwegian coast in which the *Bernd von Arnim* received three hits. The British vessel was subsequently sunk by the cruiser *Hipper.* The *Giese's* gyroscopic compass had malfunctioned, leaving her seriously handicapped in the narrow Narvik Fjord.

Later, *U 64* shows up with my Crew comrade Heinz Hirsacker aboard as executive officer. He indicated strong British destroyer forces at the entrance to the fjord. From Tranöy on they had to run submerged because of the threat. Then *U 49* reports nine enemy aircraft headed east toward Narvik. Seconds later the air raid sirens wail. Everyone runs for cover ashore as quickly as possible. I remain behind with our machine gun crew. Despite tremendous anti-aircraft fire we do not hit a single enemy plane. Fifty yards away a bomb explodes in the water just offshore and sets a shed ablaze. Only 20 yards away one of our crew is instantly killed by another bomb, while another man is simply laid flat by the blast. The crew is mightily impressed. As soon as things clear we get under way to take up our station down the fjord again. We are the destroyers' last best hope.

Yesterday and today two large Luftwaffe planes circled over Narvik. The mountain troops no longer feel as abandoned as before. One of them, a first lieutenant, comes on board. He thinks the situation ashore is not entirely hopeless. During the night we occupy a new patrol station off the island of Baröy and meet *U 51*, which is headed up the fjord. In the morning we sight the battleship *Warspite* and its escort of six destroyers, course Narvik. As we prepare to engage the enemy we run onto a shoal not marked on our charts. The top of our conning tower and our direction-finding frame antenna stay above the waterline some 1,500 yards off the *Warspite*'s beam. Full speed astern! The commanding officer aborts our attack.

Ever since that morning I have asked myself over and over whether we should have delivered the attack regardless of our precarious situation. After all, the life or death of eight German destroyers was at stake!

A short while later we hear heavy explosions and gunfire from the direction of Narvik. Aircraft overhead keep us from surfacing. In the meantime the tragedy of the destruction of the German destroyers takes its course. Late in the afternoon the enemy battleship and its six destroyers reemerge from the fjord. Our commanding officer at the periscope: "Attack impossible!" We surface at 10 P.M. Two hours later an emergency dive to evade a destroyer. Later we surface and continue recharging the batteries. At 3 A.M. we see British destroyers patrolling off Narvik. Down we go again. This time we touch bottom and give up further efforts to attack.

The Führer orders: "Narvik must be held at all costs!" We destroy our secret documents. Then we meet *U 48*. We ask: "What happened to the German destroyers?" Answer: "Sunk!" Our thoughts turn immediately to the fate of the ten crews. *U 48* tries to break through to Narvik but soon gives up because of the strong enemy presence. Submerged, we move up to Narvik and await our opportunity. The commanding officer at the periscope tries to attack departing British destroyers. Because of their zig-zagging we cannot obtain a favorable position.

In the afternoon we surface to recharge. An aircraft chases us below. A bomb explodes very close nearby. After nightfall we surface again to recharge the batteries. A destroyer passes without noticing us. A second one turns once, then steers for us on a steady course. Emergency dive! We run aground some 35 feet below the surface. Depth charges go off around us. The destroyer plays an agonizing game of stop and go. We do not dare to stir. But we need to go deeper because at low tide our bridge will become visible.

April 16, 4 A.M. Continue dive to a depth of 130 feet and lie all day long on the bottom some 7 to 10 degrees down by the stern. We have to wait until sunset. At various times during the day destroyers pass overhead. At 8 P.M. we rise to periscope depth and try to make our way into deeper waters. We touch ground again at 70 feet. Lie still until 8:30 P.M. We then surface and carefully leave Narvik Fjord at half speed.

April 17. At 3 A.M. we find ourselves off Flatöy and have to dive again when we sight a vessel without running lights. The night is too bright for a surface attack; for a submerged attack our position is too unfavorable. We resurface, only to see a submarine ahead of us. We steer toward it. The other boat dives; so do we. We spend most of the day below. At 4 P.M. we pick up the order to return to base. The crew's mood improves. At 5:30 P.M. an enemy cruiser comes in sight, dead ahead. We approach at periscope depth. The cruiser appears to move away from us. We try to catch up and gain a better attack position. It does not work. The cruiser turns away and disappears down the Lofoten Islands.

April 18, 1 A.M. Shadows to starboard: a battleship escorted by destroyers. We try to close. A destroyer detects us and chases us down into the "basement." At 7 A.M. we encounter three enemy transports with their escorts and report their position. We try to keep in contact but lose it before long. At 11 A.M. a lighthouse emerges quite suddenly out of a bank of clouds. Crash dive! This shows how frazzled our nerves have become. At 3 P.M., aircraft alarm. We finally reach the open sea, having escaped the witches' cauldron.

When our squadron commander welcomes us back to Kiel and inspects the crew, his face turns very grave. Was it the sight of our pale, hollow faces that got to him? Or sympathy for our exhausting, unsuccessful mission? Or the haunting question, "Did you really do everything possible to carry out your task, to prevent the destruction of the ten German destroyers at Narvik at all costs?"

It was my last patrol as an executive officer.

COMMANDING OFFICER, *U 57*

U 57 was a Type II single-hull boat, a "dug-out," as we called it in naval circles. Officially it displaced 250 tons, could run up to 12 knots on the surface, 7 knots under water. We had three torpedo tubes mounted in the bow and two torpedoes in reserve.

Lieutenant Commander Claus Korth turned the boat over to me with a seasoned crew of twenty-two. My executive officer was Lieutenant Kurt Reichenbach-Klinke, the chief engineering officer was Lieutenant Christ. The boat had been successful. I would have to prove myself as its new commanding officer.

As executive officer aboard *U 46* I had served on a vessel more than twice the size of *U 57*. On the former we officers enjoyed at least some privacy in quarters halfway separated from the others. On *U 57*, however, the entire crew lived, ate, and slept pressed together in a single narrow space behind the torpedo tubes on a floor of wooden planks that covered the two reserve torpedoes. Any sense of privacy was completely lost. What can you do as the commanding officer under these circumstances?

At first I had no opportunity at all to make an impact on the men, to let them know and feel who I was. I stood watch, taking turns with my executive officer and our chief navigator. En route to our operational area, on a foggy day, we scraped against a floating mine that had broken loose from its cable. We swerved to avoid a spread of several torpedoes aimed at us by an enemy submarine. Fortunately a lookout spotted them in time. One day, without warning, a bomber swooped down on us out of the clouds. The bomb failed to explode; there were fifteen small-caliber bullet holes; nobody got hurt. I seemed to have luck on my side, but it was no way to gain the confidence of my crew.

When we tried to break through the Fair Isle Passage (between the Orkney and Shetland Islands north of Scotland) we were detected by a destroyer and forced to dive. You could hear the enemy's propeller noises without using hydrophones. I kept the boat at 300 feet, steering different courses, never able to get out of the destroyer's asdic range. We gained no feeling for the true position of the enemy or his tactics. In the end we decided to come up and take a look around to assess the situation more accurately. I raised the periscope very carefully. A full moon was out. Two destroyers lay stopped some 300 to 400 yards away, exchanging signals. Very quietly we resumed our dive, our speed and engine noises reduced to a minimum. We had hardly reached our intended depth when depth charges went off around us like fireworks. I heard distinctly how the destroyers sped up just before they dropped the charges and thus had the opportunity to anticipate their maneuver and reduce our chances of being hit. As soon as they stopped their engines after their run, I reduced our speed accordingly. Everything was turned off, including auxiliary generators, to produce as little noise as possible. Even the hydroplanes were being operated manually.

Two hours later we rose to periscope depth for a look around. Nothing. "Surface!" Against the somewhat brighter eastern sky we could make out a flotilla of vessels, twenty-two according to my count. At full speed we left the scene, and since the Fair Isle Passage was obviously blocked we decided to go all the way around the Shetlands.

Now the crew knew that I was not one of those U-boat commanders who suffered from "neck pains," that is, I did not put the pursuit of honors and decorations (the Knight's Cross was worn around the neck) ahead of the safety of boat and crew and accept risks irresponsibly. That was important. I felt that we had grown closer together through this experience.

New Area of Operations: The North Channel

Crash dive to avoid air attack. We are at a depth of barely 130 feet when the bombs fall. They explode so close to the boat that the base-plates of one of our two diesel engines crack. The lights are out, darkness envelops us, and water spouts into the central control room. The boat sinks and comes to rest on the bottom of the ocean. Damage assessment. The boat itself seems to hold tight; that is the most important thing.

I consult my executive officer and our chief engineer as to our further course of action, in particular whether to continue operations or to return home for repairs. The engineer, who is responsible for the boat's technical state of readiness, argues strongly in favor of breaking off the patrol. The boat is essentially lame, our remaining diesel allowing for a maximum speed of no more than 9 knots. On the other hand, the executive officer and I want to go on with the mission. After all, the boat still has all five of its torpedoes. Decision: We can only compensate for the boat's handicap by closing in on the enemy. This means to penetrate farther south into the North Channel (between Ireland and Scotland) where enemy shipping is more concentrated.

I inform the crew of my decision and get the impression that most of the men share it. Only the engine room personnel, who are constantly reminded of our reduced speed, appear sceptical and worried, but they do not show it. The momentum they sense in the rest of us carries them along.

Diary:

Around midnight, against the backdrop of two lighthouses in the distance ashore, we move in on a convoy that is being assembled and guarded to seaward by three destroyers. We attack on the surface, hamstrung by the boat's lack of maneuverability. Three torpedoes against three targets, then suddenly the destroyers are upon us. Alarm and another crash dive!

Here the water depth is no more than 150 feet. We sink, our bows pointing down by 40 degrees and hitting the bottom hard. I try in vain to get the boat off and moving again. Through someone's mistake the boat has taken on too much water in a short period of time, and we cannot afford to run the pumps because they are too loud and would give away our position. Before we can do much, depth charges rain down on us, some eight to ten. They are right on target. Each explosion lifts the boat up by more than 10 feet before letting it fall back to the bottom. U 57 is practically defenseless because of the shallowness of these waters. We have virtually no chance to escape the depth charges because the enemy knows approximately where we are and we cannot stir. All auxiliary engines are turned off, but the destroyers have us in their grip. Powerful explosions, one after another. They cause new damage: Water leaks through in hundreds of places, sometimes a mere drip, elsewhere a jet of water or the sound of bubbles welling up. Everything is pitch dark.

The destroyers keep at it all day long without a pause. Every half hour or so one of our pursuers moves slowly across our position, listening and sounding, before loosening its load that threatens to blow us up. It seems as if the boat has come to rest in a shallow depression so that the pressure waves of the detonations pass overhead. We have no other explanation for the fact that none of the depth charges has yet torn us apart.

Unbearably slowly the minutes and hours tick away. The crew is ordered to lie down to consume as little oxygen as necessary. Each of them carries a potassium cartridge around his chest. Potassium neutralizes the lethal carbon dioxide. Every half hour I check to make sure that no one's tube has dropped from his mouth. The oxygen in the boat is almost used up.

Some men are sleeping. What nerves the boys must have! Hour after hour the air in the boat becomes more difficult to breathe. Outside the explosions go off, again and again. Slowly the enemy's propellers are milling overhead. Then a shock; the boat lifts up slightly before settling back to its former position. The men are thrown about in the dark. Something scrapes along the hull from stem to stern. The suspense is almost impossible to endure. "Search cables," the executive officer whispers into my ear. The propellers keep on milling, their sound gradually wandering off into the distance. Apparently the enemy is combing the bottom for us. In between, more depth charges. Nothing in the boat seems undamaged; cracking noises and leaks are everywhere, and none of our pumps works properly any more.

It is night again, inside and out. Inside the boat we have not seen light in 24 hours; everything is wet, cool, and the air suffocating, as if we were miners hopelessly cut off in an underground shaft after an explosion. So far we have counted more than 200 depth charges. Fortunately, none of them has hit close enough to give the boat a fatal blow.

We plan to surface at 11 P.M. Using all means at our disposal we repair the main bilge pump until it works halfway reliably. All is quiet. At 10:50 P.M. more depth charges, but farther away. We have to wait some more, at least until midnight. Things remain quiet. "Compressed air on the central trim tank!" The boat does not stir. It has taken on too much water. No buoyancy. "Compressed air on all tanks!" Still the boat does not move. Has it become a steel coffin for all of us? The men in the central control room look at me with wide eyes. Perhaps the keel is stuck in the sea bottom. I give the order to go slow speed ahead with our electric engines. A trembling goes through the boat. Our eyes are glued to the depth gauge. Slowly at first, then faster, the boat floats free and rises. Once we are all the way to the surface we adjust the air pressure. It is as if our ears are being torn apart.

The conning tower hatch flies open and we savor the deliciously fresh, clean air. The night is completely dark, the swell considerable. Astern a destroyer, little more than a faint shadow. It is too dark for the enemy to see our low silhouette. Very slowly we crawl away, using the most favorable combination of speed and noise. Our compass is still out of order and the sky overcast so that we cannot get a proper bearing from the stars. The storm still blows from the northwest, so we simply steer straight against the seas, for that must be the direction that will lead us out of this trap. All the while the crew is feverishly at work to repair the damage we sustained in our ordeal.

Toward morning we dive and load our two reserve torpedoes into the now empty tubes. Then we go up for a look around. Straight ahead an aircraft; beyond it, barely above the horizon, an inbound convoy. With maximum underwater speed I manage to bring U 57 into position for an attack on a tanker, the hindmost ship in the convoy. Both torpedoes are fired simultaneously, and in an enormous red fireball the tanker blows up, sending a huge, ever-expanding black cloud skyward. This takes away the shock the men suffered in our recent ordeal. A submarine chaser pursues us and showers the boat with depth charges, some eighty altogether. The boat bucks and shakes every time the charges go off, but we are relatively safe at 250 feet. At last our pursuer gives up and things get quiet. I let the boat sink to the bottom and enjoy along with my men an extended period of rest.

U-Boat Command orders us to return to Kiel. Off Bergen [southwestern Norway] the transmission of our remaining diesel breaks down. The engineering personnel manages to shift the "reverse" position to "forward" so that we are able to make Bergen safely. There the transmission is fixed and we replenish our fuel supply. We continue on toward the Elbe River estuary. Off Brunsbüttel we are already in touch with the signal station at the entrance to the Kiel Canal when the gates of the locks open and a Norwegian steamer slowly leaves the basin to enter the river. *U 57* is ready for the final approach to the locks. Suddenly the Norwegian vessel, its stern still inside the locks and thus without effective use of its rudder, is caught in the tidal currents of the Elbe River and pushed onto the U-boat. "Full speed astern!" But the electric motors do not have enough power; the collision becomes inevitable. Then a cry from below: "Boat is flooding!" The executive officer stands next to me on the bridge, his head turned back as if waiting for additional cries. I shout: "All hands out of the boat!"

Then I am gripped by a feeling of hopeless exhaustion. It seems as though I am floating in a vacuum. Sentiments without echo. Something terrible is happening to us in seconds, and all that in an all-enveloping darkness. Invisible forces fight it out with one another; a blind fury, an incomprehensible brutality crushes us all. All horrors, all moments of despair give way to a deep sense of bitterness, to a peculiar state of weightlessness that descends upon me like a layer of fog.

Suddenly my consciousness is reawakened by a terrible metallic crunch. The steamer's bows press and cut into our conning tower. I see the outline of its superstructure rising up above me like a wall. The boat sinks away from me—our boat that had carried us through all dangers and deadly depths. Our boat, our world deserts us and abandons us to an abysmal solitude. My life was saved, but what it had stood for, my boat, died.

Reality is stronger than all dreams and illusions. It is a parting without struggle in a way I had never imagined it. Death, whose urgent presence we had encountered and suffered so many times and who had been a constant companion to us, came here quite unexpectedly and struck its blow.

The music of the band standing by at the locks to welcome us home, its sounds already reaching our ears, dies away. Rescue parties and the coast guard are being put on alert. During the night the search is not easy. At dawn the survivors assemble. Six men are missing. One man reports that he tried eight times to leave the sunken boat and make it to the surface. The boat lay slightly tilted on its side in rather shallow waters. The man was standing in the radio room, his head precariously held in a bubble of air. Complete darkness, no sense of orientation, the first try to get out failed. Like Theseus with the help of Ariadne's thread he made his way back to the air bubble in the radio room. Seven times he repeated his quest without avail. On the eighth try he finally managed to get to the surface. Unconscious and totally exhausted, he was swept ashore and found by a search party.

That was the end of our patrol, which we had begun on a Friday.

Comment:

The official inquiry into the disaster could not establish with certainty whether the Norwegian vessel caused the collision deliberately or whether the incident was the result of inadvertent circumstances beyond anyone's control. It was also decided to raise the boat.

The salvage vessels *Wille* and *Kraft* passed cables under the boat and brought it up until the conning tower was above the surface. I was the first man to enter the boat. The sight that greeted me still haunts me in my nightmares. Two bloated corpses, grotesquely twisted in their agony, blocked my way from the conning tower into the central control room. I could not make out their identity since their faces were disfigured by the black oily slime. After we had secured the leak and pumped out most of the water, I inspected the boat for a second time. Instruments, engines, everything was covered by a blackish-gray liquid, the water still knee-high above the floor plates. Water? It was a dirty, oily fluid, a vision of the river of the underworld on which we had already embarked but which we managed to escape at the very last moment.

COMMANDING OFFICER, *U 552*

On December 4, 1940, I commissioned *U 552* at the Blohm & Voss shipyard in Hamburg.

After we had left base for our first war patrol—we were already in the North Sea—I noticed that my chief navigator, usually a lively, humorous man, seemed very quiet and looked somewhat pale. It was his turn to stand watch and I involved him in a conversation to find out why he was so quiet. At first he did not want to talk about it, but when I pressed him he finally said, "Sir, it is not important, but I forgot something at home." I asked him, "What did you forget?" After hesitating for a while he at last confessed that on all his previous patrols he had taken along his wife's wedding wreath, which he then kept under a glass cover as is the custom in many middle-class families. This time he had left the wreath at home.

I sensed that along with this talisman his confidence in a happy, successful patrol had been left behind. I gave the order to return to base, we picked up the talisman, and for the rest of the mission the navigator remained cheerful and wholly reliable.

This much I had learned from my experience on *U 57:* The personal feelings of my men—faith, superstition—play a vital role in exercising command successfully.

In retrospect, two of my many war patrols appear particularly remarkable to me: First, the operations against the Gibraltar convoy HG 84, whose escort was commanded by our distinguished opponent, Commander F. J. Walker of the 36th Escort Group; and second, the surprise attack of the Canadian corvette *Sackville* against *U 552* on August 3, 1942.

HG 84 departed Gibraltar on June 9, 1942, the very same day that we sailed from our base in St. Nazaire. The convoy's departure was reported by German spies who monitored Gibraltar from Spanish territory. On the other hand the enemy, too, knew that we had put to sea. The French resistance was quite active and had its girls in the bars of St. Nazaire and La Baule, which were frequented by our sailors. But there were also traitors in our ranks, as the following incident that happened after our departure illustrates.

One night a watchman attached to our patrol flotilla, which always escorted us out into the Bay of Biscay, observed emergency signals from a vessel out in the roadstead. He alerted the flotilla, which in turn sailed immediately to check things out. It turned out that the signals came from one of the flotilla's vessels on patrol offshore. The leading vessel went alongside; one officer and two men jumped over the railing and ran up to the bridge. Not a human soul in sight, but a peculiar chaos prevailed as if the bridge had been abandoned in a hurry. In the meantime more men had come on board and spread out all over the vessel. At the entrance to the engine room one of them discovered a man lying in a pool of blood.

What had happened? Two black men had stormed the bridge, practically sawed the commanding officer in half with their automatic pistols, and also killed the radio operator. Then they had moved on to the crew's quarters. Through a skylight they threw hand grenades into the room until everyone seemed dead and nothing moved any more. The quarters of the engine personnel were then neutralized with heavy padlocks so that no one could get out. Nevertheless, one man in the crew's quarters was still alive. When he heard the diesel engines of the boat being warmed up, he dragged himself to the entrance of the engine room. Looking inside he saw the two black men, armed to their teeth, getting the engine ready. He killed them both with hand grenades, fired the emergency signals, and then collapsed. The two were crew members who had blackened their faces with oil and soot. They had intended to get the boat under way and deliver it to the British who were waiting for it out at sea. The British secret service had planned well but had to wait in vain.

The Stalking of HG 84

U 552 was one of several boats operating as "Group Endrass" against the convoy bound from Gibraltar for England. The convoy could practically choose any course up the eastern Atlantic to reach its destination. The vantage point from the conning tower of a submarine is very low, and thus our chance that we would run into the convoy was small.

At this point the I.K.G. 40 (First Group of Bomber Wing 40) based in Bordeaux came to our assistance. One of its aircraft spotted the convoy on June 13, reported its composition, and transmitted radio signals that would allow us to home in on the enemy. It gave us the proper direction to the convoy but unfortunately not the distance. Assuming that the enemy was steering northerly courses at a speed of 10 to 12 knots, we plotted a course that would take us into its vicinity.

In the late afternoon hours of the following day we saw an airplane low over the horizon, certainly not one of the I.K.G. 40's Focke Wulf (FW) 200s. We had to be careful now. Was the convoy accompanied by an aircraft carrier? Eventually the aircraft turned away and did not return. We learned later that one of the vessels in the convoy was equipped with a catapult. It could launch Hurricane fighter planes for reconnaissance and to take on the FW 200s. Not long thereafter we observed trails of smoke—the convoy itself.

We kept in touch and radioed our position for the benefit of the other boats in our group. Active escort vessels forced us to keep our distance for a while, but we did not lose contact and managed to close in again. This game continued until nightfall. In the meantime we had taken the measure of our enemy. We knew it was a relatively small but well-protected convoy, some twenty merchantmen altogether.

June days are long days. Any attack before midnight was out of the question. The weather favored the defenders, since the escort vessels enjoyed good visibility even after dusk. Wherever the sea was disturbed by the bows of boats and ships, or churned up by propellers, the water shone in silvery-golden cascades and trails—marine phosphorescence. At a distance of about 3,000 yards we could barely make out the silhouettes of the ships, but all the more visible were their silvery wakes. Our boat, too, left behind such a brilliant trail, something we as mariners would have enjoyed and found fascinating in normal times, but which under the given circumstances burdened our attack, ideally undetected by the enemy, with additional risks. To attack with some prospect of success on a bright night and in comparatively calm seas while two corvettes patrolled dangerously close by meant a precarious balancing act.

We fired four torpedoes from our forward tubes against four different vessels, then turned around quickly to loosen a fifth torpedo from our stern tube. It would take the torpedoes some three minutes to reach their targets, long minutes indeed if you are waiting for possible hits and find yourself chased by a corvette. The latter had detected us as we showed her our broadside prior to firing our last torpedo and was now bearing down on us at full speed. We had just enough time to contemplate the fluorescent spray of our pursuer's bow wave, which was closing in ever so rapidly. We sped along with maximum speed, having even revved up our electric engines to boost the power of our two diesels. The boat trembled and shook under this ultimate performance a U-boat can deliver on the surface.

Today, through modern television we are quite used to exciting scenes where a smuggler or a criminal is being chased by a police car, the distance between hunter and hunted diminishing all the time as suspense rises to the point where it becomes almost unbearable. Then, suddenly, the pursuer has to abandon the chase for a totally unforeseen reason, perhaps because the police car's radiator gives out.

I had already sent everyone else down into the boat except myself and prepared for an emergency dive, well knowing that we would be in for a lengthy and potentially lethal treatment of depth charges, at the very least the possibility of sustaining irreparable damage. What came next sounds almost incredible. Our pursuer had slowly but persistently closed the distance between himself and us. I could already make out details on the corvette's superstructure. Suddenly an immense mountain of water, seemingly a gigantic pile of tiny pearls due to marine fluorescence, welled up behind the corvette and a terrific explosion shook our boat.

What had happened? Our pursuer had dropped a load of depth charges at a spot where, correctly anticipating our moves, he thought we had actually dived away. Of course we continued to run on top of the water, flying away at maximum speed and after a while creating the illusion (through our exhaust fumes and a veil of water vapors) that we had dived, since the enemy could no longer see us. Something else added to the enemy's confusion. The corvette—it was H.M.S. *Stork*—had us on her radar. When at a distance of some 500 yards the echo suddenly disappeared, the operator deduced that we were no longer on the surface. We would never again experience a depth charge attack at such a safe distance.

After our torpedoes had found their marks, the sky over the convoy lit up as if a fireworks display was under way. It revealed all the vessels as if they were set up on a chess board. Three of them were about to go down. Bright flares were descending slowly on their parachutes; colorful signals were fired into the air; flashlights reached out searching for us. Oil leaking from a tanker began to burn. The light of the flickering fire, reflected eerily in red-brown colors on the restless seas, reached us in frightful impulses.

The *Stork* had hove to in order to scan the sea for debris from the supposedly destroyed U-boat. Commander Walker thought he had scored his thirteenth kill of a German submarine. We opened up our distance to the convoy to load the reserve torpedoes hanging ready from their rails. At 4 A.M. the mechanics reported all tubes reloaded. By 4:30 A.M. we had regained a favorable position to strike. The convoy, at full alert, awaited our attack. The escort forces chased around like nervous thoroughbred horses, changing their courses constantly and making it hard for us to come into close range of the convoy.

Attack! Again the same launch sequence for the torpedoes. Two vessels were hit in parallel columns of the convoy. One of them simply blew up in a red-hot fireball, illuminating the vessels around, which quickly turned away. Then the same fireworks as after our first attack and the same chaotic scene, as described in Terence Robertson's book, *Walker, R.N.*:

> The chaos became complete when every ship in the convoy began firing snowflake illuminant rockets wildly and indiscriminately, lighting up every column until it became possible for an attacker to take his time about selecting a target. Walker was raging inwardly, and he almost danced in consternation when one of the ships astern opened fire with her machine-guns sending streams of tracers in a wide arc behind her, nearly hitting *Stork*'s bridge and moving round to spray the decks of the neighbouring ship in the next column. The latter, thinking he was under attack from the air, fired off everything he had at the nearest star. It was all a bit much for the escorts and, under Walker's orders, they steamed at full speed round the convoy just outside the glare of the snowflakes in the hope of catching a U-boat stalking them on the surface.

Shortly before 6 A.M. the last two torpedoes had been loaded, but no matter how hard we tried to carry out a third attack against the convoy, the watchful escorts and the breaking day frustrated our efforts. We fought an inner struggle between the desire to strike again and our responsibility for boat and crew, until the daylight hours allowed at best for an underwater attack. Miles away we tried to overtake the convoy and gain a position ahead of it so that we could dive and try our luck. This resulted in another dance with the convoy's forward escorts after they picked us up by asdic. A determined chase and depth charge bombardment caused a crack in diving tank No. IV, which at the time was filled with fuel. Some of the oil escaped to the surface and gave away our position below. Series after series of depth charges followed until we managed to surface briefly and pump the fuel into a torpedo compartment. We then flushed the leaky tank with seawater so that we would no longer trail oil whenever we dived.

Nine days later we arrived at our base in St. Nazaire. The girls at the

Bar Royal could report to their superiors that we had sunk the convoy commodore's flagship, the *Pelayo*, along with the *Etrib* and the *City of Oxford*, all of Liverpool; the *Thurso* of Hull; and the Norwegian tanker *Slemdal*.

August 3, 1942: Surprise Attack of the Canadian Corvette *Sackville*

We had used up our last torpedo to attack a convoy. All calculations had seemed perfect, but with no results. Torpedo failure. We had one more reserve torpedo in a pressure-resistant tube on the upper deck. We took it into the boat under great risk while being engulfed in a bank of fog that concealed our moment of vulnerability. We were still in the vicinity of the convoy and thus within range of radar-equipped escort vessels.

We had just taken the torpedo below, removed the gear and tools needed for the transfer, and restored the boat to full combat readiness. After taking a look at the charts, I decided to lie down for a nap while the chief engineer, after long hours of demanding work, retired to the boat's head for some private business. Suddenly a cry comes from the bridge: "Alarm!" The shrill sound of the alarm bell jars everyone awake. I jump up and run into the central control room. When I arrive there the men of the watch are tumbling down the conning tower from the bridge, falling all over one another. What's going on? The technical personnel on duty has already secured the ventilators. A look at the depth gauge shows that the boat is going down slowly. The chief engineer dashes by me to turn one of the valves. I see the terrified face of our chief navigator, the last man to slide down from the bridge into the control room. His only word of explanation: "Destroyer!"

There is no time to ask questions now. Our bow is raised up instead of pointing down. "All hands to the forward compartment," howls the chief engineer. The men chase down the center passageway to the forward torpedo room. Everyone acts according to our standard emergency procedures, practiced a thousand times and taking but a few seconds. There is nothing for me to do but to go along, especially since I have no idea yet of our overall situation. Our depth gauge shows 30 feet. The conning tower must be above the surface.

At this moment the boat is rocked by an immense blow. It shakes and then the lights go out. The dim lights of the emergency back-up system reveal that the upward movement of the boat has been arrested and that it has begun to sink like a stone with a strong forward inclination. "All hands aft!" We must regain control. Depth charges! Water in the engine room! The chief engineer at last manages to level out at 586 feet.

What had happened?

The Canadian corvette *Sackville* had picked us up on her radar while we found ourselves enveloped in the fog bank. Guns at the ready, the enemy had then rushed toward our position. Passing us on opposite courses at a distance of a mere 50 yards, the corvette started firing as soon as we became visible. Fortunately we were too close for her guns to hurt us, the rounds passing harmlessly overhead. But just as the *Sackville* turned and was about to disappear into the fog again, one of her 4-inch guns scored a hit on our conning tower and blew a hole in the shaft that supplies our diesels with fresh air. One man of the watch on the bridge was hurled against the tower hatch by the explosion, but nobody else suffered injuries. Crash dive! The boat sank like a rock because the air shaft had run full of water, and the usual depth charges were next. We probably trailed some oil, and it was quite likely that pieces of the super-structure had come loose and were drifting on the surface.

American newspapers picked up the *Sackville*'s claim that she had sunk us, and the story reached Germany by way of Switzerland. Tears and sorrow among parents, relatives, and friends when they got the word. Rejoicing, indeed doubly so, when we turned up after all at our base after the patrol.

The *Sackville*'s commanding officer, Alan Easton, has described this episode from his point of view in his book, *50 North: An Atlantic Battle-ground.* Easton happened to be eating lunch when first the corvette's as-dic operator and later her radar picked up echoes of the German submarine. A dense fog lay over the sea.

> I was craning my head over the dodger trying to see through the murk. My heart was beating fast.
>
> A dark smudge appeared dead ahead. In three seconds it revealed its shape—long and low, high amidships. A submarine!
>
> She was crossing our course with slight closing inclination going from starboard to port. Her bow wave made it evident she was making eight or ten knots.
>
> "Hard aport. Full ahead. Open fire!"
>
> The submarine was on the port bow now a little more than a hundred yards off. The ship was swinging to port—but not fast enough—the U-boat was inside our turning circle; we could never reach her. Would the gun never fire! Eighty yards . . . seventy only . . . broader on the port bow now.
>
> At last!
>
> With the gun on the depression rail and the ship swinging fast, it fired at point blank range, scarcely a ship's length away, two hundred feet, the en-emy broadside on to the line of fire.
>
> On that instant a gaping hole appeared at the base of the U-boat's con-ning tower, squarely in the centre. It was accompanied by a hail of fire from the port point-fives and the Vickers machine-guns. The high explosive shell burst, ripping the near side of the conning tower out. I saw pieces fly and then the yellow smoke of the projectile rising within.

She was visibly diving. Another round went out of the gun but went over; her bow was under water. A depth charge from the port thrower sailed through the air, fell with a splash into the water but was short of its mark. The boat went down fast and was beneath the surface before the fog closed over the place where she submerged.

The local military administration provided a villa for Endrass and me, beautifully located under pine trees at La Baule les Pins near St. Nazaire. It belonged to a Parisian opera singer and was fully and exquisitely furnished, including paintings by Watteau, Guillaume, and other French artists.

By then Endrass and I had become the closest of friends. Among comrades we were only referred to as Castor and Pollux. We had been executive officers in the same squadron and had received our own independent commands at about the same time: he *U 46*, a Type VIIc boat on which I had served earlier as a watch officer; I *U 57*, a small boat. Between patrols we lived together in that wonderful house in La Baule les Pins. We organized parties for our friends and invited our girls there from Paris: Monique, the singer from Belgium, and Pati, the Russian dancer. We had first met them at the Sheherazade, a famous restaurant and nightclub run by Russian emigrés. As it turned out, we were two pairs of friends who found each other. Monique was the daughter of a Belgian physician; Pati's father was a Russian general. Both were highly educated; in fact, they knew more about German literature and music than we did.

Endrass fell on Christmas 1941 while operating against a convoy bound from Gibraltar to England. Having learned of his death, Monique refused to perform for three months. When, after returning from my patrol, I heard of Endrass's death, I boarded the train for Paris to report to Dönitz at U-Boat Headquarters. I arrived in Paris late that evening. At the station the staff of the Sheherazade was waiting for me, including Pati and Monique. Apparently Dönitz's aide-de-camp, who also frequented the restaurant, had tipped them off. Without saying a word we went to the Sheherazade, which had already closed for the night. Here a Russian love-feast, a lavish banquet, had been prepared, set up under candlelight by Russian waiters in their national costumes. It was a memorial dinner for my friend Endrass.

Today all that is gone, irrecoverably, forever. "The flames have died away, and so have the tides, the games."

In their mythology the ancient Greeks developed a powerful symbol for friendship, the Dioscuri. When Castor falls in battle, Zeus decrees that he and Pollux are to spend half their time in Hades and the other half on Mount Olympus. Only now, in the tension between these two worlds, do they become an immortal pair of friends, just as they still gaze down on us as a constellation from the night sky.

Pairs of friends and circles of friends are well known throughout history. They have their special place in the annals of our civilization and have always exerted a considerable influence upon those around them. Socrates, for example, was constantly surrounded by a circle of friends. The Greek school of philosophy is a school of friends. Maecenas and his friends, Virgil and Horace, have become part of our language—Maecenas the patron.

How profound the idea of friendship has been in earlier times—indeed, how institutionalized—we can still see when we study life at the French royal court in the late Middle Ages. Here the *mignon en titre* represented the notion of friendship alongside that of the authority of the state. Today in our materialistic world, when a storm of opposition threatens to blow away all ideals, friendship has lost something of its former luster but nothing of its meaning and significance. We may be more careful in using the word on a daily basis, yet its significance has not changed. When we call someone a friend we do so as a recognition of mutual confidence, aware that there can be no secrets and no taboos between us, that we can discuss matters without barriers whatsoever, without calling into question respect and tolerance toward one another. I am convinced that being confident about one's friends remains an important commitment, for it offers an island of calm and stability in the quick and shallow currents of our days.

On September 5, 1984, I took leave of another friend, Teddy Suhren. We had shared duties as watch officers in the 7th U-Boat Flotilla, had commanded boats at the same time in the Battle for the Atlantic, and had later trained submarines and their crews for frontline deployment in the 27th (Tactical) U-Boat Flotilla in the Baltic. During all this time we were aware of our differences in character, strengths, and appearance, but our military duties and our common appreciation of how they should be carried out had brought us close together.

Fate had dealt Suhren a series of harsh blows. Having served as chief of U-boat operations in the Arctic Sea, he suffered dearly under the arbitrary treatment and revenge the Allies meted out after the war. He came to know the inside of Norwegian prisons very well. His wife left him to live with an American soldier who at the time brought home higher pay. His parents and his sister committed suicide rather than fall into the hands of Russian troops in the East. Suhren never talked about all this, but it tore him up inside. On his last journey I wanted to be with him.

The funeral took place in Hamburg at the Ohlsdorf Cemetery. My train from Bonn arrived late. Under sunny autumn skies and through the cemetery's greenery I walked up to the terrace outside Hall B, where I found other mourners waiting for the ceremony to begin. Halls A and C were occupied, one funeral after another.

I recognized many of the faces around me: Godt, Kretschmer, Korth,

Bargsten, Cremer, and others—after all those years they looked somewhat strange to me. The Knight's Crosses on their gray suits did not quite seem to befit the occasion. Indeed, they looked macabre to me as we took our place in death's waiting line. Here and there I overheard banal comments about Teddy's recently published book, *Nasses Eichenlaub.* The West German Navy was also represented—their highest ranking officer present being a *Flottillenadmiral*, the equivalent of a brigadier general.

At last the gates to Hall B open. We barely hear organ music playing in the background, not live but from a record. I sit down in the third row. The coffin is surrounded by wreaths and flowers and flanked by an honor guard of *Bundesmarine* officers. The music stops. The representative of Teddy's graduating class, Crew 35, is the first to speak. After a brief, undefinable organ interlude he is followed by the honorary president of the Naval Association whose address seems lively and loud. Then it is the turn of the submarine commander under whom Teddy served as executive officer. He speaks hesitatingly, searching for words, visibly moved. Finally, the spokesman for the Association of Submariners. Using the famous lines of the Flanders Flotilla of World War I, he suggests that on account of Teddy's usually unkempt appearance and overall bad deeds St. Peter would likely send him to a special heaven for U-boat commanders where they can continue their old ways of singing, drinking, and merrymaking.

For all who spoke, Teddy seemed to be representing the stereotypical *Landsknecht*, the soldier of fortune of bygone days who made merry with his friends as their drinking buddy, whose sense of humor was legendary, and who did not always stop at the limits of the possible. For example, when entering Brest after a war patrol and approaching assorted dignitaries of the naval base waiting to welcome him and his boat home, no other man than Teddy Suhren could have raised his megaphone and inquired across the water, "Are the Nazis still in power?"

The picture I had of Teddy was quite different. To me he was a friend with whom I had gone through this damned war, a man marked by the terrible fate of his family. I saw his exaggerated honesty as something designed to hide his true feelings. I listened to his colorful humor, but it too only masked the cynicism of a lost existence, the endorsement of unpopular views.

The words that filled the room failed to reach me. A trumpeter played *Das Lied vom guten Kameraden.* When it was over the curtain came down after this last act in the dramatic life of my friend Reinhard Suhren. We mourners left Hall B through the crowd that was already waiting outside for the next funeral. Teddy's relatives left in a car that had been standing by with its engine running. I could not even express my condolences to them. I was told there was to be a get-together of the old-timers. I was

too disappointed, too depressed, to participate. Ali Cremer took me back
to the station. Eleven hours on the train, Bonn to Hamburg and back.

I paid my friend Teddy Suhren my last respects. Forget, friend, if you
can, what they made out of your last hour.

No one knows how Endrass fell. But he died in the zenith of his life.
He was spared the agony of decline.

When I reported after my last patrol to Admiral Dönitz, the Commander-in-Chief of the U-Boat Command, I used the opportunity to suggest that my successor on U 552 should make the South Atlantic his
principal area of operations because it was a region far less dangerous.
Dönitz accepted my suggestion. My men went out on four more patrols,
and they survived. Their very last frontline assignment was as a floating
weather station in the Arctic. Then the boat returned to Germany and
was scrapped in Wilhelmshaven at war's end. One night a naval officer
in civilian clothes entered the shipyard and sawed off the head of the
boat's periscope to keep it as a souvenir.

Five years later the man phoned me and said that it would burden his
conscience to keep this memento of my boat for himself. He begged me
to accept it as a gift. Since that time the periscope head through which I
made so many observations during the war has been in my possession.
Occasionally my children and grandchildren pick it up and look through
it for fun. The world they perceive is so colorful, so different from the
one I associate with that periscope, from the haunting pictures of an era
long gone by.

In the fall of 1942 I left the 7th U-Boat Flotilla, their bases in France,
and the band of brothers of U-boat commanders who, although operating on practically all seven seas, were never far from us because we knew
about them by monitoring their and the U-Boat Command's radio traffic.
We lived with them and celebrated their successes. We mourned them
when their silence indicated they would not come back.

Each of them had his own history. I should mention and introduce all
of them, especially those whose names are forgotten today but whose
faces and words are fresh in my memory. Some of them actually made
history: Werner Hartenstein, for example. I met him for the first time in a
French bar. He sat by himself, oblivious to those around him. When I sat
down next to him, he said in an unfriendly voice, "My name is Hartenstein. I don't care who you are." He was a newcomer in the circle of well-
known names. He did not hesitate to repulse intrusions into his reserved
behavior with some vehemence, an attitude grounded more in a sense of
humility than a desire to hurt others. His experiences and the way he
overcame challenges made him someone special.

Hartenstein's boat had been dispatched into the Gulf of Mexico to shell an oil refinery. The boat surfaced at dawn, its gun crew manning the 4-inch deck gun. In the excitement the gunnery officer forgot to have the stopper removed from the gun. The first round was set off, exploding in the barrel. The gun crew suffered light injuries; an ensign was severely wounded. Hartenstein issued orders to have the useless portion of the barrel sawed off, readjust the gun's ballistic characteristics, and resume the bombardment of the refinery. Later the boat stopped at Martinique, an island loyal to the Vichy government, to have the ensign treated in its hospital. Years later, after the war, my French friend Admiral Jean Sabbagh, who was then also a submarine commander, told me that he had met the German ensign and had been able to assist him in that emergency. Thus this story has come full circle.

After his return to France Hartenstein made the customary personal report to Admiral Dönitz in Paris. The patrol had been successful and Dönitz was in a good mood. "Hartenstein, is there anything I can do for you while you are here in Paris?" "Sir, if I only had a car, I would love to do some sightseeing." "But of course, Hartenstein, my personal car is at your disposal." Thus, later that afternoon Hartenstein, along with Karlchen Thurmann who had returned from patrol at the same time, were off in the Admiral's limousine. Around 8 P.M. the Commander-in-Chief asked his aide whether the car had been returned. The aide: "Sir, did you place the car at the two U-boat commanders' disposal?" "Yes, but of course not for so long. It is always the same story. If you offer these types your little finger, they'll grab the whole hand." Thus, the admiral had to call for a smaller car to take him to a scheduled visit to the city commandant of Paris. When he returned to his headquarters, his first words were, "Where is the car?" "The two submarine commanders have not yet returned." "As soon as they come back they are to report to me at once." Long past midnight, having done their share of bar hopping and gotten thoroughly acquainted with the city, Hartenstein and Thurmann returned at last. The aide-de-camp informed them, "You are to report to the Commander-in-Chief at once!" But when he realized that the two were far from sober, he added, "Well, I suppose this can wait until tomorrow." Hartenstein, however, felt himself called by his commander's voice. He straightened himself out, put on his uniform, and made his way to Dönitz's quarters. Dönitz, who was in the habit of working long into the night, was still up and complained bitterly that the two had taken advantage of his generous gesture. Hartenstein listened to the tirade unmoved, then saluted his commander and replied, slightly altering the famous lines attributed to Börries Baron von Münchhausen, "On many a flag have I laid my hand swearing loyalty in this wicked war, many an admiral have I served . . ." before he simply turned around and left. The next morning at breakfast Dönitz retold the whole story to everyone's amusement.

Hartenstein commanded *U 156* when she sank the *Laconia* off North Africa. The latter turned out to be transporting Italian prisoners of war, and when Hartenstein realized that the ship's lifeboats were far too few to accommodate passengers and crew he set in motion an international rescue operation. He alerted U-boats and merchantmen of other nations in the vicinity to the developing catastrophe by open messages on the international emergency frequency. Hartenstein himself took as many of the shipwrecked men aboard his boat as he could. To indicate the humanitarian nature of their actions, he and the commanding officers of the other submarines covered their boats' forecastles with huge Red Cross flags. This, however, did not stop U.S. "Liberator" bombers flying toward and over the scene from dropping bombs onto the U-boats and their shipwrecked guests. Clearly, this action not only violated international law but also went against the unwritten obligation to come to the aid of those in distress.

The behavior of the Americans in this incident led to a controversial German countermeasure, namely, the order not to render help to shipwrecked sailors for fear of endangering one's own ship and crew. The Allied prosecutor at the International Military Tribunal in Nuremberg after the war characterized these instructions as an order to kill—an accusation that in the end could not hold up in the face of evidence. To illustrate this episode, I would like to quote an extract from a Führer conference at the Reich Chancellery on September 28, 1942, at which Admirals Raeder and Dönitz were present:

> Hitler continued: "I now want to address a matter we have dealt with in the past few days by way of radio-teletyper and telephone—the *Laconia* affair. To rescue the crews of sinking enemy vessels does not only endanger our own boats because of the ever-present threat of air attacks, but it goes against the very objectives of U-boat warfare. We must keep in mind what impact it has on enemy morale: He who sails for England must know he sails straight into death."
>
> At this point Hitler became more vehement: "It is absurd to supply shipwrecked sailors in their lifeboats with additional foodstuffs, as has come to my attention, or to provide them with sailing direction to the nearest coast. I hereby give the following order: Vessels and their crews are to be destroyed, including crews who happen to be in lifeboats." Hitler had uttered these words in a most determined tone and commanding voice. General Keitel, who stood next to Hitler, took out a notebook, placed it on the table, bent over it and recorded Hitler's directive. After a few moments of silence Hitler regained his composure and asked calmly: "Are there any other matters to discuss?" At that point Dönitz stepped back from the table, stood at attention, and said, "No, my Führer. It violates the honor of a sailor to shoot defenseless shipwrecked men. I will not issue such an order. My U-boat men, all of them volunteers, are carrying out a struggle

with very severe casualties in the knowledge that they are fighting fairly for a good cause. The envisioned order would undercut their fighting morale. I beg you to withdraw the order." Hitler, again calm and using his Viennese dialect, replied: "Well, in that case you can do as you please. But no more aid and sailing directions." Keitel produced his notebook again and struck out the sentences he had taken down earlier. Throughout this episode only Hitler and Dönitz spoke, nobody else among those present.

This version of the conference is based on notes taken by Dr. Ing. Waas of the Navy's Construction Department immediately following the meeting. Its key points are also reflected in an entry of the Naval High Command's War Diary in December 1942: "The killing of survivors in lifeboats is not desirable, not so much because of humanitarian reasons, but because of damage to the morale of our own crews who would expect a similar fate for themselves if roles were reversed." With few exceptions U-boat commanders followed these instructions.

COMMANDER, 27TH U-BOAT FLOTILLA

In Gotenhafen on the Baltic (today, Gdynia in Poland) I was responsible for the tactical training of German submarines before they joined combat squadrons for frontline service. To simulate Allied convoys I had at my disposal six to eight merchant vessels displacing between 6,000 and 10,000 tons; the U-boat tenders *Wilhelm Bauer*, *Waldemar Kophamel* and *Saar*; and as escort forces the ex-Norwegian torpedo-boats *Löwe*, *Tiger*, *Leopard*, and *Panther*, as well as three minesweepers. In addition we could call up Luftwaffe squadrons from the nearby air base of Rahmel to provide air cover.

About every two weeks, eight to ten new U-boats joined the flotilla. With them we practiced day and night attacks against the convoy and its escorts, which cruised in waters between the Danish island of Bornholm and Libau on the Latvian coast. To render conditions as realistic as possible we were at sea in any type of weather, and the ships did not show their running lights. We used hand grenades to simulate depth charges. Our tactics reflected as accurately as practicable the experiences we had undergone in the Battle of the Atlantic.

We were quite concerned over the question whether our training program took into account the changing conditions of the U-boat war at sea. We knew our losses were mounting. While early in the war, until June 1942, we had lost on average two to three boats per month, corresponding figures for the period since July 1942 had gone up frighteningly to about a dozen boats per month. In May 1943 no fewer than forty-two boats failed to return. By the same token, Allied losses declined. In the early years of the war we had sunk more vessels than Allied and neutral shipyards could replace with new construction. This changed by the end of 1942, as the measures that President Roosevelt had announced in his famous speech of May 17, 1941 (before the U.S. entry into the war) began to take effect. He had said: "The Nazis are sinking three times the number of ships that British yards can build, and twice the number of British and U.S. shipyards combined. Our response must be: acceleration of the U.S. shipbuilding program and efforts to reduce our losses at sea." This led to the so-called Kaiser Program, the construction of the "Liberty" ships.

What turned the U-boat war around? The reasons are primarily scientific and technological, but they also have to do with matters of organization and productivity. The whole question has been analyzed at some length. Here I would like to limit my discussion to a brief summary.

Allied radar, used since 1940 aboard aerial surveillance aircraft and soon thereafter on escort vessels afloat, greatly hampered U-boat wolf-pack tactics against convoys and in the end made them unfeasible altogether. High frequency direction finding devices, also known as Huff/Duff, could pinpoint the position of a U-boat within a radius of 25 nautical miles as soon as the boat went on the air to guide other submarines toward the convoy. The Allies also obtained the approximate position of a U-boat by automatically comparing radio bearings picked up by listening stations located around the Atlantic. In this way convoys could be routed away from likely U-boat concentrations.

The "Leigh Light" system, combining radar and a powerful flashlight, enabled Allied aircraft to attack submarines at night when the latter surfaced to recharge their batteries. The "Hedgehog" allowed escort vessels to fire off a whole salvo of up to twenty-four depth charges with contact detonators, thus showering submerged U-boats with a hail of explosives. As U-boats sought greater depths to escape pursuit, the Allies dropped depth charges of higher destructive power to maximize effects. The asdic, or sonar underwater locating device, at first only useful if the searching vessel reduced its speed to below 10 knots, was improved to allow for its use at speeds of up to 18 knots. Moreover, the Allies vastly increased the number of escort vessels and surveillance airplanes and assured their cooperation in the search for U-boats. This effort culminated in the formation of so-called hunter-killer groups built around aircraft carriers.

But by far the heaviest blow against the U-boats came when the Allies cracked the German radio cipher *Schlüssel M*, or Cipher M. From about mid-1941 on, indications mounted that the enemy was reading some of our traffic, that is, he had access to our system of enciphering and deciphering. Again and again the men at the front alerted higher authorities of their suspicion. The leaders, however, clung to the view that *Schlüssel M* was absolutely secure because of the multitude of different combinations the cipher machine allowed. If the naval leadership had taken these warnings seriously, relatively simple changes in the cipher procedure could have rendered it much safer, such as a superencipherment or the use of maritime positions as reference points rather than in absolute terms. At any rate, radio messages for or from U-boats should have been decoupled from ordinary naval traffic to increase cryptographic security.

Already in March 1941 a British raid against the German patrol boat *Krebs* had garnered two of the rotor wheels used in the *Schlüssel M* cipher machine. A similar surprise attack against the weather observation ship *Lauenburg* gave the British cryptographic material whose true nature has never been revealed but is referred to as invaluable.

On May 9, 1941, Lieutenant Commander Fritz-Julius Lemp's *U 110* delivered an attack against a British convoy before damage due to depth charges forced the boat to the surface. All hands abandoned ship after Lemp ordered explosives with time-delay fuses to be attached throughout the boat in order to scuttle it. The explosives failed to go off and the boat remained on the surface. When Lemp tried to swim back to *U 110* to assure its destruction, he was shot dead in the water by the British who had closed in on the boat in the meantime.

A specially trained British boarding party under Lieutenant David Balmé entered the German submarine despite heavy seas. In the course of four hours Balmé and his men transferred to the destroyer *Bulldog* by way of a small dinghy all the cryptographic material they could find, the boat's naval charts, the cipher machine with all current settings, the callsign book, the encipherment instructions, and the radio log, as well as the spare rotor wheels of the cipher machine. While this operation went on, the *Bulldog* hove to in order to prevent the Germans in the water from observing what was going on and possibly sending word back home. During their years in captivity the crew of *U 110* remained isolated from other prisoners of war to forestall any kind of communication. Until the end of the war the German Naval High Command never learned about this incident.

Throughout his daring exploit, Lieutenant Balmé faced the constant threat that one or more of the explosives aboard the boat might blow up and kill his entire party. The raid would have far-reaching consequences. It meant the beginning of the Allied victory in the Battle of the Atlantic. Balmé's name is rarely mentioned. At the time, in Bletchley Park in England, a group of British and Polish experts under Alan Turing, joined by Jewish emigrés, developed the concept of a machine we would today describe as a computer. The latter enabled the enemy to break into *Schlüssel M* and begin to read virtually the entire radio traffic not only of the German Navy but of the Wehrmacht in general. The British were able to decipher German messages for the remainder of the war, except for most of 1942. The process became so advanced that most signals were read within two to three days of their transmission. The British thus gained a precise picture of enemy dispositions. Convoys could be routed away from our U-boat patrol lines while Allied hunter-killer groups were ordered to move in on them.

The "Enigma" cipher machine was originally developed for civilian applications. Patents for it had been obtained in several countries, including England in 1926. It could be bought on the open market. The military version of the Enigma contained a number of special features, but its basic principles were known. This circumstance substantially helped the Polish mathematicians make their initial technical analyses. Until the end of the war, German experts simply assumed that the incredibly high number of different rotor combinations for encipherment purposes rendered the Enigma safe to use. Even if one machine fell into enemy hands, the decipherment process was likely to be so time-consuming that the information learned would be of no use because events had moved on. While the German radio intelligence service could boast successes during World War II, the results of British efforts in the field remained a quantum leap ahead.

What made the British so superior? They created a novel form of cooperation between the military and the scientific community. They called it operational research. The U.S. equivalent would be operational analysis. These groups of experts contained scientists from a variety of disciplines: physicists, chemists, mathematicians, astronomers, economists, psychologists, and the like. This, for example, was the composition of the team at Bletchley Park who worked together with experienced naval officers in the area of "operational and special intelligence." They collected all information they could possibly assemble about German U-boats, their tactics, armament, level of training, number and duration of war patrols, and even the personalities of the commanding officers. So-called mixed teams evaluated the information and passed their conclusions on to the forces engaged in anti-submarine warfare. After the war in Spain I happened to meet a former British intelligence officer who at one time had been in charge of tracing my and my boat's activities. He still remembered details about my war patrols that had long since slipped my mind. And what did we know about those who opposed and fought against us in that war? Practically nothing.

The operational research teams developed these methods at a steady pace and kept them so secret that, while feeling their effects very clearly, we had no idea about their technological and operational dimensions.

How did the U-Boat High Command react to the increasing effectiveness of enemy countermeasures; what was its response to the declining successes in the Atlantic? In May 1943 Dönitz called together the commanders of all U-boat flotillas operating out of bases on the Bay of Biscay for a conference. Anyone who has attended similar meetings knows how strongly Dönitz's charisma affected those under his command and how unlikely it was for serious criticisms to be brought forth. In this case Dönitz's view and thus that of his flotilla commanders can be summarized as follows. To withdraw the U-boats from the Atlantic would free thousands of Allied aircraft, which in turn could be used against German cities. Likewise, hundreds of escort vessels could be diverted against German coastal shipping in the North Sea and cut off German supply lines to Norway. Churchill would be able to realize his dream of breaking through the Baltic approaches. A later argument would add that under such circumstances the evacuation of two million refugees across the Baltic at the end of the war would have become impossible. On May 31, 1943, Dönitz flew to Führer Headquarters to consult Hitler about the problem. Hitler concurred with Dönitz's views and added: "The Atlantic is our western perimeter. It is better to fight the enemy there than along the shores of Europe."

A retrospective analysis of Dönitz's arguments reveals that the types of Allied aircraft employed in anti-submarine warfare would have been impossible to use as strategic bombers against Germany, or only following extensive modification, on account of their flight characteristics and weapons systems. But why would the Allies go to any such trouble if their production of long-range bombers was quite sufficient to meet demands? To break through the Baltic approaches would have required major fleet units, not patrol craft or escort vessels. And finally, the continued U-boat offensive in the Atlantic could not prevent the Allied invasion of the continent. But even if one lets Dönitz's arguments stand, it would have been wiser to bind Allied naval and air forces in the Atlantic by sending U-boats out on sporadic rather than massive missions, especially snorkel-equipped boats that could run their diesels even when cruising at periscope depth.

Which measures did the German side take to reduce submarine losses and boost their successes against Allied shipping? Since the fall of 1942 most boats carried a so-called Metox, which was originally developed by the French radio industry. It was an improvised device designed to measure—and alert U-boats against—incoming Allied radar signals. The contraption consisted of a primitive wooden frame antenna on the bridge (the so-called Biscayan Cross), which was connected by a cable to the receiver inside the boat. It turned out to be useless in heavy weather and an impediment whenever the boat had to crash dive. In addition, the Metox device sent out electromagnetic waves of its own that could be picked up by the enemy.

Other such measures followed, such as the "Naxos" device that reached the front in September 1943 and was supposed to interfere with enemy radar reception. "Aphrodite" was a balloon some 25 inches in diameter and carrying three 12-foot-long dipole antennas. Trailed by a U-boat on the surface, it was meant to confuse the enemy as to the boat's real position. "Bold" was a container filled with calcium hydrate. It could be expelled from a submerged submarine through a special tube, remain suspended in the water, and fool pursuers by producing a second sonar echo on their screens. "Alberich" became the code name for a special rubber coating, some 4 millimeters thick, that was put on submarines to reduce the likelihood of reflecting radar and sonar impulses.

Torpedoes, too, underwent modification. The so-called FAT and LUT models could be preprogrammed, for example to run loops through an enemy convoy until they hit a target. The "Zaunkönig" torpedo featured an acoustic listening device that responded to engine and propeller noises of enemy ships and detonated the torpedo at a pre-set distance. The snorkel, an air tube projecting beyond the surface, allowed a boat to use its diesel engines while running submerged, primarily for the purpose of recharging its batteries. Last, the "Bachstelze" was a heavy, manned kite that could be trailed by a U-boat at higher speeds up to an altitude of some 300 feet. Difficult to handle, it supposedly increased the boat's observation radius but for all practical purposes could only be employed in distant waters devoid of aerial surveillance.

Except for the snorkel and the new torpedoes, all these measures constituted improvisations that did not even begin to compare with the enemy's enormous scientific and technological advances. They did little to reduce U-boat losses, nor did they help destroy more enemy vessels. To the contrary, fewer Allied ships were sunk than ever before in the war, while our losses averaged twenty boats per month in 1944.

At the latest, the Normandy invasion of June 1944 nullified all arguments for a continuation of submarine warfare with traditional boats. Nevertheless, between January 1, 1945, when the Americans reached the Rhine and the Russians stood in East Prussia, and the end of the war on May 8, 1945, more than 100 additional U-boats were lost. Only the new Type XXI and XXIII boats afforded their crews a better survival chance and held out the possibility of limited successes when using improved tactical procedures. But quite apart from the fact that these boats came too late, they did not constitute a miracle or secret weapon that could have altered the course of events.

We leaders of the U-boat flotillas knew about our staggering losses at sea. For us the statistics meant more than just cold figures. Each boat lost implied the sacrifice of human beings, of comrades and friends. Crews whom we had trained in the Baltic days or weeks before did not return from their first war patrol. Living in ignorance of the enemy's growing technological edge, we assumed that our casualties had to do with inadequate training and preparation on our side, and in this respect I felt much personal responsibility. We chief instructors in the training flotillas decided to present Dönitz with our demands for improved equipment for our own escort forces, for the allocation of more aircraft, and for a more thorough training schedule before the new boats left for the front. But who should go to Berlin and challenge Dönitz on these points? Teddy Suhren suggested we should draw lots. I as the man ultimately responsible for the tactical training of our boats decided that it had to be me. When I returned from that meeting in Berlin I felt disappointed and annoyed because my views had been rejected practically out of hand and I was not even given sufficient opportunity to argue my case. Teddy said he had always warned against the arrogance of certain staff officers—an attitude confirmed by another veteran of tough convoy battles, Ali Cremer. Once, after he had returned from a war patrol, he described to the staff in Berlin an abortive attack he had made with the newfangled "Zaunkönig" torpedo, which in theory could locate its target automatically with the help of its acoustic warhead. It was the last best hope U-boat men had at the time. By every appearance the torpedo in question had completely malfunctioned and run out of control. But for the staff officers the answer was obvious: "Well, Ali, why don't you simply admit that you missed your target?" For those men, nothing could ever happen that was not supposed to happen.

One explanation for the staff officers' behavior could be that they needed to radiate optimism even when things were going badly. Moreover, they lived and worked in the presence of Dönitz's charismatic personality, which retarded dissention and created certain Byzantine arrangements at the top at a time when many of Dönitz's closest advisors lacked experience and insight into the true conditions at the front. At any rate, no one can claim that the U-Boat Command did not have access to critical information, observations, and assessments.

Of 39,000 German U-boat men in World War II, some 30,000 went down with their boats. After the summer of 1943, of every three boats that sailed from their bases two would not return. How can we explain that crews who had barely escaped death on their last outing were ready to go at it again? Did it have to do with the principles of duty and obedience? Was there still a strong will to fight? Was it the result of superior leadership qualities on part of the officers that assured the loyalty of their men? How did one bridge the gulf between the far-from-enticing task of binding enemy forces in the Atlantic and the vague hope for better weapons systems, which, in their heart of hearts, everyone knew would come too late and make no difference?

Everyone felt that successes became fewer and fewer while losses and danger increased all the time. U-boat commanders experienced this tension with particular intensity. The following example stands for many from that time of declining fortunes. Operation Order "Kanal Nr. 1" for U-boats operating against Allied naval forces in the English Channel states:

Every enemy landing craft, even if it carries only 50 soldiers or a single tank, is a target that deserves the U-boat's full commitment. You are directed to attack it even if it means exposing our boats to possible destruction. . . . A U-boat that causes the enemy casualties during the landing is fulfilling its highest mission and justifies its existence even if it is lost in the process. . . . Commanding officers and chief engineers who do not exhibit the necessary enthusiasm for attacks will be subject to disciplinary action upon their return to base.

Of thirty-six U-boats sent up to the Channel from their bases along the Bay of Biscay, only nine were equipped with snorkels. The Allies had reinforced their Coastal Command with aircraft of all kinds so that their radar surveillance reached well into the Bay of Biscay. Boats without snorkels were picked up by radar, forced under water, or attacked so that none of them ever reached the Channel, several were sunk, and the rest returned in poor shape. The snorkel-boats enjoyed minor successes while losing some of their own as well. Between June 6 and the end of August 1944, our boats sank no more than five enemy escort vessels, twelve ships of about 55,000 tons, and four landing craft: twenty-one out of a total of 5,000 Allied vessels of all types involved in the operation. Of thirty German U-boats operating in the Channel during this phase, twenty were destroyed.

There is a principle valid in all navies that allows the commanding officer of a warship to decide on the spot and after weighing all options whether or how his vessel should engage the enemy. The Naval High Command violated this principle when its orders insisted on kamikaze-like actions under threat of punishment in case of noncompliance. Nothing like it had ever occurred in the German Navy before. It is testimony to the degree to which the Naval High Command had taken over the vocabulary of the political leadership, who tried to reach its goals through a kind of fanaticism that made a mockery of human values.

The later Operation *"Winkelried"*—so named after a Swiss soldier in the Battle of Sempach in 1386 who allegedly drew the bulk of the enemy's attention upon himself to give his comrades the break that would lead to their victory—was based on similar notions. Here German members of coastal commando units (midget submarines) actually signed a form by which they pledged to accept death as a military necessity. Stripped of its rhetoric, the demand was simple: either success or death.

When war came in 1939, there were some 3,000 men serving in the U-boat branch. By the end of 1941 Germany began to suffer an acute shortage of trained officers and petty officers. A special personnel program addressed the problem and solved it by early 1943. After the summer of 1941 the principle of voluntary service in the U-boat branch was phased out. Instead, fitness became the only criterion. However, to the end of the war the U-boat service continued to attract relatively high numbers of volunteers, especially among its officers.

There is something unique about the relationship between the crew of a U-boat and its commanding officer. The latter, in contrast to his counterpart on surface vessels, is completely integrated into the shipboard community without privileges of any kind. Success or failure of a boat hinges on the abilities and performance of every single member of the crew as well as on the aggressiveness of its commanding officer. A U-boat crew must function as a "band of brothers," to borrow Admiral John Jervis's famous dictum. Obviously it was easier for a successful U-boat commander to lead his men than for one who was less distinguished. But it was especially important that every crew member thought of himself as a link in a chain, as a part of a people's community destined to achieve great deeds. At the outset of the war we envisioned a European continent under German leadership. When victory became increasingly elusive, all efforts centered on the avoidance of unconditional surrender. As defeat became inevitable, we in the Navy retreated to a position of "Don't give up the ship!" Those who desired to free themselves from the chain drew upon themselves draconian reprisals.

By 1943 the average U-boat commander was twenty-three years old, just two years older than the mean age of his crew. These men had gone through the Nationalist Socialist education system, their views reflecting the social values of the regime. Their ideals prominently included a deep commitment to the fatherland, to the concept of a people's community, discipline, and the leader principle.

Proper leadership was inspired from above. After each war patrol a U-boat commander had to report in person to U-boat Command Headquarters and describe his latest experiences to the commanding admiral and his staff. This procedure brought personal ties whose value is diffi· cult to exaggerate. In addition, many organizational measures eased and enriched the life of the crews while their boats underwent refits. Two well-known examples include the special train sailors took on their furlough home, and the excellent and well-supervised recreational facilities near Germany's major submarine bases in France. This special care extended to certain amenities aboard. We always had coffee and chocolate, and sailors on recreational leave could expect to take along to their families a package containing high quality food items.

Propaganda, too, contributed to our self-image. U-boat men considered themselves members of an elite outfit as Admiral Dönitz's special forces, a "free corps Dönitz" so to speak. Such feelings, in turn, tended to encourage individuals to show themselves worthy of such a reputation. In this time of general and increasing uncertainty—aerial bombardments, threatening defeat—a U-boat man enjoyed the comfort of sharing life with his crew and comrades. Such interpersonal relations could become so intense that they sometimes overshadowed one's natural instinct to survive.

There is yet another explanation for the type of comradeship one encountered aboard a submarine. For what exactly is a U-boat? It is a craft that operates in three dimensions. This experience is vital for the men aboard. They live in the sea. The sea becomes a natural part of their lives. The men have to sharpen their senses; intensify their perceptions; react to sounds, vibrations, the salinity of the water, or temperature changes. They have to develop means of cooperation if they want to survive. You have to get to know your comrades to fathom their weaknesses and their strengths, for it is vital to predict where a chain of mutual dependency is likely to break, a chain that in the end controls everyone's life. Whenever a U-boat man leaves his base, when the escape hatches to the world above are shut, he leaves behind life in all its color and variety, the familiar companions of the sun, the moon, and the stars. He reduces his existence in that steel tube to but a few principles, among which comradeship and the will to survive rank the highest.

In our training flotillas the presence and example of successful U-boat commanders and enlisted men acted as an incentive for the new boats and their crews. This leadership by men who had fought at the front became especially crucial because psychologically the general spirit of the times, or *Zeitgeist*, reinforced its effects. By ensuring that general societal values, standards, and behavioral norms always matched those of the U-Boat Service, we rendered our leadership decisions plausible and through open and mutual cooperation preserved the soldiers' readiness to fight. Thus, exemplary military leadership combined with the overall attitude of the population to make it possible to continue the war even when it had been lost beyond any doubt.

I once was privileged to engage in a conversation with Professor Esau who at the time headed the Reich Institute for Physics Research. Our talk acquainted me with the scientific situation that, on the one hand, had enabled the enemy to be so successful against our U-boats and, on the other hand, limited our abilities to respond to the enemy's measures. He told me that the Procurement Office of the Army had completely misjudged the significance of radar and set other priorities instead. Moreover, he complained about a misguided personnel policy. Experts in the natural sciences along with radio amateurs had been sent to the front rather than to scientific laboratories, while highly qualified researchers of Jewish extraction had been banned altogether. He further told me that additional developments of Professor Hahn's experiments toward nuclear chain reactions and an atomic weapon lay in the distant future. Such efforts would require huge investments in terms of personnel and material resources and were quite unfeasible under the prevailing conditions. In telling me all this he chose his words very carefully, not only because these were secret matters but also because he wanted to avoid the impression of pessimism and resignation, which might undermine the fighting spirit of Germany's armed forces and could draw the death penalty.

Another scientist with whom I came into contact was Dr. Aschoff. He was a torpedo specialist, and we had long talks about the so-called homing torpedo. The latter eventually reached the front under the code name "Zaunkönig" and led to certain successes against Allied escort vessels in the convoy battles.

Dönitz tried to push the technological development of U-boats and their weapons ahead by forming a scientific group under the direction of Professor Küpfmüller. A member of this group was Professor Cornelius, also an expert on torpedoes and special weapons. He taught at Charlottenburg Polytechnical University, and I was a frequent guest in his house. He believed such research was a step in the right direction but that too few experts had been allocated to the project and that cooperation between civilians and the military left much to be desired.

Three times during my military career I was invited to Führer Headquarters. The first time was in April 1942 when I was asked to report to the "Wolf's Lair" compound in Rastenburg (East Prussia) to be awarded the "Oak Leaves" cluster to my Knight's Cross. Hitler presented the decoration to me in the presence of his naval aide-de-camp, Captain Karl-Jesko von Puttkamer. Hitler thanked me for my missions in the Atlantic and asked me to join him and his other guests for lunch. During the meal Hitler dominated the conversation almost completely, stressing that he would do everything in his power to make life easier for Germany's soldiers. Anything that impeded military success would be weeded out mercilessly, especially delays in the production process, financial corruption, and all forms of sabotage. Under National Socialism, according to Hitler, the German people had left its past behind and set out for new shores.

As a soldier I liked what Hitler had to say, but I took silent exception to his verbal excesses and the way he put forth his views. In particular I found his disrespect for our enemies abhorrent. For him, Churchill was an alcoholic and Roosevelt's chief quality was his physical paralysis. Among Hitler's entourage I met Field Marshal Wilhelm Keitel and General Alfred Jodl, as well as his personal physician, Dr. Theodor Morell. Jodl impressed me as a clear-headed soldier concerned about the welfare of his subordinates. I remember Morell as an ungainly man who cared little for his appearance. His dinner manners raised eyebrows around the table. Whenever he spoke, however, he came across as knowledgeable, not as the quack that later analysts have often characterized him.

He was a general practitioner of considerable experience who consulted specialists whenever his own expertise was pushed to the limit.

I also made the acquaintance of the Secretary of the National Socialist Party, Reich Leader Martin Bormann. He had married the sister of my Crew comrade Walter Buch. Mentioning this connection, he invited me to be his guest at the Platterhof in Berchtesgaden. Three months later Teddy Suhren and I decided to accept the invitation. We first put in a stop at Pullach near Munich, the regular residence of the Bormanns. We were welcomed by Mrs. Bormann, the daughter of the Supreme Judge of the Party Tribunal, a very attractive and likable woman. She was surrounded by no fewer than nine children to whom she had given birth in intervals of about twelve months. From Pullach we were taken to the Obersalzberg near Berchtesgaden where we stayed at the Platterhof, the guest quarters of the Party leadership. Here we spent three interesting and refreshing weeks of vacation.

We could roam the entire Obersalzberg without the least restrictions. One night we were invited by the Bormanns, together with the famous movie personalities Willy Fritsch and Herta Feiler. Miss Feiler would eventually marry the actor Heinz Rühmann. Bormann had established an entire model farm on the Obersalzberg, which he was proud to show off to us. On one occasion he approached one of his prized bulls, grasped it by the ring through its nose, and led it around for us to admire. Willy Fritsch used that moment to whisper into my ear, with obvious reference to Bormann, "the steer of the Obersalzberg." Not only did Bormann look the part with his stocky, bull-necked build, but he played it, too, in a different sense. With his background in agriculture he would speak to us at length about his successes as a cattle breeder. Then, back at his house, he made it clear that his own procreative qualities had not been limited to fathering his numerous legitimate offspring but had resulted in a number of illegitimate children as well. Fritsch's observation had been right on target.

That evening I was also introduced to Eva Braun, a young woman with a pretty, albeit somewhat expressionless, face. She invited us to call on her at her place the next day. Teddy and she got along splendidly; he even induced her to abandon completely the reserved attitude that was her usual trademark. She, the Führer's mistress, suffered greatly from the fact that she could not participate in any official functions. When Hitler and she had eaten breakfast and the first visitors arrived, she had to retire. Hitler made it plain to her that he could never marry her because it would damage his public image. It would be inappropriate for him to reveal he had a private life. Instead, he was to be at his people's service day and night.

Through Eva Braun we also made the acquaintance of Magda Schneider, the mother of the actress Romy Schneider. She struck us as

an accomplished and sometimes bubbly socialite. Together we undertook a trip to the tea house, or "Eagle's Nest," as the Americans dubbed
it after the war. A winding road led all the way up to an altitude where
trees could no longer grow. We arrived at a rocky promontory that had
been made into a terrace, then walked through a tunnel to an elevator. It
took us up another 300 feet into the interior of the so-called tea house. Its
walls made of mighty blocks of natural rock, the house consisted of a
large living area as well as several guest and utility rooms. The living
room opened on three sides onto the majestic world of the Alps by way
of oversize, undivided windows. It was a most impressive panorama indeed.

I visited Führer Headquarters for the second time in the fall of 1942 to
receive the "Swords" in addition to the "Oak Leaves" cluster of the
Knight's Cross. At that time the headquarters was located in Vinnitsa in
the Ukraine. On the way our flight had a layover in Prague, where I had
an opportunity to get to know that old imperial and university city. We
were guests in the house of the German city commandant.

In Vinnitsa I ran into the same faces I had encountered at the "Wolf's
Lair," except in very different surroundings. As the open staff car took us
to Hitler's headquarters we passed through a vast, fertile country. Here I
saw Russia for the first and only time in my life. A sense of melancholy
lay over the land and its people. It was not just caused by the fury of the
war that had visited this region, but it had to do with the very essence of
the country. Since that visit I have felt a closer affinity to the works of
Dostoevsky and Tolstoy.

At Headquarters I made the acquaintance of Heinz Brandt, who had
won the gold medal in equestrian show-jumping at the Olympic Games
in Berlin and who later served as a colonel on the General Staff. He sat
next to me during lunch. We all listened to Hitler's words, which hit us
like so many blows with a metal object. Perhaps it was the proximity of
the front lines that induced Hitler to choose as his topic for the occasion
Heraclitus's dictum that war is the father of all things. Hitler's arguments
jumped back and forth across 2,000 years of history. He cited Darwin's
notions about the struggle for existence and the selection of the fittest.
According to Hitler, only peoples who were strong had survived. Ever
since the German people had entered the stream of history it had been
threatened from the East by Huns, Mongols, and Russians. There had
been only a few moments in Germany's past when a Führer had arisen
to unite the German people and to meet the external challenges. Thus,
Hitler argued, Germany's struggle was against a modern-day Genghis
Khan who in turn enjoyed the backing of the international Jewish community.

And then Hitler went on to say something that must have been in the
back of his mind all along, namely, that the collapse of the eastern front

would bring chaos for a thousand years. For a moment I was caught in reflecting about this unexpected association of a 1,000-year Reich with a 1,000-year Chaos so that I missed a portion of Hitler's subsequent utterances. Today I can only recall fragments, such as the tension between *Lebensraum* and population density; notions about emigration and birth control; and the conclusion that Germany's average population density of 135 persons per square kilometer required the acquisition of additional *Lebensraum* to ensure proper food supplies. We had been prepared for this kind of thinking by Hans Grimm's book, *Volk ohne Raum* (People without Space), which we had devoured when it came out in 1926. Had there not been other peoples in history in search of living space? What about the British Empire? Or France? Or the Dutch colonies? It was not a question of international law or humanitarianism; in fact, the subject did not even come up. Since our school days we had been too engrossed in Darwinian notions. And yet I felt a sense of uneasiness about Hitler's presentation, a sense deepened by my recent experience of learning more about the Ukraine and its inhabitants.

In his conversations with me Brandt came across as quite critical of the situation, an attitude that reflected the mood of the Army's operational staff. But this did not mean active resistance against Hitler, as some analysts would imply after the war to the amazement of those who had been there and knew better. Brandt lost both legs in the explosion of July 20, 1944, that failed to take Hitler's life. He died a short time later. To this very day Brandt's possible association with resistance groups remains a matter of debate. Brandt was promoted posthumously to the rank of major general. The Army planned an official state funeral for him, but the event was cancelled without further explanations. Instead, he was put to rest with only a few of his relatives in attendance. The coffin was sealed and the whole ceremony closely watched by the Gestapo.

My third visit to Führer Headquarters, now back at "Wolf's Lair," came in the summer of 1943. On that occasion I received the official diploma to go along with the decoration of the "Swords" to the Knight's Cross I had been awarded earlier. Three other distinguished U-boat commanders joined me on this visit: Captains Wolfgang Lüth, Robert Gysae, and Teddy Suhren. After the official part was over, the four of us stayed on as Hitler's dinner guests. At the time there was much talk about the new secret weapons, and Hitler entertained us with a monologue about technological developments. I still recall him raving about a newfangled accumulator based on some chemical caustic solution. It supposedly would free Germany from its dependence on lead, a raw material in very short supply. Now that the V1 had gone into production and the V2 rocket was being developed, and I myself had seen prototypes of the revolutionary Walter propulsion system for U-boats, I was impressed by Hitler's words. Everything appeared quite plausible. Nevertheless I retained my skepticism, especially after listening to a presentation in Danzig by Hans Fritzsche, a high official in the Propaganda Ministry. He talked about the development of new weapons systems. Next to me sat a Luftwaffe officer. When Fritzsche came to the topic of new technology for the air force, the Luftwaffe officer whispered into my ear, "Exaggerated, completely exaggerated!" As Fritzsche moved on to address the subject of the new electro-boats of the submarine branch and quoted Dönitz to the effect that the new boats would be as effective in convoy battles as their predecessors had been in the old days, it was my turn to whisper back, "Completely exaggerated!"

The next day we were the guests of General Adolf Heusinger, chief of staff of the Army's operations division. On that occasion I met the brother of my Crew comrade Baron Haus-Diedrich von Tiesenhausen, Captains Wolfgang Schall and Wolfgang Köstlin, and once more Lieutenant Colonel Brandt. All agreed that conditions along the eastern front had become very critical and complained that Hitler interfered in matters of insignificant detail entirely unjustified by the overall assessment of the situation.

We were also invited by the operational staff of the *Waffen-SS*. This invitation resulted from the fact that SS Leader Heinrich Himmler assumed the official sponsorship of Gysae's boat. Gysae, known throughout the Navy for his sometimes careless remarks, said on this occasion quite sarcastically, "Yesterday we were still losing the war, today we are winning it again." The SS leadership, notorious for its constant opposition to Army officers, wasted no time in passing the remark on up the chain of command. General Heusinger was asked to see Hitler about the matter. Heusinger was briefed by his own officers about our conversations, and we, too, were requested to contribute our version of the incident once we had returned to Gotenhafen. We felt very awkward being under the suspicion of having passed on confidential remarks in such a manner. Lüth and I composed a letter in which we described the incident and the conversations from our point of view in defense of the implicated Army officers. Many years later, in 1982, Major General (ret.) Köstlin brought up the affair once more when I met him one day in Spain. He recalled that as late as July 1944, after the attempt on Hitler's life, the whole incident was brought back into the limelight and used to accuse Army officers of lack of loyalty and sabotage.

Another interesting man I met during the war in Berlin was Herr Girardet, the well-known newspaper publisher from the Rhineland. After the war I ran into him again in Bonn when he gave a speech as President of the Association of Newspaper Publishers. Afterwards we sat together and he refreshed my memory about an incident in connection with our first encounter during the war. He had just returned to

Berlin from the eastern front and was relaxing with friends in a bar when I was introduced to him. On that day I had come back from Führer Headquarters. When I extended my hand to greet Girardet he remarked half-moved, half-jokingly that my very hand had touched the Führer's only the day before. He also asked for any details of my meeting with the Führer and what kind of impression he had made on me. Girardet expected that, as so many others, I would indicate how fascinating the encounter had been. He felt almost taken aback when I remained quite critical about Hitler and his monologues at the dinner table. At the time, Girardet considered me arrogant and felt disappointed in me. But when we met so many years later in Bonn, he confessed that I had been one of very few people who had not fallen victim to Hitler's charisma and the personality cult surrounding him.

I have already mentioned that I showed up from time to time at the U-Boat High Command in Berlin (code name: "Koralle") in order to inform myself about the latest developments or to present concerns I had about the discrepancy between the effectiveness of our training in home waters and the realities out in the Atlantic. On one occasion I witnessed an Allied air raid against Koralle. One of the attacking planes was shot down. Its crew descended on their parachutes. One of them got caught in high-voltage electrical wires. A German chief petty officer thereupon cut him loose and proceeded to mistreat him. I immediately intervened and asked the petty officer to explain his actions. He replied: "My family was killed by American air raids." Later we discussed the incident in our mess. Opinions were quite divided. Only a few of my fellow officers shared my view that this prisoner deserved protection from those who had captured him, the same treatment we would extend to a shipwrecked sailor. The majority of those present said they could well understand the petty officer's emotional reaction. How far the war had already succeeded in confusing otherwise rational minds!

In Gotenhafen I lived aboard the U-boat tender *Wilhelm Bauer*. When Teddy Suhren became my second-in-command and I had to direct only every other training exercise, I had to give up my quarters because the *Wilhelm Bauer* always went out to help simulate Allied convoys. Instead, I received a stateroom on the *Wilhelm Gustloff*. This was not just a single cabin but a whole suite consisting of a reception area, a dressing room, a bedroom, and a huge bathroom. I still recall the beautiful built-in closets, furnished from rare woods. When you opened them, lights went on inside automatically, a great luxury indeed in those days.

Before the war the *Gustloff* had been in the service of the National Socialist organization charged with looking after the recreational needs of workers and employees throughout Germany, also known as *Kraft durch Freude* (Strength through Joy). The ship had taken vacationers to Madeira and the Canary Islands. The club rooms and the cabins were exquisitely furnished. Altogether the vessel had undertaken only a few cruises, but you could still see reminders of those days. The parquet floor was marred by burn spots where people had extinguished their cigarettes; there were stains caused by red wine all over the carpets; and some of the wall panelling had been damaged. But one must say that the state in pursuit of its goal of a people's community had done something for the "workers of the fist" who in turn supported the new regime. Perhaps we were indeed headed down the path prophesied by Petty Officer Maltus, the "Tiger of the Baltic," so many years ago on the *Gorch Fock*.

In August 1944 I became Director of Testing and Training of the new Type XXI and Type XXIII "Electro" U-boats. Carl Emmermann, a Crew comrade of mine, assisted me in the assignment. Our primary task was to test the new superboats with their huge batteries under tactical conditions and to write up the manual for operations against the enemy.

We received the first boat of the larger Type XXI series. Her commanding officer was yet another Crew comrade of ours, Adi Schnee. Gerd Suhren served as chief engineer and Conny Lüders as executive officer. We went through all traditional tests and individual exercises and then practiced attacks against convoys along with the other boats of the 27th Tactical U-Boat Flotilla. The results were impressive. The new boat displayed superb characteristics when operating alone. It also enjoyed far greater survival chances when hunted thanks to superior maneuverability both laterally and vertically. But the boat did by no means live up to the boasts Dönitz had made to Hitler and us U-boat officers. Dönitz had ordered mass production of the new boats under the assumption that they would enable him to resume successful convoy battles as in the earlier parts of the war—indeed, that we would inflict losses and damage upon the enemy far in excess of our achievements at the height of the Battle of the Atlantic in 1942. Compared to the older Type VIIc boats, the new Type XXI version undoubtedly represented progress and innovation. But it could never by itself have turned the tide in the war at sea, let alone in the overall conflict. The new boat enjoyed considerable improvements when measured against standard submarine designs then in use in other navies. After the war, for example, the Russians developed their "Whisky" class boats out of our Type XXI. Even the 209 Model built more recently for export by the German shipbuilding giant Howaldwerke/Deutsche Werft (HDW) in Kiel depended for its basic features on the Type XXI design.

My life in that last phase of the war was dominated by political and military events that absorbed my undivided attention. I will again let my journals tell that story. But quite apart from these developments, I experienced something entirely new in my inner attachment to another human being, something that in its exclusivity and strength I had never felt before.

On February 19, 1943, Teddy Suhren, Claus Korth, and I were invited to the apartment of another U-boat commander and his family in Gotenhafen. At the darkened entrance to the building we were searching for our host's name and the appropriate button to ring his doorbell when a lady walked up, her face covered by a scarf. She said to us, "Well, if you also plan to visit the Heinsohns, I might as well press the button for you." The door opened; we left the dark entranceway and stepped into the lighted elevator our host had sent down for us. The lady then pulled back her scarf, I looked at her, she looked at me, and from that moment on to this very day a relay mechanism began sending impulses back and forth between us—a relationship that has kept me in suspense and excitement, has enriched my life and made me happy. For on that day I met my future wife.

I do not recall what we talked about in that elevator. Knowing my wife, she probably dominated the conversation and said many funny and clever things. At any rate, when we reached our host's apartment we sat together, danced all evening long, and had so much to tell each other that the world around became lost to us. Next to me sat a woman who enchanted me with her natural charm, her lively and cheerful temperament, and also her wit. And she came across as perfectly natural without the least pretensions. Whatever she said was marked by openness, warmheartedness, and intelligence.

I still remember that I jotted down her address and telephone number on my starched shirt cuffs. She also suggested that everyone present should sign a postcard to Mrs. Korth, who had been unable to attend our party. We agreed and she signed the card as "Ilse Topp." When she passed the card to me, I said," Now wait a minute, we are not that far, yet!" The others, glancing over my shoulder, just laughed. She then added with her usual charm, even though the situation appeared somewhat embarrassing to her, "Well, Mr. Korth, let's just leave it as it is. Your wife will think Mr. Topp is married." Later my friend, the artist Erich Klahn, would comment, "Ilse must have a sixth sense for such matters."

THE END OF THE WAR

Diary:

January 3, 1945
Today we listened to a radio address by Gauleiter Hanke, the Party official in charge of the besieged city of Breslau in Silesia. Manly words without ballast, exhorting the inhabitants to fight to the last. His words culminated in a quotation

from the Silesian clockmaker and philosopher, Jacob Böhme: *"Wer nicht stürbe, ehe er stirbet, der verdürbe, wenn er stirbet"* [He who has not tasted death before he dies, will be miserable when he dies]. In other words, those who have not been prepared to sacrifice their lives will be gripped by the fear of death when the time comes and die as weaklings, miserably, their spirits broken.

Böhme's words took me back to the convoy battles at sea. How many times did we gain back the gift of life when we had already given up all hope? In those cases we had thrown everything overboard: things that normally had been highly desirable to us; things we had striven for and fought over appeared suddenly unimportant and empty to us in the face of the final struggle. But as soon as the first ray of hope touched us we began to recover our old system of values, and once we had planted our feet solidly on the shore, now weighted down by all the usual ballast, we immersed ourselves again in the most ordinary and mundane matters.

Hanke was not prepared to fight to the last. Cowardly, he fled to safety and abandoned Breslau and its population to its horrible fate: murder, rape, destruction.

Letters:

January 28, 1945

You have not heard from me in some time. Yesterday I returned to Zoppot [near Gotenhafen], but you had already left to be safe from the Russians. I breathed a deep sigh of relief. When I collected the few things that are left I witnessed the misery of the refugees first hand. Huddling for eight hours in the drafty train depot at temperatures near 15 degrees below zero centigrade and not eating a bite for 24 hours has been quite a lesson in humility for me. All around me mothers with crying babies. Misery, distress, people in need of relief.

January 30, 1945

A short time ago the *Gustloff* went down while taking a load of refugees to the West. The seas were heavy and temperatures below the freezing mark. She had some 5,000 people on board; a catastrophe without precedent. The commanding officer of a torpedo-boat just received orders to go out and render assistance. I saw how the man turned pale when he got the news. His wife and three children had sailed on the *Gustloff*. What must have gone through that man's mind, knowing only too well that chances for a rescue are nil? I feel very small when I realize in all this misery that my own family is safe. But I cannot help it. Only yesterday I read in a book about Magellan the famous motto of Jão de Barros: "He who lives for glory is not afraid of danger." Yesterday I could fully identify with him. Today those are like so many hollow words. Who among those 5,000 human beings thought of glory for even one single moment? No, they yearned to stay alive and died full of fear.

There are crowds of people near the steamers in the port, all hoping to catch a ride to the West. The policemen have their hands full trying to keep matters under control. Trains arrive full of wounded soldiers stretched out on dirty, soiled patches of straw, their grayish faces emaciated and half frozen from the cold. And yet they have the will to survive. Our will to live is after all the most profound of all human instincts.

Air attack. Now the planes are even chasing people in the streets. Anti-aircraft fire does not seem to bother them. I happened to be near No. 11 Hindenburg St. (how long will it be before it is renamed?) when I entered our old home to find shelter from the flying shrapnel. I was also curious to learn what had happened to it. In each room a refugee family, nameless misery. Huddled closely together, they live, cook, sleep, and generally try to survive. All the toilets are clogged up.

I am glad you did not have to go through all this. On the other hand, I wish you could at least have had a glimpse of it to steel yourself for the times ahead.

February 2, 1945

Today, after a three-week trek with three carts and fifteen horses, Lieutenant Sauer's parents arrived in Zoppot. I offered them to stay at our place. The attitude of these people is remarkable. He is seventy, she sixty years old, both temporarily depressed but unbroken. Admirable people, indeed. Already in the last war they lost everything and became refugees. Now again they had to abandon to the Russians two flourishing estates. All they have left now are three carts full of household items for a family of eight, and their steadfastness. Two human beings like them, who have shared a long life together and exist only for each other, can hardly be touched by want and misery.

February 8, 1945

I am aboard the small torpedo-boat *TF 5* on our way from Gotenhafen to Kiel. A long-neglected compass had us end up in Swedish territorial waters, but we were fortunate in noticing our mistake before the Swedes did. Visibility is poor, allowing us to make out few reference points ashore to get an idea where we are. Suddenly the order: "Both engines full speed astern!" At the last moment a lookout had spotted a shadow ahead that turned out to be the coastline of the Danish island of Bornholm. We finally anchored after almost colliding with a fishing vessel in dense fog. Yesterday we heard enemy planes humming overhead on minelaying missions. Today we must wait for our minesweepers to clear the channels so that we can proceed to Kiel, where I will take over command of the new boat.

COMMANDING OFFICER, *U 2513*

From Notes:

Before I took over *U 2513* on April 22, 1945, I served for a few weeks as commanding officer of *U 3030* (also a Type XXI boat). Along with a few other experienced sailors on board, I used every available hour to train the new crew. We placed emphasis not only on knowing one's own battle station and area of expertise but also on acquainting oneself with the responsibilities of comrades in order to have some reserves in case of casualties. This meant, for example, that experts in the area of batteries and generators could fill in for diesel mechanics in the engine room, and vice versa. Throughout these drills we kept up our normal shipboard routine. To simulate realistic conditions we often had to pull switches and levers. We usually turned off the electricity or, if this was impossible, put up warning signs for the men to be especially careful.

One day the petty officer in charge forgot to post these warning signs while we were running our electric engines for underwater propulsion. A young enlisted man got accidentally caught in the machinery and was fatally injured. A court martial followed, and the petty officer was sentenced to fight in a penal company at the land front against the advancing Allied troops. The petty officer not only admitted his negligence but was deeply shaken by the consequences of his action. To tear him away from our shipboard community at this point would have meant death for him. I protested the finding of the court martial. The petty officer stayed with us on board, for here too he fought at the front.

April 25

We U-boat commanders find ourselves in a heated debate with members of the staff of the U-Boat High Command. Should the city of Flensburg on the Danish border, full of refugees and wounded soldiers, be defended or declared an open city? Should the midshipmen presently training at the Naval Academy in Flensburg be flown to Berlin to form a last line of defense around the Führer? We U-boat men are quite prepared to do our duty to the last, but for such nonsense we will not stand. We left the room in protest.

April 27

I report for the last time to the Chief of U-Boat Operations, Admiral Hans-Georg von Friedeburg. Once he had been my commanding officer on the *Karlsruhe*, a man whose dark eyes under bushy brows, although always veiled by the smoke of an expensive cigar, had radiated trust and confidence to everyone around. Today he is no more than a shadow of his former self. Aware of the absurdity of giving further orders to continue the war, he betrays himself by choosing words he no longer believes in, by becoming a link in the chain of nonsensical decisions that mark life in these final days. He says that if we can no longer defend our fatherland we must continue the struggle from our base in Norway until all is over. He and his staff would fight to the last bullet, and he expected the same from us. He shook my hand, full of confidence as always, but also full of grief. When he turned away he had tears in his eyes. He knew he would never see me again. (A few days later, after he had signed Germany's unconditional surrender, he took his own life.)

April 28

A last meeting with the Navy's Commander-in-Chief, Admiral Dönitz. His tone is as cordial as always. No sign of nervousness. But he still believes that proper fighting spirit can do wonders against tanks and aircraft. He talks about taking control of all German forces in the northern area while Hitler will continue to lead the other armies from his Headquarters in Berlin. Implied in these remarks is the notion that things can still be turned around. Rumors of differences between the British and the Russians give rise to such last hopes.

Then a handshake, stronger than von Friedeburg's. But no answer to the question that seems to hang in the air: For what or for whom are we still fighting and risking our lives? Dönitz had retreated behind a veil of unconvincing moral considerations and irrational arguments to justify his actions even though he cannot have believed in them very deeply. I was reminded of a picture that graced at that time so many living room walls of Navy families, sometimes even the pillowcases on their sofas. It showed "The Last Man" clinging to the wreckage of his vessel in heavy seas and proudly holding up his nation's flag.

But this was no time for sentiments. At stake was the survival of my crew of fifty human beings. According to our sailing orders, we were supposed to leave Kiel in company with several other boats on our way to Norway. I consulted with my chief engineer and we agreed to fake engine trouble to delay our departure. Our foresight paid off. The enemy's intelligence service did not fail to notice the other boats' movements. We followed them half a day later and were spared the attack of British fighter-bombers that sank or damaged several of the other boats.

April 29
We monitor a radio announcement that our front lines will be shortened and withdrawn in the west. In a way it is a last respite to allow the Americans, British, and French to take over responsibility for Europe's future.

April 30
British forces have crossed the River Elbe near Lauenburg and are closing in on Lübeck. I feel relieved, and not because of some macabre sense of sarcasm. For I know now that my family will not fall into the hands of the Russians. The German people are in a state of deadly exhaustion.

In the evening I invite some comrades over: Wächter, Wahlen, Grau, Lambi, Hilbig, Bielig. Am reminded of Deeping's dictum, "Happiness is work and a comrade." Each of our boats carries fifty such comrades. It is the task of us commanding officers to shepherd these men safely and without pathos through the last inquisitorial round without ending up in an auto-da-fé.

May 1
We depart for Horten in Norway, where I had briefly stopped over on my last "war patrol" in 1942. At 10 P.M. we learn of the Führer's death. The dream of a Greater German Reich is over. Dönitz assumes control over what is left of it. In his radio address he stresses the same things as in his farewell speech to us submarine commanders on April 28.

May 1–3
South of the island of Anholt we run into enemy activity but remain on the surface. As we enter the Oslo Fjord an aircraft moves in to attack. We dive. After-

wards we make Horten without further incidents. We are still under orders to engage the enemy. While docked in the naval base we continue to do repair work on our antennas and otherwise improve our survival chances.

In the meantime we receive the following news: a cease-fire in Northwest Holland; Hamburg, Kiel, and Flensburg have been declared open cities; negotiations about an armistice are under way with the British Field Marshall, Sir Bernard Montgomery; Northwest Germany and Denmark surrender. But the U-boat war continues until we receive the code word "Rainbow." The core of the fleet is being scuttled. Soon thereafter "Rainbow" is cancelled. The boats of comrades are being bombed and sunk. We are powerless.

May 7

The "minister in charge," Count Lutz von Schwerin-Krosigk, announces the unconditional surrender of the entire Wehrmacht. There is not to be any more bloodshed. This I learn in Oslo when I visit my chief engineer Heinz Peter in the hospital. He also warns me that the British have assembled a force of forty-eight naval units off Lervik. I return to my boat on the double. On the trip back I discuss all possible options with Dr. Nordmeier. We give up any plans to seek out the enemy because it is too late. Instead, we prefer to scuttle our boat since we are ignorant of any instructions to the contrary. All of this is then cleared up by the Grand Admiral's unequivocal order neither to scuttle nor to destroy the boats because we may save the lives of hundreds of thousands of Germans if we faithfully observe the armistice conditions.

We have a meeting of all submarine commanders aboard the torpedo-boat *Panther*. As senior officer present I make sure that we act in unison. Someone raises the possibility that Dönitz's instructions may have been issued under orders from the Allies and that therefore we should scuttle our boats independently to save the honor of the flag. This notion is flatly rejected by the officer in charge of U-boat operations in the west.

May 8

We solemnly lower our flag. I assemble the crew and inform them of the latest developments. Then we move out into deeper water and jettison all secret materials as well as our torpedoes.

May 10

The U-boat basin is well guarded on all sides. In the evening the boat next to ours flies a German flag suspended from a balloon. Bad taste. Also a question of proper leadership. I decide to retreat with my boat to Smörstein. Our own good discipline is endangered by being too close to the other boats. Once bad habits are formed, they are difficult to overcome. In Smörstein we live ashore in rural surroundings. We organize activity groups, including instruction in the English language. In the evenings we huddle around the fireplace. Unforgettable. Walter Flex, old songs and new ones.

The corps of engineers supplies us with electricity and a landing craft. Long discussions whether we should send a part of the crew home on the landing craft. We decide against it for disciplinary reasons. The crew must stay together.

We must obey the Allied instructions in all their ramifications, no matter where that might lead us. Deep down I feel, however, that our behavior will make no difference with regard to the treatment we Germans will receive. It will be degrading in any case.

May 12

The Allied Armistice Commission announces: All U-boat crews must be reduced to essential engine personnel only. Again we debate whether to send some of the men home. At the same time we are to indicate whether we will be seaworthy for a period of fourteen days. Evidently the boats are to be transferred to England. In the afternoon all commanding officers meet for coffee in Smörstein. Adventurous designs are being hatched, such as leaving Horten in single file with black flags flying. Or simply taking off for Kiel and thus presenting the Allies with a fait accompli. But what next? Another idea is to have *Panther* take all nonessential personnel to Kiel.

May 13

Franke and Meier bring orders that all nonessential crew members have to disembark except for the commanding officer, the executive officer, the chief engineer, the chief navigator, the two chief machinists, and twenty-nine others, mainly engine room personnel. I address the crew, which will now be torn apart. Who is to leave us? One man volunteers. When I make clear that more will have to go, several more raise their hands reluctantly. I was proud of them all. At 7 P.M. those selected are sent off with cheers echoing back and forth. A few have tears in their eyes. They know that an important part of their life has come to an end.

May 14

Life goes on. We enjoy our last days in freedom surrounded by pastoral beauty and haunted by uncertainty about our future. Smörstein is pleasant and relaxing. Only when we think of our loved ones at home does apprehension take over. May fate be kind to them.

May 16

The British arrive at 2 P.M.: Captain Wingfield and several other officers, accompanied by the ubiquitous Norwegian home guardsmen. The greeting is quite formal. Afterwards we assemble on the *Panther* to answer questions. Toward the end of our meeting Captain Wingfield expresses his admiration for the German U-boat force as well as understanding for our present predicament. Nice gesture. The English inspect the Type XXI boats and seem greatly impressed. "Fine boat." They are considerably worried about the boat in Smörstein outside their direct control.

May 17

Brilliant sunshine here in Smörstein. In the afternoon we weigh anchor and transfer to the pier at Holm, newly built by German engineers. We are the first German vessel to dock there and receive a most cordial reception. Celebrations continue until 5:30 A.M.

May 18
   The winds have freshened up. The boats are difficult to handle. We receive orders to transfer at once to Holmestrand. We break camp not without a sense of nostalgia. After all, we had enjoyed real freedom here for the last time in a long while. In the evening there is a meeting of all U-boat commanders.

May 19
   We pick up a radio message from the U-Boat Command's operations division that all boats are to follow the Grand Admiral's instructions. Anything else is considered irresponsible. Boats still at sea are to surface and surrender. At noon we get under way. Several British officers embark on Franke's boat. In line ahead, we enter Oslo harbor under the threatening guns of British destroyers.
   For Whitsuntide we have decorated the boat in festive green. British marines board Franke's boat. At noon I meet Wiegand. Franke's staff surgeon joins us. Guns at the ready, the marines had robbed them of watches and fountain pens. "Just" times have arrived. In the evening I try once more to get through to Germany on the telephone. No success. For the first time we begin to realize what it means to lose our freedom. On the other shoreline people move back and forth without the least restrictions. At least we can still look at them through our binoculars. Soon we will be surrounded by barbed wire.

May 26
   A farewell party for Wiegand, Brauel, Petersen, and Hauber, who are to sail their boats to Scotland. Much singing, music, drinking. Until 4 A.M. we are engaged in discussions about Russia, about socialism at home, about the mistakes that have cost us the war. I have to think of an evening aboard the U-boat tender *Wilhelm Bauer*. On that day the National Socialist Gauleiter Forster made the most arrogant comments about the Poles. I remember the atmosphere at Führer Headquarters, so full of hubris. Our conversations move between a desire to justify what we have done and a sense of self-scourging as we would witness it in the future. For the most part the discussions remain very superficial.

May 27
   At 7 P.M. we take leave of the four boats bound for England. There are flowers, as if they were off to a war patrol. The remaining crews honor them by taking up formation, singing the national anthem, shouting hurrahs, and waving their arms. "Comrades, when will we meet again?" Some of the departing men had joined voluntarily after the British flotilla commander promised them that they would return home immediately after transferring the boats and training British personnel to handle them. This promise was broken. We saw them again only after they had suffered through two and a half years of captivity in British camps.

May 28
   At 9 A.M. we move the boat over to the Tygesholm Pier, very close to the British destroyer *Campbell* whose guns are pointed menacingly at us.
   Suddenly, at about 4 P.M., I am wanted on the upper deck on the double. Our boats are now being guarded by British marines armed with rifles and bayonets.

Each boat is being visited by two British officers and several enlisted men. We know what this means. A document is handed over to me. The entire crew is to assemble at once on the pier. There will be an opportunity later to gather private belongings.

In the meantime the British soldiers ransack the boat. After only four minutes I am missing my Knight's Cross, 500 Norwegian crowns, and some scarfs. Whatever is left of our belongings we pack under the supervision of a British officer. I get the impression that the officers have lost control over their men. Tin cans with food are being opened indiscriminately, our stock of alcoholic beverages plundered. Only after I lodge a formal protest with Captain Wingfield do these excesses stop. When I return to my boat it flies the British flag.

Briefly saluting my boat, I leave the last piece of German soil in Norway. The only Germans remaining on board are the chief engineer and the six senior members of the engine personnel, among them Steimle. I shake each man's hand. Steimle has tears in his eyes. Trucks take us to the train station. I ride in an automobile.

The train trip lasts twenty hours. Enlisted men in freight cars, officers in a regular passenger car. The men look impossible in their mixture of civilian clothes and military uniforms. There was no time to dress properly. Is this part of the British plan? A harsh and cold night. The Norwegians refuse to give us water even though they have plenty of it. We are defamed, slandered, despised, hated. The enemy's propaganda has done a solid job. Our pain and suffering begins.

We arrive at the Krageröy campsite. No one had expected us. The place is overcrowded. Men are sleeping in sheds. We devote the first days to the task of finding decent quarters for our men.

June 1

A first clash with riotous elements in the camp. One man is arrested for failing to obey orders. Several hours later a noisy crowd moves threateningly through the camp. "Kill Topp!" What might be going on in Germany at this time? I think the camp leaders are too soft. The men of the 18th Patrol Flotilla refuse to work. Each of them carries a stick. Red scarfs turn up. The yeast is rising.

June 3

I have been promoted to the post of detachment commander and call my men together for a straight talk. I try to explain to them as clearly and logically as I can what the situation is all about. It is in the interest of each individual to behave in a calm and orderly manner. We cannot relax discipline until we are safely back on German soil. It is our goal to take the men back as good Germans who will be able to help reconstruct their country and who will instinctively do the right thing, untouched by the propaganda they are exposed to from all sides.

Comment:

I think back to my last days in Germany. Thanks to the good services of Admiral (ret.) Carls, my wife successfully made it to the west and found shelter in Blumendorf Castle. This haven lasted only a short time because she had to move on when the English decided to make the castle their headquarters. So we packed up again and drove in an old car powered by producer gas to Travemünde on the Baltic Sea near Lübeck. On the way we were attacked by British aircraft that fired their machine guns at anything that moved. A human being! Hunt him down! We scrambled out of the car and sought shelter in a ditch. Bullets whistled overhead. In Travemünde the authorities directed us to the house of Consul Kröger, where we reluctantly accepted shelter.

Three days later, one day before my departure for Norway, a pinnace docked alongside *U 2513*. It was my wife. At the last moment I could prevent her from boarding our boat because sailors have always believed that a woman on board will bring bad luck. But for me the visit meant a last and happy meeting with my wife before I sailed into an uncertain future. How had my wife managed to get to Kiel? In Travemünde she had talked her way aboard a steamer bound for Kiel with a potentially lethal cargo of mines and torpedoes. The trip must have been not unlike that of a tank truck loaded with kerosene going along roads peppered with land mines. But love can make you take incredible risks. My wife made it safely back to Travemünde, just one day before the British occupied the place.

We sailed the next day for Norway. Had we stayed only one day longer we would likely have been sunk, as so many other vessels were in Kiel harbor. The last act of the tragedy began. What was and is going on beyond the Elbe River's gray curtain can only be compared with visions from Dante's Inferno. The echo of those ghastly events touched us in a bad way. And yet, no kind of suffering is unique.

I had to think of a Russian lady I once met in Paris. Two of her brothers fell in World War I, the third one in the Revolution. Her father took his own life. Her mother? Perhaps also dead? Gone mad? A cleaning lady? She herself fled via Siberia and China to Japan. With her last remaining funds she bought real estate. She was barely back on her feet when an earthquake destroyed everything. Her sister was pulled dead from the collapsed house; she survived as the last member of her family. Friends did what they could for her. She lived from hand to mouth and carried the burdens of life, so unfair and so harsh, as an inspiration for others.

I met this lady in Paris, rue de Liège, at the Sheherazade. She, a former Russian grand duchess but now old and white-haired, sat on a small chair in the basement where the gentlemen took a last look at the fit of their ties and ladies checked on the color of their lipstick. That is where she told me her story.

Diary:

June 4, 1945
It has been eight days since we arrived at the reservation at Krageröy, also known as a camp for prisoners of war. Barbed wire is all around us. I share a

room in the barracks with a naval construction official. The roof still leaks, but we have managed to put together a bookshelf and even found some literature to stock it with. We are thinking of Germany and how we can reconstruct all that has been destroyed. We form activity groups and try to prepare ourselves for the civilian life ahead. None of us is giving up.

June 20

I am back in camp after two weeks on the road. In the end I was not sorry to return. When I saw my comrades again and moved back into the now familiar quarters in the barracks, I almost felt at home. In the meantime I had an opportunity to see parts of Norway, a beautiful country populated by sturdy, handsome people. On the way to Bergen we got stuck in snow drifts 10 feet deep over a length of several miles. We stayed in a place called Haugestöl. Several Alpine hares crossed the road. People told us there are also snow foxes and ptarmigans in the area.

We heard of the peculiar habits of the lemmings. Our guide told us about the harsh conditions in the wintertime; how he must use snowplows to keep the roads open; how a blizzard can undo in hours the work of many days. He also spoke of his men and his dogs. It was obvious that the man enjoyed seeing some unfamiliar faces in his neighborhood. He had been up there for three years now. Not easy, if you have a family at home.

Then we came down from the mountains and experienced once again the change in vegetation. There were dwarf pines, different kinds of moss, then small birch trees slowly growing taller as we descended, finally the dark forest that surrounds, along with colorful meadows, the many lakes—this is the face of Norway. I also visited other camps, encountered disciplinary difficulties, witnessed how crowded the conditions are.

And then always the same thoughts run through my mind. It will be difficult to bear the reprisals that the Allies will undoubtedly mete out against the conquered. We did, after all, expect total surrender at the end of this total war. But what hurts perhaps the most is that on our own side we display discord and a lack of unity. Was the notion of a "people's community" no more than a phantom never to be attained? Camp life can make you mad. The behavior of some men is incomprehensible. Why would a soldier turn against a comrade with whom he has fought and suffered for five long years? Lack of instinct. Seduction by extreme, radical ideas.

Yesterday the construction official read an article by Eugen Roth from a Munich newspaper published at the time of the bombing terror. He distinguished between the highest and the deepest misery. Only love can help you overcome the deepest misery, love of other human beings and of the gift of life itself.

June 21

Summer solstice. A mighty bonfire on top of the bare rocks. We have a nice view down a lovely valley to the west. Above the dark mountain huts the sky is still bright even at midnight. Not so many years ago, as members of the youth movement in the 1920s, we would sing *"Flamme empor"* full of faith and hope, and even jump through the flames as a symbolic act of purification.

Motionless and huddled together, the men sit around the fire and stare into

the flames that seem to recall once more the war, the destruction, and all the horror. The torch is lowered. I gather myself up and say a few words of encouragement in our present situation, which is marked daily by humiliation and hatred. I
stress the values that we soldiers have retained throughout and beyond this terrible war, values such as individual commitment and solidarity, which will be
sorely needed to rebuild our destroyed country. But neither the flames nor my
words pierce the darkness above and all around us. Quietly we walk back to our
barracks.

June 27
    The days go by with little change. And yet we find occasions, a special hour, to
lift our spirits. Today we listened to a concert with the Spanish cello player Pablo
Casals from Albert Hall: Beethoven's "Fidelio" Overture and Schubert's Con-
certo for Cello in A minor. Instead of images of friends and foes, we felt for the
first time that which has always bound the European peoples together.
    After 10 o'clock we are no longer allowed to be seen outside the barbed wire.
We are told it would disturb the moral feelings of the Norwegians. We feel like
lepers. Damned for all time to come? Even in this lousy fishing village of Krageröy we can feel it. From now on we are taken down to the waterfront as early as
7 A.M. to go swimming, just when the sun rises. Oddly, we like it better this way.
To experience the breaking day in all its purity and stillness is like a morning
prayer.

August 1
    I find myself in a tent in between forests and lakes. In two days we are sup-
posed to leave for Germany. Along with twenty men of my crew, Lieutenant Peter, and the construction official, we have managed to get relief from the crowded
conditions in the camp. We are cutting wood in Norway's inexhaustible forests,
two thirds for a local farmer, one third for use in the camp. Eight days we have
been out here under brilliant, sunny skies. Our tents are pitched in a valley between two lakes along a trout stream. We live as in the old days. We rise at
6:15 A.M. and work from 7 A.M. until noon. At first we were not used to this kind
of work, but things go more smoothly now. If only our food were better! Inside
the camp rations have been shortened again. Two and a half slices of bread. Yesterday the farmer brought us dried cod and potatoes. That should help some.
    The other day, after I had used their telephone, I sat down with the farmer and
his wife for a while. They spoke very reasonably about the war. But what will
certainly taint us are the horrors committed in the concentration camps. I simply
cannot believe that it all happened. Today one of the Norwegian home guards
said that Germans should be banned from setting foot on Norwegian soil for ten
to twenty years. The hatred of the peoples around us encircles us like a strong
wall. If we want to survive we must maintain our solidarity and help one another.

August 12
    This is my last day here. I leave my men behind. It is a most painful farewell
because with them I leave everything behind that has meant anything to me over
the past few years: my hopes, my pride, my joys, and my home. I could stay on

if I wanted to. But better a quick cut than a long agony, as one man after another will be going home in the weeks ahead.

Comment:

The remaining parts of my journal were stolen from me after a degrading bodily inspection along with the rest of my personal belongings. Virtually every German in captivity came to know this systematic and organized form of humiliation. The nights we spent without blankets on canvas sheets on the slimy, soggy ground. Interrogations under bright flashlights while the inquisitors remained in the dark. Body checks of the officers, naked in front of jeering British soldiers or hired hands from our own side who could now compensate for their inferiority complexes. The German soldier was spared nothing.

On August 26 we finally stepped on German soil again. Gray skies mirrored the cheerless welcome we received. Only a few people took notice of the 3,000 prisoners who marched in long columns to the processing camp from where they would be released to their families. Bent down and daunted, as if burdened by a heavy load, they shuffled along. The only cheerful noise came from a group of young German girls who strolled along arm in arm with black Allied soldiers. Their babbling and screaming died suddenly when they became aware of our gray caravan. In contrast, the men who followed the Grand Admiral's orders and handed their boats over to the enemy to save the lives of hundreds of thousands of Germans (as the radio message had stated) were sent to work in Belgian and French coal mines and kept behind barbed wire for up to another two years in spite of promises of an early release.

That is what the end looked like.

U 2513 was transferred to England by one of my engineers, Lieutenant Brunner, and from there to the United States. In 1973 I spent some time as a guest in the house of Jim Bradley, who had once been the U.S. liaison officer at the Military Assistance and Advisory Group (MAAG). In his "captain's cabin" he kept photographs of all the ships and boats on which he had served as an engineering officer. Among other pictures I detected one showing a submarine very similar to our Type XXI boats. As it turned out, it was not only a German boat but my very own U 2513. Bradley had served as chief engineer on the boat when it was being used up, mainly as a target boat, at the anti-submarine warfare school in Key West, Florida.

But one day U 2513 took over a very special task. After the war the Americans experimented with nuclear propulsion systems. To test a novel steering mechanism for those boats, U 2513 was selected as a guinea pig, so to speak, because of all conventional boats it enjoyed the highest underwater speed. This speed could be boosted for a short time to 24 knots by a special switching arrangement of the batteries. The project was so crucial that one day the President of the United States, Harry Truman, announced a visit to see it work. One day he showed up on board accompanied by the usual number of secret service agents. The boat then got under way, reached deeper waters, dived, and began the experiment. The president and his bodyguards stood in the central control room. To demonstrate the steering system in all its effectiveness, the boat's speed was increased to 24 knots. Suddenly, as a result of the heavy demand, the electrical system blacked out and complete darkness enveloped the men in the control room. The boat slowed down and the chief engineer repaired the short. When the lights came back on they illuminated the following scene. Guns drawn, the secret service agents had completely surrounded the president to protect him from harm. It is not difficult to imagine what had gone through their minds. In fact, this first time on a submarine had allowed their imaginations to run wild. After all, they had heard so much about German U-boats during the war and about mysterious missions after it had ended. It all came together when the lights went out, instilling in them the belief that a coup d'état was under way. Thus my boat made history one more time. Later it was sold for scrap.

Extensive experiments with *U 2513* induced the U.S. Navy to modify its building program for fleet submarines in favor of so-called Guppy boats (Greater Underwater Propulsion Power). These boats had larger battery capacities, stronger electric engines, and an improved hull design for higher underwater speed. The six *Tang* class submarines were essentially modernized versions of the Type XXI boat. Also, the teardrop shape of the later nuclear submarines goes back to a German prototype, the Type XXVI design with a Walter propulsion system. The British, French, and Russians, too, used German models to redesign their submarines after the war. The British submarines *Explorer* and *Excalibur* stood in the succession of the Walter boat, while the Russian "Whisky" class and the French *Narval* borrowed heavily from the Type XXI boat. It would be no exaggeration to say that the great navies of the world improved and developed their conventional submarines after the war on the basis of German wartime experiences. Indeed, Germans were leading in the construction of conventional boats and their propulsion systems during the war and have retained that role in the post-war period.

Our stay at Krageröy gave us plenty of opportunities to contemplate our situation. Our parental homes and our educational institutions had failed to provide us with the guideposts that would have allowed us to steer a steady course in troubled times. We had been set adrift, left the proper channel, and run into shallow waters. For example, neither on the *Karlsruhe* nor at the naval academy did we learn that ever since the *levée en masse* during the French Revolution war is no longer the prerogative of those who prefer the military profession to other pursuits. What was left of the much-touted "warrior class of the nation"?

The total war had touched everyone indiscriminately, soldiers and civilians, women and children. We also did not know that to die for a country or a principle became a senseless act of heroism if country, principle, and all good patriots went down in an all-consuming catastrophe.

How did we see the entry into the war? On January 26, 1934, Hitler had concluded a nonaggression treaty with Poland. But the people's hatred was later fired up by supposed or actual actions by Poles against the German minority. Eventually we heard about the murder of hundreds of Germans at the hands of the Poles, about the raid against the German radio transmitter at Gleiwitz, and finally about that "Bloody Sunday" in Bromberg—all reported in gory detail by the regime's propaganda machine. Those measures as well as certain diplomatic complications had finally led to the German invasion of Poland from the west, while the Red Army moved in from the east in accordance with the Nazi-Soviet Nonaggression Pact. Tied to Poland by their treaty obligations, England and France thereupon declared war against Germany. Why not against Russia? This question remained unanswered for us.

Today we know that Germany's invasion of Poland at 5:45 A.M. on September 1, 1939, was not an act of self-defense; it had little to do with violated rights, protection of minorities, Danzig, or the Corridor. The invasion grew rather from a long-planned and now brutally enforced scheme to push Germany's borders eastward. In Krageröy, behind barbed wire and isolated from the latest news, we could not find answers to many of these questions. When Hitler marched into Russia, did he feel compelled to add expansion to expansion? Was the attack on Russia a preventive measure? How great was the gap between propaganda and reality?

We had believed that Hitler's personal dynamic force as well as that of his government would create a New Order in Europe and that this second attempt under German leadership—the first one under Napoleon had failed—would be successful. At the same time we saw ourselves as liberating Europe from the Bolshevist menace. For those who organized this "Crusade," a drive for power linked up with political and racist ideology, an attractive mixture to which volunteers from all over Europe felt drawn. We may recall here that when Bernard of Clairvaux in 1147 spoke out with great eloquence in favor of a second Crusade against the infidels, he did not forget for a moment that he would deliver the elite of France's nobility to almost certain death and thus strengthen the Church in its power struggle against the secular forces in the country. And as we contemplate the actions of crusaders then and today, we should also bear in mind that many of them got caught up in the opportunities of the moment rather than in the pursuit of noble aims for the future. Perhaps some of our modern crusaders thought it wise to let their flags catch the prevailing winds in time so as to be better placed in a Europe under German rule.

The "Crusade" became a war of annihilation on both sides with 17 million military casualties and 18 million civilian victims. Even when the guns stopped firing, murder in Europe continued in reprisals against refugees, against collaborators, against Quislings. "Oh Liberty, what crimes are being committed in your name!" These were the last words of a French freedom fighter before she was guillotined during the Terror of the French Revolution.

I have no intention to somehow balance the dead and murdered on both sides, nor do I plan to downplay the National Socialist crimes for which Auschwitz will remain forever a terrifying reminder. All the past has become a shadow, that of the others as well as mine. Every good and every evil carried its own yardstick. The three old men who, we are told, at the Teheran Conference drew some lines on a map of central Europe in an old school atlas and thus affected the fate of millions of human beings, cannot escape the shadow any less than we can. But we are alive, and for that reason we must hang on to the shadow. We do not want to forget, for we know that Nemesis, the guardian of all true measure, has a historical dimension that judges in terms of centuries.

One question is being raised again and again: How was it possible for a nation that has made such outstanding contributions to culture and world civilization, for a people that produced men like Kant, Goethe, Schiller, Humboldt, or Beethoven, to commit such crimes, to lead a war of destruction that entangled so many in guilt? But then, what do we mean by guilt? In a religious sense every human being is guilty. Of this the doctrine of original sin and the tragedies of classical antiquity remind us all the time. In the context of this inescapable conflict I, too, feel guilty. Perhaps all the more so because denying guilt is always a critical obstacle in its removal and remission. Yet a confession of guilt can never be a collective one. Every single individual must check for himself how deep and how knowingly he was involved in the injustices and crimes of the National Socialist era and then decide on the proper standards by which to measure his personal guilt and responsibility.

I reject the notion of a collective guilt or liability, for it includes those who were not involved and threatens to burden even those who were not yet born at the time. Above all, we must guard against efforts to make us objects in the political games of the present and likely of the future as well, games that demand as players German citizens plagued by neurotic feelings of guilt and prepared to exercise self-humiliation and suffer like flagellants.

Naturally, we emerged from this terrible war as pacifists. But we did not subscribe to the view that governments should simply follow the will of the population, lay down all arms, and thus usher in eternal peace. No, our love of peace is strong, manly, knowing—the kind of love that has been a European tradition from Erasmus via Leibniz, Kant, and Max Weber all the way to Albert Einstein. We did not yet know that in a total nuclear war hundreds of millions of people are likely to die and that the question of life or death may be a simple function of the wind direction. It would also mean the death of millions of children whose opinion about freedom or oppression is immaterial to the decision makers. Today this frightful burden rests on those who feel responsible for our welfare. But those of us who are familiar with our history and mythology know also that the apocalypse has been threatening us at all times and that the seven-headed monster of the sea and the two-horned beast of the earth have always been there.

I find it impossible to sum up the sense of loss, disappointment, bitterness, and despair at the end of the war—a war that had consumed all our energy and left us nothing but chaos and debris. To draw subtle lessons of experience from this war after thirty-five years, to describe them in all their color and complexity, is the task of historians. For me the years since the war have not softened anything; they may have eaten up the words, but they cannot stem the tide of images and visions that rushes through my mind. Perhaps a few lines from Buchheim's book, *Das Boot*, will help, if only to demonstrate how inadequate words remain when one tries to capture the craziness and grotesque dimension of those images: "A feeling of unreality overtakes me. This is not the old earth. We slide along on a layer of lead, on a moon orbiting dead and cold through space. Are we the same as in the old days? What does all this mean?"

The men of *U552*.

Final inspection of the crew prior to sailing.

Engelbert Endrass welcomes me back after a war patrol.

Commanding Officer, *U552*.

The C.O. at the periscope.

Anxious men in the central control room while a depth charge attack is under way.

Entering St. Nazaire after my seventeenth war patrol. Note damage to conning tower caused by the Canadian corvette *Sackville*.

Reception at the naval base.

Deputy Inspector and
Chief of Staff of the
West German Navy.

German liaison officer
at SACLANT (Supreme
Allied Commander, At-
lantic).

My aunt, Anna Topp, before and after
Theresienstadt.

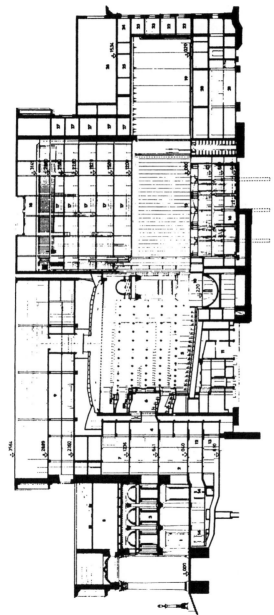

Our award-winning blueprint for refurbishing the National Theater in Munich.

4

After the War

There was a great stillness after the war. We had been silenced. My generation had lived a two-faced life. At first we pressed forward, eager, full of hope and energy. After the crash of Icarus, which touched us all, we turned inward, resigned, bewildered. We were survivors, carrying along our errors and trying to come to grips with them so that we might slowly step away from the shadow that had been cast upon my generation.

The small circle of my immediate relatives revealed how hard we had been hit by the war and the regime. Both of my parents, who had lost their house in Hanover in a bombing raid, died shortly after the war, victims of a measure by the British occupation authorities. Gas for cooking purposes was a precious commodity in those days, and the British decided to activate the supply system for German households only in unpredictable intervals for short periods of time. One day, after opening the valve in the kitchen and while waiting for the gas to come, my mother fell asleep. She and my father did not wake up again after the gas finally arrived.

My family lived and suffered through this war like most other families who, actively or passively, became a part of the struggle between the peoples on both sides: They were locked up, bombed out, became refugees. The war left its mark on all of them. Vicariously for them all, allow me to single out the fate of my wife's sister, Erika von Köller.

She married into a family whose values and lifestyle had been shaped by Prussian traditions. Her husband's sister, Cornelia von Köller, was named after Goethe's sister Cornelia who was her great-grandmother in the female line. Cornelia had married Gerd von Tresckow, a cousin of Henning von Tresckow who headed the resistance movement against Hitler. In the Prussian civil service and as military officers, the male members of the family served their kings for generations. The greatest Prussian ruler, Frederick II, once put his credo into these words: "Our life consists of a fleeting transition from our birth to our death. During this period a man has the obligation to work for the benefit of the society to which he belongs."

Erika von Köller gave birth to her third child, Gabriele, on December 22, 1944, in the hospital of Cammin in Pomerania, not far from the Köllers' estate at Schwenz. On New Year's Eve she was released and taken back home on a horse-drawn sled. At the time, horror stories multiplied about the unchecked murders and rapes of German civilians by the approaching Red Army. This behavior was encouraged by brutal public addresses such as those of Ilya Ehrenburg:

> If you have killed one German, kill a second one. For us there is nothing more enjoyable than to see German corpses. Don't count the days, don't count the kilometers. Just count the Germans you have killed! Kill Germans! Your aged mother begs you to do it. Kill Germans! Your children urge you on. Kill Germans! The soil of your mother country calls out to you to do it. Do not hesitate! Make no mistake! KILL!

But the Pomeranian nobility retained its steadfastness inwardly and outwardly. Servants wearing white gloves continued to serve the meals. A Köller does not leave her native soil. Everyone acted in a disciplined way and did his duty, even toward the state that nobody loved. And the state had decided, under the threat of severe punishment, that nobody was to join the trek to the west without the Party's permission. Everyone knew what that meant. After all, Erika's sister-in-law Cornelia had already had a run-in with the authorities. She had listened to foreign radio broadcasts, which was strictly forbidden. Someone denounced her. Two Gestapo officers showed up to investigate. She had grown up with Prussian moral convictions; freedom and truth meant much to her. Frederick the Great himself had once said, "Newspapers, if they are to be interesting, must not be interfered with."

For Cornelia the radio was like a newspaper. She not only expected freedom and truth from others but she also told others openly what she thought and did. Yes, she had listened to those foreign radio stations. When her two inquisitors shouted her down and added the rhetorical question, "You knew that it was against the law," she replied honestly and proudly, "I thought that applied only to ordinary people." For this enchanting but naive confession vis-à-vis her tormentors she paid with doing time in a penitentiary. Because of her frail health she was soon transferred to a regular jail, which looked more like a concentration camp, from which she was finally released, a broken woman, after a year and a half. Not long thereafter she committed suicide. Even before her death she had been divorced from Gerd von Tresckow, who happened to be in Italy when the attempt was made against Hitler's life. Since his arrest seemed imminent, a friend of his, a physician, offered to hide him in the hospital he was running. But Gerd was a Tresckow and turned himself in to the authorities. Before long word arrived that he had died of angina pectoris. In reality he had been executed.

Early in January 1945, three days after her release from the hospital in Cammin, my sister-in-law Erika had to be readmitted because of high fever. Complications resulting from her difficult childbirth and the lack of medication forced her to stay in the hospital for the next two months. By early March she could hear artillery fire from the front some 20 miles away. The patients were told that the noise came from Germans blasting holes in the ice-bound Oder River. Then a female physician took Erika aside and told her, "Get out of here as fast as you can! "

Weakened after her two-month hospital stay, Erika gathered her three children, one of them not even three months old, and got ready to head westward. The roads were clogged with crowds of hungry human beings; they were being strafed from the air by Allied fighter-bombers, all the while fighting for their very survival in the face of unimaginable terror, rape, and murder. In Cammin all hospital patients assembled on the market square. There were no cars available since they had already been commandeered for the Party bosses and their families. At that point Erika with her three children was fortunate to run into a military column. A sympathetic physician—her last operation had been just two days before—offered to take her in his staff car to Divenow and on back roads to Swinemünde where she caught a refugee train bound for Schleswig-Holstein. With many interruptions, mainly caused by air attacks, the train moved slowly westward loaded with many casualties, dead and injured. Near Kiel she at last found emergency shelter.

After the plunge into the abyss, I tried to analyze how these terrible events had come about.

On January 30, 1933, the popular and respected Reich President Paul von Hindenburg had installed the new government. He did so essentially for two reasons. The previous cabinets had failed to gain majority support in the Reichstag, and after the elections of July 1932 the National Socialists had emerged as the strongest party. In the beginning, Hitler as Reich Chancellor led a coalition government that also contained conservatives.

Today we often hear the expression, *"Wehret den Anfängen"* (Catch evil early before it is too late!). It implies that already the Party program and

Hitler's *Mein Kampf* should have signalled the dangers ahead. Well, in the 1920s and early 1930s there were more than twenty political parties. As today they not only made many promises to the voters but accused one another of dirty tricks. Libelous remarks were a daily occurrence. Educated people read party platforms only with strong reservations. Few had studied Hitler's *Mein Kampf* in any detail.

All foreign nations recognized Hitler and his regime as Germany's legal government. They concluded internationally valid treaties with him. The Vatican took the lead in July 1933. All nations except the Soviet Union participated in the 1936 Olympic Games in Berlin. Even the Soviet Union maintained normal diplomatic relations with the Third Reich.

After Hitler became Chancellor, he said in many public speeches that National Socialism meant no threat to peace. For example, on May 17, 1933, he spoke about disarmament and stressed Germany's readiness to forego military equality with other countries for another five years. He also declared that Germany was not interested in offensive weapons and invited an independent commission to inspect Germany's paramilitary forces. Only a few realized at the time that these and similar moves, while leading indeed to a certain détente in international relations, were nothing but diplomatic tricks to alleviate the mistrust of Germany's neighbors and to camouflage a massive rearmament program.

In June 1935, England and Germany concluded a naval agreement that froze the relative size of the two fleets according to a ratio of 100 : 35 and promised eventual equality in the category of submarines. In November 1936, Japan and Germany signed the Anti-Comintern Pact, joined a year later by Italy. This pact against the menace of communism strengthened Germany's prestige abroad. We all agreed proudly with Hitler when he announced on February 27, 1937, in Munich's Hofbräuhaus: "Today Germany is once again a world power."

Hitler enjoyed further successes, as we saw them. In the spring of 1938 Austria was added to the Reich. In the Munich Agreement of September 30, 1938, Hitler induced England, France, and Italy to grant his request for one-third of Czechoslovakia's population, the Germans of the Sudetenland, along with important industrial and strategic areas. When Hitler occupied the rest of the country, the western powers did nothing to prevent it. Later in 1939 Hitler forced Lithuania to return the Memel district to the Reich, and on August 23 he concluded the Hitler-Stalin Pact.

Skillful propaganda prepared the German public for these actions in the arena of foreign policy. I vividly recall a poster you could see everywhere, in train stations, in public buildings, in hotels and restaurants. It showed profiles of Frederick the Great and Bismarck, both overshadowed by a profile of Hitler. The poster symbolized the notion of historical continuity. It was not difficult for us to come to the conclusion that Hitler's successes in foreign affairs also involved a strategic dimension, namely, a united Europe under German leadership. If this was indeed the case, how could we possibly withstand the attractiveness and momentum that such a vision entailed? Doubts first arose when this strategic dimension became intertwined with ideological pseudo-values, such as the idea of the master race. But such doubts did not go so far as to make us reject force as a political means. Had not at all times invaders exhibited brutality to intimidate the attacked people and to force it to surrender? We did not necessarily feel uncomfortable in this atmosphere of anti-intellectualism and moved around in a fog of political ignorance. Struggle was glorified as a desirable, manly experience; war was seen as a perfectly legitimate instrument in international relations.

In the beginning, actions against Jews stayed within publicly accepted bounds. Only some of them had to give up their positions in the civil service without losing pension benefits. These measures intensified with the Nuremberg Laws of September 1935. Now marriages between Germans and Jews were outlawed, Jews could no longer hold public office, and in addition they lost the right to vote. But at this time they were still legally protected in their persons and possessions. Jewish officials who had been fired could draw their pensions.

The idea of dividing human beings into superior and inferior races struck me as absurd. I neither believed in any special quality of the German or English races nor in a divinely chosen Jewish one. The painter Oskar Kokoschka once observed, "There are only two races: one characterized by spirituality, the other not." I agreed. The mixture of different races had blessed Europe with the most beautiful achievements in culture and art.

After witnessing the hate campaign of Jewish newspapers against Germany on our visits abroad, we were prepared to interpret the Nuremberg Laws as political countermeasures without realizing the consequences they entailed. In November 1938, after the crisis over the Sudetenland, the illegal seizure of Jewish property began. Only in November 1941 did the government draw up the formal legal regulations that allowed for the seizure and confiscation of Jewish property. Now not only Jews who had emigrated abroad but also those deported to concentration camps outside the borders of the Reich lost their citizenship and their possessions. But beyond all such legal and legalistic measures lay the activities of the Gestapo. Already in the fall of 1938 its men torched synagogues in the infamous "Night of Crystal"; plundered Jewish stores; beat, tormented and killed Jewish people; and forced German Jews to pay a collective fine of one billion reichsmark. We were at sea and only received news filtered by the Propaganda Ministry. If we had doubts about these activities we were quite prepared to rationalize them by suggesting, for example, that these were transitional problems, or that all revolutionary movements sometimes get out of hand.

The creation of concentration camps was made possible by a governmental decree on February 28, 1933, one day after the Reichstag Fire. It laid the foundation for arrests without subsequent trials and due process of law. The decree was still signed by Hindenburg. It was primarily aimed at curtailing communist activities. Article 48 of the Weimar Constitution provided for the restriction of basic rights in case public law and order were being seriously disturbed or threatened. Even the U.S. Constitution allows for such measures in the event of domestic unrest or war. Under the National Socialist regime, the method of arresting citizens without judicial review developed into a political terror weapon not only against communists but against any opposition elements. The conservative wing of the Nazi Party, some sections of the armed forces, representatives of the diplomatic service, as well as certain industrial leaders spoke up against the boycott and confiscation of Jewish property. Given the diminishing influence of these groups in Germany's public life, such protests enjoyed only limited success. Leading echelons of the Wehrmacht opposed the development of the SS into an armed force and the political indoctrination and infiltration of the officer corps by the Party.

In view of such muted protest, one must assume that any such activities under a totalitarian regime had to remain submerged below the level of everyday affairs. One must know that no open protest could succeed once the National Socialist regime became entrenched. The print and broadcast media would never have published pieces critical of the regime because editors and interviewers knew full well that it would have meant the end of their professional careers. Many Germans ended up in concentration camps because they spoke up openly or even clandestinely against the government. One must be clear in one's mind that the terror was not restricted to Jews and foreigners but likewise was directed against all German political opposition.

About 2 million Germans fell victim to the regime, among them women and young people whose "crimes" consisted of little more than admitting fear and despair. The woman and mother who loses her child in an Allied aerial bombardment releases her pain and terror in the cry: "The Führer is responsible for all this!" She is denounced and executed. For protest to be effective requires organization. But all existing organizations in Germany were disbanded as early as the spring of 1933. This included professional groups like labor unions or the association of medical doctors. Or the old, independent organizations were merged with their National Socialist counterparts, as in the case of student fraternities. Associations with international connections, for instance the Rotary Club or the Freemasons, were suppressed altogether.

A frequent accusation holds that Germany's collective conscience should have been awakened in view of mass murder in the concentration camps. But today we cannot even begin to imagine the curtain of silence that shielded the concentration camps against curious eyes and minds.

Neither I nor any of my acquaintances recall a single case where a released concentration camp inmate dared tell others about his or her suffering. Of course, silence can be eloquent, but it cannot tell you much about cruel reality.

The Red Cross visited the camps and reported about conditions inside them. But these visits were rigged, the inspectors seeing merely the spruced-up facades while falling victim to a brilliant system of deception whose cleverness was revealed only after the war by surviving inmates. The controlled German press, for instance, carried articles from time to time in which authorities were praised for stopping "excesses" in the concentration camps. At the same time foreign propaganda, to which few had access, often disseminated deliberately exaggerated or outright false information. It was easy for the German propaganda to expose such stories as lies.

Even for the most critical minds during the war, let alone the masses, knowledge about the regime's excesses remained very limited. It was known that one could be arrested without due process of law and that Jews had been systematically deported since the fall of 1938. Neither the approximate number of inmates nor the organized mistreatment and mass murders in the concentration camps were generally known. The mass murders, as we know today, fell primarily into that phase of the war when Hitler had realized that he could not conquer Russia and instead devoted his attention to his other goal, the destruction of the Jews. One must also bear in mind that during this time of massive aerial bombardments it was not uncommon for Germans to live for weeks and months without knowing the fate of their own closest relatives. Under the pressure of constant air raids, they found their lives in permanent danger and were less disposed than normally to pay attention to the suffering of others.

I should also stress that the National Socialist movement would have been unthinkable without the social upheaval that World War I brought to Germany. The majority of the people had lost faith in the traditionally leading social and political circles to solve the problems of the time. The democratic center had lost power politically, socially, and economically. Newly emerging groups slowly pushed the remaining conservative forces from power. These emerging groups, however, lacked both political knowledge and experience, while thriving on ruthless vitality and a lust for power. One cannot properly understand the ascendency of National Socialism as a historical and psychological phenomenon without seeing it as a part of a broader social revolution.

Today's popular view of equating National Socialism alone with the misdeeds of the regime during the war and in the concentration camps stands to be revised by future historians. Whether we like it or not, National Socialism represented a popular movement. Hitler knew how to

bind the hopes and interests of the overwhelming majority of Germans
to his movement. In the beginning, his successes met the expectations
he had raised. Soon after Hitler's seizure of power, over the span of six
months, the number of unemployed workers dropped by 50 percent
from its peak of 7 million. Businesses prospered again. The new state-
run or semi-official organizations revitalized previously idle economic
forces. For example, the autobahns, the building boom in the housing industry, and the Volkswagen project all proved that the long years of depression were over. After 1936 Germany enjoyed, for all practical
purposes, full employment. With the sad exception of Jewish citizens,
everyone who wanted work and was able to work found a job. Average
wages kept up with the cost of living. There were paid vacations. Recreational time off was supervised by the "Strength through Joy" organization. Passenger liners undertook cruises for the workers down to Gran
Canaria or up to the Norwegian fjords. This method of regulating vacations also enabled the regime to exercise means of ideological manipulation, something people were prepared to endure and in some cases
actually welcomed. Workers and peasants became fully integrated into
the people's community. The old demand for the equality of classes and
estates was transmuted into a quest for equality of opportunity. Such demands rested, of course, to a great extent on political opportunism.

In the eyes of many Germans Hitler became a man of mythical qualities. One Reich, one People, one Führer! At first this was not just an
empty phrase. And how did foreign countries react? Even Hitler's critics
abroad had to acknowledge his diplomatic successes. Churchill admired
the way Hitler had rekindled German patriotism. The Swedish legal authority Nyrén promised he would "help reevaluate the new Germany
and the man who as Führer is providing such great leadership." There
were many such positive assessments.

This was one side of the National Socialist regime. The other showed
the totalitarian state. By 1934 the foundations of this totalitarianism were
in place everywhere. In February 1933 the so-called Law for the Protection of State and People gave the National Socialist ministers of the interior in the various German states complete freedom of action and
practically abolished guarantees of citizens' individual liberties. The
"Enabling Act" of March 23, 1933, in effect set aside the constitution and
gave the government the right to enact legislation by decree without any
of the traditional guidelines and constitutional restrictions. The regime
also manipulated the formerly independent legal system, and not only
after creating in 1936 its chief instrument of legal terror, the People's Tribunal. Already by mid-1933 all rival political parties had been outlawed.
As of July 14, 1933, the Nazi Party was the only legal one in Germany.

The next step came on January 30, 1934, when the "Law concerning
the Reorganization of the Reich" delivered the coup de grace to Ger-

many's tried and popular federal system. In its place Hitler created his totalitarian state of national centralization. To perfect this system the Führer had to accomplish two more things: rid the Party of internal dissenters, especially the proponents of a permanent revolution; and gain the loyalty of the armed forces. The supposed "mutineers and traitors" within the Party were executed without trial in the course of the infamous Röhm Putsch in late June 1934. To integrate the Wehrmacht into the system did not require bloodshed. When Hindenburg died, Hitler simply combined the offices of Reich President and Chancellor in his person. On August 2, 1934, the entire Wehrmacht swore a personal oath of loyalty to the Führer.

In a democratic society even criminals enjoy an alternative, a fair punishment based on legal prescription and enforced by the proper authorities. This alternative does not exist in a totalitarian state. Here the legal system becomes the regime's slave. Without the possibility of redress it deprives its victims of their freedom, their property, and their lives. Only complete association with the regime or complete self-denial prevent people from ending up as victims. One could even argue that those who are forced to take the lives of others are among the victims.

Hitler did not exercise a monopoly over totalitarianism, but his variety certainly attained a high degree of perfection. It makes little sense to establish a relative ranking of totalitarian experiences. Totalitarianism existed before Hitler and there has been totalitarianism since the war, not just in Europe but everywhere in the world in all kinds of ideological disguises, even religious ones. Every totalitarian regime has its own unique humanity-despising characteristics. Neither the number of victims nor the methods used are ultimately crucial for the totalitarian experience, but rather the principle of unlimited, institutionally exercised power against which the individual is impotent.

Illegality and inhumane totalitarianism also touched our family. My aunt Anna Topp and her daughter Else became its victims. When the National Socialists seized power on January 30, 1933, their lives changed forever. Neighbors and friends, except for very close ones, now avoided them. After Else Topp had been employed for a while by the *New York Herald Tribune*, she changed jobs to work for a construction firm. Her boss knew that she was half Jewish. A fellow worker tried to blackmail her. "Either you turn your coat and your camera over to me, or I will report to the police that you are Jewish." The boss came to Else's rescue and offered continued protection.

The firm did construction work in connection with the fortified lines of the "Westwall" and later the "Atlantikwall." One day it received instructions to do work in Auschwitz as well. The firm sent a delegation to Auschwitz to find out more about the project. It came back with the warning, "Terrible things are going on there!" The firm declined the contract with the excuse of being overburdened by other projects. In this way Else and her mother learned for the first time about a termination camp. They now stood on the edge of the abyss that threatened to swallow them at any moment.

Anna Topp, virtually penniless after her family had lost all they had in the great inflation of the 1920s, and too proud to accept handouts from her relatives, used her knowledge of Hungarian and French to become a telephone operator for international calls. Throughout those years she knew that her deportation to a concentration camp could come at any time. When Berlin suffered its first air attacks, Else and Anna Topp, as Jews, were forbidden to seek refuge in air raid shelters. Instead they hid in the backyard of the little house that Else, being only "half Jewish," had been allowed to rent. Her mother, "fully Jewish," could stay with her. Oddly, their house was the only one in the Kaiserallee to survive the bombardment intact.

In May 1943 Else was in her office when her terror-stricken mother called with the long-feared news. The abyss had opened its chasm at last. Anna Topp was to report immediately to the central assembly point for the transportation of Jews in the Grosse Hamburger Strasse. Else ran home, helped pack the suitcase, especially warm clothing, and then took her mother to the collection point. A train stood ready. Its cars carried the instruction, "6 Horses or 40 Persons." A huge crowd had assembled alongside the train: men, women, and children. Heart-rending farewell scenes were everywhere. Then orders were shouted, the doors to the cattle cars opened, and the people were pushed inside. In the confusion Else lost sight of her mother. All she could remember for the next two years was her face—stoic, as if etched in stone.

The lexicon tells us about Theresienstadt: "In Czech: Teresien. A town in northern Bohemia in the administrative district of Aussig. Population 2,500 (1948); 6,800 (1938). Between 1780 and 1882 a military fortress; from 1941 to 1945 a concentration camp for Jews." The town was named after Empress Maria Theresa. Theresa is a name that reminds us of women who brought love and care to their fellow human beings—St. Theresa of Avila, the greatest of Christian mystics, for example, or Thérèse de Livieux, canonized in 1925. The Nazis rendered the name into a symbol for hatred, human degradation, suffering, and death.

As of February 16, 1942, the chief of the security police in the Reich Protectorate "Bohemia and Moravia" decreed that Theresienstadt henceforth become a ghetto for Jews. One paragraph of the decree reads: "All measures necessary to construct the Jewish settlement are to be taken through administrative channels." The Nazis would develop Theresienstadt into a showpiece camp to fool foreign visitors, including Red Cross delegations, about the true treatment of Jews. One witness, Jochen von Lang, remembers: "According to Nazi terminology it was not a concentration camp. There were no gas chambers. But its inmates, crowded together in incredibly confined quarters, were unfree like criminals, exposed to any kind of arbitrary chicanery, and constantly under the threat of death." Many inmates had used up their life's savings for a place in the so-called Retirement Home for Jews. It was anything but a retirement home. The inmates lived and ate under the most miserable conditions. Thousands of the "retirees" were deported to death camps. For those fortunate enough to stay, a Jewish Council oversaw all daily activities. In the town, the stone barracks were so overcrowded that many inmates had to sleep on the ground. In the winter months, given inadequate heating, this led to painful bladder and kidney infections.

Anna Topp was issued a registration number that enabled her to receive packages from her relatives. But the relatives, too, suffered dearly and did not have much to share. Anna Topp was allowed to acknowledge the receipt of the packages on preprinted postcards. Any additional personal messages were forbidden. Indeed, any contact with the outside world was strictly outlawed under pain of severe punishment. Anna Topp benefitted from her command of foreign languages, Hungarian and Czech in particular. This enabled her to work as a supervisor and interpreter.

After Germany's surrender the camp was dissolved. Anna Topp regained her freedom in July 1945. The picture on her release papers speaks for itself. She had not been mistreated physically, but mentally she had suffered torment, as her stony face would show forever after. She never talked about Theresienstadt. Even though she found employment for some time on the staff of the Foreign Office and was active in the Organization for Persecuted Persons, she remained an outsider in her public life as well as to her family. She was a broken human being, without dreams or tears, and lived her life apart from the rest of society. Her physical appearance and mental state deteriorated visibly. In the end she was admitted to a hospital where she took a turn for the worse, bodily and mentally. Anna Topp died on March 10, 1965. Her face in death, freed at last from her inner fears and pain, showed the profile of a beautiful woman.

All this I learned after the war, which had allowed us virtually no time off for family affairs. During the entire conflict I saw my parents only once. The same holds true for my cousin Else. She kept silent in order not to implicate me. But I could have found out earlier about the fate of my Aunt Anna. It does not give me a sense of relief to suspect that her family ties to the famous U-boat commander Topp probably saved her from deportation to a death camp. I also fear a personal intervention on my part, had I known her fate, would have made no difference.

In my house I have decorated an entire wall with a panel of twenty-five pictures painted by Erich Klahn, all of them showing details of Odysseus's wanderings before his return to Ithaca. The goal at the end of all his wanderings, the motive for all his acts of commission and omission, is to return home, to return to the basic values of the human existence. Like Odysseus we drifted through the days and nights, through the years of war, not to seek glory but to bear life such as it is in a manly fashion. The final picture shows Athena warning Odysseus against any desire of carrying on his struggles forever: "Son of Laertes and the gods of old, Odysseus, master of land ways and sea ways, command yourself. Call off this battle now, or Zeus who rules the world will be angry."

The Greek poet Nikos Kazantzakis wrote his *Odissia* in 1938. He takes up Dante's interpretation of a man being restlessly tossed here and there, a man conquered and overpowered, lonely and without hope, but nevertheless determined to fight on. In Alistair MacLean's book, *H.M.S. Ulysses*, I discovered many parallels to my own war experiences. The British cruiser *Ulysses* is engaged in seemingly endless missions, escorting Allied convoys through the Arctic Ocean to Russia. Weary and torn by suspense, the ship's crew must not only overcome, again and again, the challenges of the icy polar nights and merciless winter storms, but must also battle the German enemy who endures heavy losses himself while attacking the *Ulysses* with aircraft and submarines in order to destroy the convoy. Without asking the purpose of their mission, the men transcend the limits of ordinary suffering. Bitter, worn out, and on the verge of mutiny, they grow to undergo a metamorphosis that leaves them doing their duty stoically under the onslaught of events. Their commanding officer could offer no explanation for this transformation of his men, nor was he able to make the Admiralty comprehend the situation. He was overwhelmed by the realization that nothing he said made the slightest impact on his superiors.

In Giovanni Pascoli's *Ultimo Viaggio*, Odysseus, after his safe return to Ithaca, takes off for one last voyage in search of perfect happiness. Whatever happiness may be—love, wisdom, truth—Odysseus is looking for it in vain. Instead, what overwhelms him at the end of his voyage is the notion that man in his endless wanderings between truth and error remains unchanged. He is still apprehensive about apocalyptic rejection and painfully aware of the fateful limitations of the human condition, a burden we have to bear daily.

I have always felt a special affinity to Homer's *Odyssey*. This includes the many added interpretations and variations presented to us over the span of 2,000 years by men like Virgil, Dante, Kazantzakis, Tennyson, James Joyce, Pascoli, and others.

Back from Norwegian internment, I find myself in Bremerhaven on a campground closed off by barbed wire. After several hours two old friends, the writer and war correspondent Wolfgang Frank and the former PT boat commander Friedrich Wilhelm Wilcke, both working for the Americans as interpreters, come to see me. They invite me to accompany them to the American officers' mess. Soon I am surrounded by mountains of butter, bread, and meat. I notice how American soldiers sitting next to me empty their half-eaten meals full of nutritious food into the trash cans. My friends tell me the German population is starving, not because there is a lack of food but as punishment for having followed Hitler into the war and for having fought to the bitter end. Our long-suffering people, exhausted and bled white, must now starve as a form of punishment! The winners appear to have forgotten in this arbitrary treatment that they entered the war out of humanitarian concerns in the first place. Suddenly I have lost all my appetite.

I return to my tent at the campground. The next day I am released. Wilcke accompanies me to the employment office, where I receive the proper papers to transfer into the British Zone, for my destination is Travemünde. I assume that is still my wife's place of residence. I am joined by an army major, both of us in uniform and with our decorations. We are told that the wearing of decorations is no longer allowed. We don't care. That night Wilcke invites us to the half-destroyed house of an uncle of his in one of Bremen's suburbs.

In the still intact living room a well-laid table awaits us along with the best the kitchen and cellar have to offer. We eat by candlelight because there is no electricity. Besides the host and his wife, their two sons, thirteen and fifteen years old, are present. In his words of welcome, directed more toward his sons than to us, our host expressed much of what was on his mind. It must be unique in the course of history, he said, that a whole people—soldiers and civilians, women and children—had fought for six years under the greatest deprivations and with terrible losses, only to discover in the end that it had fallen victim to political leaders who pretended to punish crimes but in reality were more than anyone guilty of committing them. He added that this realization in no way diminished the feats of the soldiers. These words were obviously directed at the major and me. I have never forgotten this encounter. Those words, and the friendly atmosphere in which they were spoken, seemed like an anchor tossed out into troubled waters.

The next day the major and I hopped on a coal train bound for Lübeck. There we parted company. He went on to see his family in nearby Schwartau while I found a truck driver who took me along to Travemünde. At last I stood in front of Consul Kröger's house where I had taken leave of my wife. I soon learned that only hours after my wife had moved into the house, the British had forced her to leave again. My wife sat literally on the street not knowing where she might spend the next night with her two little children. Finally a sympathetic soul saw her misery and offered my pregnant wife shelter at her house. Thus my wife lived with Mrs. Hinrichsen until friends helped her move to Celle where, protected by my parents, she could await the birth of our son. I followed her atop another coal train.

In Celle I encountered the following situation. Shortly before the end of the war my parents' house in Hanover had been completely destroyed in an air raid. What few belongings they could salvage they took along to Celle, where they now lived in extremely modest and crowded conditions. Here my wife had joined them after an adventurous trip by truck over roads in bad need of repair. It is a miracle that she did not lose her child during this ordeal. We finally saw each other again in that house at No. 6 Trift, which was to become both our home for the next seven years and a source of constant torment.

Words cannot recapture our feelings when we saw each other again. For my wife all worries that had burdened her in the past fell away. Once more she had me as her protector, for she needed protection not only to give birth to our child but also to survive in an environment full of hostility and need, and short on understanding. For me it meant the end of immediate dangers to my life, the reunion with my family, and an invitation to move on to new shores. It also meant a complete reassessment of our situation.

Celle had been spared by Allied bombs, but all around roads and towns lay in ruins. Hanover, my native city, was a heap of rubble. Factories that had survived the bombing were dismantled. All food was rationed; it was too much to starve, too little to live on. Any deeper analysis about the war and the recent past had to be postponed until we won the struggle for our daily bread. We thought of little else besides the necessities of daily life. To ponder professional options for the future was a luxury I could not afford. Protecting and feeding my family came first. Any intellectual ambitions had to take a backseat for a while.

A friend of mine recommended me for a job with the "Nordsee" Fishing Company in Cuxhaven. As an ordinary seaman I would go out into the North Sea on trawlers and other fishing boats that had originally been destined for the scrap heap but were now deemed good enough to visit the fishing grounds of the Dogger Bank and the Fladengrund.

ORDINARY SEAMAN

A letter:

Cuxhaven, November 1, 1945

Things around here are somewhat adventurous. I assume the letter I wrote from Hamburg has reached you. No sooner had I dropped it into a mailbox when a car stopped and took me down to Wischhafen. There I sat on the road again with all my luggage. Then a motorcycle drove by, bound for a German POW camp nearby. I thought I might find better transportation there and hopped aboard, again burdened down by my heavy load. After a few incidents we arrived safely at the camp, and indeed the next morning I caught a ride on to Cuxhaven. By chance I met my former executive officer, Lieutenant Klug. I was able to talk him out of a sack of white cabbage for you. So don't be surprised if it shows up at our place in the near future.

Cuxhaven looks exactly the way I had imagined it from a book of seafaring stories I had devoured as a boy. But if I had imagined myself so far to be a true mariner, there were still lots of new things to learn, such as the financial arrangements, the muster roll, or keeping a registration book. I received my gear and clothing in a house guarded over by a stony-faced old fisherman. Rubber boots up to my belly, oilskin clothing, a sou'wester, a knife and gloves to kill the fish, and many other things. I threw everything into a huge seabag, which I slung over my shoulder and carried aboard.

Then everything went very fast. On November 1, I joined the crew of the *Max M. Warburg*, a fishing trawler of 184 tons. There are nineteen of us on board. I lodge with eleven others in the forecastle. Things are primitive, but we will manage. We will sail at 7 A.M. on November 4. We will be away for twelve days, stay in port for 36 hours, and off we go again. That will be the routine for the foreseeable future. Ashore I have rented a decent room in the house of a construction official who works for the city. The house is about 30 minutes from the train station. I include the rest of my ration stamps along with a postage stamp on which you will recognize without difficulty your U-boat man. Until now I did not know about this stamp.

Best regards from your ordinary seaman.

Diary:

My first day aboard the *Max M. Warburg*. It was still dark when I left Groden, where I live, to march to the harbor. The watchman hands me my seabag, which I had left with him while telling me all about his heroic deeds during the war. I barely listen to him. By means of an almost vertical ladder I climb on board. Mariners are known to be taciturn. I enter the deck. "Morning." No reply. "I am the new seaman." A few men raise their eyes from whatever trivial activities they are engaged in. Nobody stirs. It turns out there is no mattress for me. Reluctantly, a locker is cleared so that I can stow away my belongings. After half an hour, as I am about to leave the deck to go outside, a question: "What's your first name?" Apparently the ice is broken.

Work begins. We drag nets around, roll barrels full of salt, and do other chores. In the meantime we have gotten under way, crossing the Elbe River to Brunsbüttel where in 1940 I lost my boat *U 57* in a collision. There is no time to dwell on those events. We demagnetize the vessel. My formerly clean suit is a mess already, as if we had been out here for days. The men work hard, but their manners are coarse, their utterances unfriendly. A soft soul would not be able to stand it for very long. The men, having somehow learned that I am a former U-boat commander, do not quite know what to make of me. They address me by my first name as they do with everyone else, but they hesitate to shout me down the way they do it to our cabin boy, the former naval ensign von Seydlitz. By the way, he is a nice young man. I will look out for him. In the evening they begin to ask me about my past. The atmosphere becomes more friendly. Deep down they are as simple as children.

Letters:

It is Saturday afternoon and I owe you a report before I will go to Kaltenberge with my former chief engineer, Lieutenant Peter, to spend Sunday there.

But back to the adventures of your seaman. As I walked through the darkness to the harbor, everyone was still asleep except a few others who likewise had to be aboard their vessels early. I realized for the first time that I had joined a different social class. I now belong to the working class.

The ship was ready to sail when I arrived. My work station was on the forecastle and I handled the forward lines as we got under way. Soon we were on the Elbe headed for the Dogger Bank. There are no time-outs for ordinary seamen. We repair the nets, get them ready for the catch, stand watch. Perhaps it was good that I had no time to think things over. After 24 hours we reached the Dogger Bank and brought out the net. At the same time a storm set in—it is November, after all. It would not abate for the remainder of our outing.

When we lowered the net for the first time, one member of the crew got caught in the steel hawsers and was dragged overboard. While the boat lay stopped, we hauled the net back in. The man was unconscious, his foot crushed. The captain's reaction from the bridge: "You idiot!" Nothing else. We took the man to our deck. There were no medications on board, only rubbing alcohol to ease the pain and prevent infections. My limited medical knowledge from my U-boat days helped a little. We put the foot in splints and tried to straighten out the bones. Everything is up to the healing process and the goodwill of Hippocrates. There are no coastguard cutters that might be called in. To break off our fishing trip was out of the question. Human lives are of little value around here. The man remained on board for the next ten days. We cared for him as best we could. Not once did the captain show up to take a look at the man.

About half of our catch is commercially usable. We fall into an exhausting routine. We haul up the catch, empty the net onto the deck, bring it out again, then sort, kill, and stow away the fish before we repeat the entire process. You asked if we get any sleep. Practically none. While the fishing routine is under way there is no time off. For ten long days we are wet and cold, our hands bloody and worn, toiling like slaves without respite. Every once in a while we process the old catch before the new one is heaved aboard. On those occasions we collapse for a half hour's rest. While we wolf down our meals the net stays out just a little longer than usual.

Our mess deck is dirty. Nobody has time to wash up or to brush his teeth. Perhaps it is not necessary anyway since we swallow so much salt water involuntarily. Whenever we get some sleep we never bother to undress because it would mean wasting time. I always wake up bathed in sweat because right next to my place is the stove that keeps us warm. That is our world for twelve days at a time.

I am back again. While looking for a new place to stay I made the acquaintance of a simple woman full of humor. On one occasion she said: We Germans are in the habit of pursuing one goal at a time, using up all our energy. In the process we forget that to the right and left of our path there are beautiful things that alone make our lives worth living. As a result we usually collapse in a state of exhaustion before we even reach our goal.

Today I received a telegram informing me that I will not be able to enroll at the Technical University in Hanover at this time. I have decided to stick with the fishing business for another while. After all, I am pretty good at negotiating with people and organizations.

Once more your sailor has solid ground beneath his feet. We docked at 1:30 P.M. right near the huge fish-processing facilities and began to spit out the catch we had stowed away in the ship's belly over a period of ten days. We seamen are ready to go ashore, freshly washed and shaved, in civilian clothes that look little different from what we wear at work. Our next task is to smuggle our goodies past the guard on the pier, for the situation is this:

As soon as the vessel makes port it is taken over, along with its entire cargo, by the fishing company. A guard is posted near the gangway to make sure that no fish that is not accounted for leaves the vessel. Every crew member—except the captain, who enjoys special privileges—is entitled to 5 pounds of fresh fish, or 10 pounds if he is married. In reality everyone tries to beat the system. Your sailor, knowing his feeble wife at home needs all the food he can lay his hands on, managed to take ashore, besides his ration of fresh fish, a few cans of cod liver, two bottles of cod liver oil, and a small barrel of salt herring. If you consider that the *Warburg* returned from this trip with 115 tons of fish, you will forgive your sailor that he cheated the guard after his very first voyage.

Loaded down by my heavy seabag, the bottles neatly stored among the fish, I stumbled up the gangplank and showed the guard my receipt for 10 pounds of fresh fish. It took a good deal of acting on my part to convince the man that nothing fishy was going on. When I handed my ticket to the British soldier at the gate, he only said: "Fish? O.K." He did not seem interested in the least in my heavy bag. It took me three quarters of an hour to make it home instead of the customary 20 minutes. The flounders and the cod I will give to Peter and my landlord for the nice treatment they have extended to me. It would be impossible to send you the fresh fish, given our inadequate means of transportation, but everything else is on the way.

Then your husband had to see the doctor. You need not panic; it is all taken care of. It simply goes with the life of an ordinary seaman on a fishing vessel that his hand will be torn up from handling the steel hawsers and the fish. Result: blood poisoning, but nothing really serious. The doctor has forbidden me to use the hand for a while. This means I will have to sit out the next voyage. I regret it because in spite of all the difficulties I had begun to find my way around. So for the next two weeks I will stay ashore and try to learn a little more about the business side of the fishing industry.

I am sitting in my little room in the attic, covered by a blanket, and I feel good and warm as I exchange these words with you. The hand still bothers me a little bit. For that reason, and because I have a cold, I will keep my letter short. You can imagine how often I am thinking of you. The cold, the wetness, the pain, the lack of sleep, the loneliness among strangers—I am prepared to bear it all if it can buy us a halfway secure livelihood. The price is very high, the struggle bitter and hard, much harder than I had feared.

Diary:

After a short time this much was clear to me: until the end of the war I had lived and worked among comrades, among friends who shared my values and attitudes; now I stood alone. Around me I saw people whose ambitions in life were limited and who barely concealed their aversion against anyone with a different face, different priorities, and different ways of expressing himself. This was something new for me and I, as a former officer, became an obvious target of this aversion. It made little sense to try to avoid this confrontation. I was determined to remain steadfast and to face this social problem.

And yet I kept imagining that I could become active in a creative sense, to construct something with my own hands. This kind of sorting out, organizing, and registering that loomed ahead, this atmosphere of fish heads, was not to my taste. Had I not already been busy creating something? Right next to the destructive side of mastering the art of war there had been the challenge of forming and leading human beings. And not just any kind of human beings, but those who went out to sea into the very teeth of death.

How wonderful it would be to be able to study architecture after all! It simply must work: complete concentration on that one goal; saving every penny; the help of others who might open doors for a friend in need.

December 3, 1945
At the suggestion of a businessman, I saw today the secretary of the free labor unions in Cuxhaven. The result was as planned. My step will make it more difficult for the workers' councils to discriminate against former military officers. The secretary is a lowly figure, but honest. He suffered terribly in the concentration camps for his unflinching views. For him the Social Democrats are the only acceptable political party. These people move themselves to tears. They are very much convinced of their own importance and are patronizing toward others.

December 21, 1945
Just finished our third voyage. As far as physical challenges are concerned, it was worse than the first one. The seas averaged force 6 to 7. We kept on fishing except for one day when the storm was too bad. The men are being pushed to the limits of their endurance. Even the older men among us seem to have had enough. One day I was almost swept overboard but could hang on to a piece of the stern at the last moment. We are forever wet and cold. I feel something is not quite right with my kidneys. Bending down to kill the cod is very tiresome and makes my back hurt badly.

This time our crew enjoys a more congenial composition. Above all, Otto from East Prussia is a fine companion. Von Seydlitz, too, is with us again, this time promoted to apprentice seaman. There is also another former submarine commander. The original members of the crew are more open to us newcomers after they realized that I had rejoined them. The surprise their faces betrayed was like a small triumph for me.

Finally home again! And there I find my wife's telegram informing me that I have been accepted to begin my studies at the university!

My journal and the letters show how steep my fall was from the position of a celebrated U-boat commander to that of an ordinary seaman before the mast.

STUDYING ARCHITECTURE

On January 4, 1946, I attended my first lecture at the Technical University in Hanover, Professor Wickop's course on construction theory. When I entered the classroom I was under the impression that I was pretty good at drawing things. But the professor's proficiency and speed of producing ground plans and perspective views on the board was a difficult act to follow. I would have become very depressed in a short period of time had it not been for a fellow student who gave me helpful hints. He had returned from the trenches with a shot-up hand.

How had I as a U-boat commander and "war criminal" been accepted by the university? I later learned that several professors on the board overseeing admissions had put in a good word for me as a native Hanoverian. Perhaps they recalled that my crew and I had been official guests of the city and even had signed Hanover's book of honor. Naturally there had also been opposition, which became more vehement when I was elevated to the position of scientific assistant.

The School of Architecture, housed in the Schlosswenderstrasse, was half destroyed. It was wintertime. In the workrooms we used stoves to keep warm, but they were far from tight. Smoke filled the air and we sat bent over our drawings with red and watery eyes. Those of us who had been soldiers were in the habit of studying more intensively than the rest because we were eager to pass our exams as soon as possible to be able to provide for our families. We helped each other as much as circumstances permitted. Professor Wickop confided in me later that he had never before or later encountered students who devoted themselves as fully and as eagerly to their assignments as our group. I lived during this time in an old trailer once used by lumberjacks in the woods. It had no insulation against either cold or heat and belonged to the construction firm Bosse in Stadthagen, where I had worked as an intern. Our trailer stood in the courtyard of a parsonage. Inside there were two bunks, one on top of the other. The upper bunk belonged to Mr. Bosse's son, who was also a university student in Hanover. Our furniture consisted of a small table, two chairs, and a tiny closet. In a corner we had a sink with a ewer beneath it. We had to get our water from an old pump in the yard. Whenever temperatures fell below the freezing point the water would freeze in the sink.

After her life-threatening trip from Lübeck to Celle, my wife tried to find appropriate accommodations in view of my impending release from captivity and the birth of our son. Two weeks before the expected birth of the child she had the following encounter with our local housing director, a communist. "What do you want? Who are you?" "I would like to be assigned to the room that the family of Mr. S. has kindly placed at my disposal. Here are my identification papers." "You cannot get the room; it is too large for you." My wife: "I expect the arrival of my husband as well as a child." The director: "I would not count on the return of your husband. He is a war criminal. You won't see him again." My wife, who at that point had not yet heard from me, was close to passing out. But she composed herself in order not to appear weak in front of this creature and said: "You are wrong, Sir. I do have news from my husband." Hereupon the man became unsure of himself and signed the papers.

I saw this room a few days later when I returned to Celle. In the end we gave it up again and exchanged it for two smaller rooms with outside walls. A disadvantage was, of course, that we had more trouble keeping the rooms warm with our little stove. We had no heating fuel, neither wood, briquettes, nor coal. I got in touch with a forest ranger who allowed us to cut wood in his district, which consisted mainly of torched trees. The British, in search of Germans hiding in the woods, had burned everything down with their flame-throwers. All families in our house pooled their resources and together we cut enough wood to last us through the winter.

I knew almost all the residents in our house from my school days. The proprietor owned a machine tool manufacturing plant specializing in oil drilling equipment. His sister had married a Luftwaffe captain, a former dive bomber pilot who was now enrolled as a student in Celle's teachers' college. On the first floor lived a couple. He worked as an insurance agent in Hanover. Since he often took time off from work, one day a commission showed up to investigate his frequent absences. It turned out that he was indeed working hard, but only for his family. He was fired the next day. But the man showed himself flexible. It was the time of the massive Berlin airlift, and one of the airports involved was Fassberg near Celle. Along with the American soldiers came the German prostitutes, a real land plague. But for the former insurance agent this meant the chance of a lifetime. He would provide transportation services so that the soldiers and girls could get together. He took them out into the hay, waited until the business was properly conducted, collected his fee, and then drove them back to town.

Also on the first floor lived a widow with her son, and next to her an employee of the city construction office. He was originally from the zone now occupied by the Russians, and he had left his wife behind. Eventually the two were reunited. He had graduated from a specialized school for construction personnel and was in the habit of complaining that people with an academic background knew nothing about the construction business. Deep down, however, he was clearly envious of those who had earned a university degree. We all shared a common kitchen downstairs. It was an ideal place for exchanging gossip, telling jokes, and hatching intrigues.

My family lived in a city that had been spared the bombing terror and among people who had suffered no material sacrifices. One day, after asking in vain for help from someone in the house, my wife hired two men from the shelter for homeless men to build a wooden partition in the basement for us to store our few extra belongings. Even though the owner of the house ran a machine tool outfit, we asked in vain for the use of a hammer. A few days later, someone broke into the basement and stole some sixty cans of meat belonging to the owner of the house. My wife was convinced that it was the work of our two bums, for whom she had even prepared a potato soup from our meager supplies to thank them for their assistance.

We lived on the edge of starvation. One day my wife had to be taken to the hospital suffering from edema caused by hunger. As refugees we had no reserves. For reasons beyond our comprehension the owner of the house stored a considerable number of sausages right above the passageway to our two rooms. They knew that we were starving. It cannot have been ignorance, as in the case of Marie Antoinette before the French Revolution. When Parisians one day were clamoring for bread, she is said to have responded without meaning any harm: "Let them eat cake!" No, for our landlord it was a matter of cold chicanery, of undisguised egotism.

But not everything in Celle was touched by a sense of sadness. Next to us lived the Reinhardts. He had once worked for the industrial giant Rheinmetall and now ran a factory in Celle together with a partner. And he who produced something also had something to eat. Mrs. Reinhardt was a generous woman. Since our children were forbidden to play in the backyard of our house, they played instead with the Reinhardt children in theirs. As a result, the children of both families grew up together in considerable freedom. We also had friends whom I knew from my school days, for example Dr. Jessen, our family physician. After the currency reform, when our savings had all but disappeared, his son-in-law Dr. Nebelsieck offered to lend us money so that I could finish my studies. Fortunately, the availability of financial loans through the university enabled me not to have to take him up on his generous offer. Also, my old music teacher, Professor Fritz Schmidt, in whose choir I had once sung

Bach's St. Matthew Passion and the Mass in B minor, had an open house for us in the Kalandgasse, the old Latin school.

I also belonged to a round table discussion group organized by the painter Erich Klahn. I had come to know him and his work through the Schmidts. Besides Klahn and myself, our group consisted of Professor Plassmann, a specialist in Germanic studies; another former naval officer; and Peter Seeger, who would later become director of the Pelizäus Museum in Hildesheim. In our discussions, and inspired by Klahn's works, we tried to rescue what was still of value in the ruins around us, notions that would stand the test of time. Who were we? Where could we detect relationships and contexts?

It was clear enough that visible phenomena were little else but the result of underlying forces beyond our immediate detection. To pinpoint these forces became the basis of our inquiries. To get us going, one day Klahn wrote the ambiguous French phrase *Sans Celle Rien* beneath the likeness of the goddess Fortuna standing tall atop the earth on an engraved plate. It could either mean that we could achieve nothing without the help of fortune (*Celle* = Fortuna), or that we were nothing without Celle, our town, our home, our discussion group. We shared the demand of the hour: to understand and tame the forces that operated behind and between the things around us; to do so with the materials that have been entrusted to man; to create artistically complete forms—in architecture, through painting, or through the other arts—without expectations, but also not without hope. We wanted to juxtapose true shape and form against the substitutes of a civilization dominated by technology and industry. We desired to prevent the further loss of substance—indeed, to see ourselves as the ultimately important substance and to base our creations on that experience. In some ways our discussions reminded me of the debates we had engaged in so many years before as members of the youth movement. The chief difference was, of course, that we had gained experience, had matured, had fathomed life in all its heights and depths like the knight in Dürer's etching, accompanied by death and the devil.

Through Dr. Spandau, who as a major in Gotenhafen had presented talks about German history for the officer corps, I made the acquaintance of the professor of physics, Pascual Jordan. He introduced me to key aspects of the theory of microphysics. According to Professor Jordan, changes in our scientific knowledge, spearheaded by microphysics, have brought about changes in the very way we are thinking. As an analogy he compared the revolution of modern physics to man's earlier realization that the earth is round. As long as man saw the earth as a gigantic disk he could hope to explore and explain everything on it because of its clear limitations. Columbus, whose discovery ultimately changed only our perception about the parts of the world that were unknown until then, destroyed this hope forever. Since that time we know there are many questions in the world that we will never be able to answer no matter how far we travel, for the answers lie beyond our grasp in the realm of infinity. In a similar way, modern physics has shown that we should never expect to be able to deduce the entire field of possible knowledge from a limited set of experiences: for instance, the way Descartes had done it when, starting from his *cogito ergo sum*, he built up an entire ideology. Today we find ourselves in a situation similar to that of Columbus, who possessed courage enough to leave behind everything that was known to him in the hope of finding more land beyond the seas. The way modern physics has pointed to the limits of classical physics has also removed the basis for explaining the world through the principle of dialectical materialism. From the insights of modern physics a new type of philosophy must one day come that restores the unity of our view of the world, which we have lost over the past centuries.

Our discussions naturally also touched on the Nuremberg Tribunal and its effect on the population. We were particularly interested in the two indicted Grand Admirals Raeder and Dönitz. Words and phrases like "Free Corps Dönitz," "U-boat spirit," "Comradeship," and "Loyalty" had been associated with the U-boat arm in broad circles of the population. Now their Admiral stood accused and his followers were silent. That was an impossible situation. At the time none of us knew how deeply Dönitz had become involved with the National Socialist regime, which had since been recognized and branded as criminal. Certainly he had not hesitated to become Hitler's successor. On the other hand, we were familiar with what Dönitz as Commander-in-Chief of the U-Boat Command had instilled in his men in terms of soldierly virtues and that such virtues lost none of their value if they had been misused by others. Dönitz was also prepared to make sacrifices. After all, he lost his two sons at sea.

I had intended to gain and maintain distance from these matters and not become engaged in public discussions after the war. In this case, however, I could not remain on the sidelines. I was well aware of the personal risk I was taking. The very completion of my studies was at stake. And always in the background I had to be mindful of the British "Education Officer"—what arrogance the word alone conveyed—before whom I had to appear every three months and who queried me about my democratic disposition. On those occasions we—that is, two former army officers serving on the General Staff and I—had to stand in front of a British officer who was dressed in breeches and as outward indication of his opinion about us held a riding crop across his knees. Oh yes, we had learned well to camouflage our feelings.

But in Dönitz's case something needed to be done if we wanted to live with a clear conscience afterwards. Thus we began the tiresome process of drafting and circulating a petition on behalf of Grand Admiral Dönitz. It was a difficult process because our means of communication were very limited. We had no telephones. You needed special permits to move from one occupation zone into another. We had no paper, let alone a typewriter. After I had drafted the appeal, Dönitz's defense council, Kranzbühler, made sure that the wording was in line with the terminology used by the Nuremberg Tribunal. Then we arranged that all living and prominent U-boat commanders signed the document. We translated the petition into English, French, Russian, and Latin (for the Vatican). I harbored no illusions about the impact of our action, but I felt I had to do it no matter what.

Even today, after having studied Dönitz's achievements and mistakes in great detail, and not unaware of his human weaknesses and political delusions, I stand behind my decision of 1946. I seem to be in good company. In his book, *Pour rétablir une vérité,* the former French President Georges Pompidou cites General de Gaulle's assessment of the Nuremberg Trials: "In Nuremberg they got everything confused. They executed the generals, that was the mistake."

To the
Allied Control Council of Germany

Re: Review of the Nuremberg Verdict against Grand Admiral Dönitz

As representatives of the German U-boat arm in the past war we hereby address the Allied Control Council and appeal to its human and military conscience. We act as spokesmen for the former members of the German U-boat force who we know are united in their thoughts and feelings about this matter. We gain this conviction from the fact that most officers and enlisted men of the U-boat branch were either trained by us or served with us at sea. We know the hearts of these men. They think the way we do. Our appeal stems from our collective quest for justice.

We hereby ask for the review and repeal of the verdict against Grand Admiral Dönitz because we are deeply convinced that the crimes he has been accused of do not exist.

The U-boat war was begun according to the rules laid down in international law and, once our enemies intensified their countermeasures, carried on under orders from the Grand Admiral, as detailed by the defense council Fleet Judge Kranzbühler. The war was fought consistent with our own conscience and our sense of justice. We were never asked to do more than what a soldier's ethos will allow anywhere in the world.

There never was an order to kill shipwrecked sailors. Already at the trial this fact was attested to under oath by a great number of U-boat commanders. Those, however, who violated the principle of coming to the aid of shipwrecked persons after ensuring the safety of their own boat and crew, did so against the standing orders of their superiors. Those who took the *Laconia* order or other utterances of our Grand Admiral to mean that they had license to kill shipwrecked sailors, can only have acted in such a way based on their own psychological complexes. Their interpretation went against the very spirit of the U-boat service. Their number is very small in comparison to the vast majority of U-boat men who stayed within their orders.

We do not know all the details of the indictment or how far time limits apply to the accusations and charges expressed at the trial. Nor can we speak to the kind and weight of the political accusations that have been lodged against the Grand Admiral. Press reports have been vague in these matters. But we know the personality of our Grand Admiral, and we have come to learn what kind of man Dönitz is in five years of fierce fighting. Not once has this man asked us to do anything dishonorable. His intentions and his principles always reflected highest moral standards and restraint. We are deeply convinced that he, too, never acted in a dishonorable fashion.

We believe we speak out in the name of a universal military conscience. Soldiers and sailors do not understand when one of them is being convicted because he has fought for his fatherland and thus for a good thing, and has done his duty. After all wars soldiers have been the first to reach out to their former enemies because soldiers respected one another with a clear conscience. We know that the verdict has also painfully touched the sense of fairness, justice, and chivalry among Allied soldiers.

Given our personal experiences in this war, given our understanding of the principle under which this war at sea has been fought, and knowing the personality of our Grand Admiral, we ask that you do not defame with the verdict against this military man a service branch that has proved through its high percentage of casualties that it fought a just and honest struggle.

We also ask that the clean record of these dead as well as of the living not be tainted by marking the person of their highly revered superior and his actions as criminal.

In Germany, September 1946

[Signed by: Junior Captain (ret.) Erich Topp; Junior Captain (ret.) Reinhard Suhren; Commander (ret.) Otto Schuhart; Commander (ret.) Carl Emmermann; Captain (ret.) Viktor Schütze; Commander (ret.) Hans Witt; Commander (ret.) Georg Lassen; Commander (ret.) Ulrich Heyse; Commander (ret.) Otto von Bülow; Commander (ret.) Ali Cremer; Junior Captain (ret.) Heinrich Lehmann-Willenbrock; Lieutenant Commander (ret.) Karl-Heinz Wiebe; Junior Captain (ret.) Victor Oehrn; Junior Captain (ret.) Rolf Rüggeberg; Junior Captain (ret.) Hans Eckermann; Commander (ret.) Ernst Bauer; Commander (ret.) Wilhelm Schulz; Junior Captain (ret.) Albrecht Brandi; Commander (ret.) Adalbert Schnee; Lieutenant Commander (ret.) Hermann Rasch; Lieutenant Commander (ret.) August Maus]

One day, while attending a lecture on art history, I was picked up by the British military police. This caused great excitement among my fellow students. A jeep took us to the former home of the Nazi district leader Hartmann Lauterbacher, now housing the British Intelligence Service. When I inquired what this was all about I was told, "You will find out soon enough." Since it was lunch time, I was first taken to the basement.

Then a door opened and I was pushed into a dark room. When my eyes had become used to the darkness I faintly recognized several men sitting at a table. They were eating. Perhaps one's sense of smell is particularly sensitive in the darkness, but I perceived a terrible stench pervading the room. Its cause, as it turned out later, was a bucket hidden behind a curtain that was being used for basic human necessities.

Someone asked me to join them at the table and to take off my coat. I told them: "That won't be necessary. They will come and get me out of here in a few minutes." Roaring laughter. "We were told the same thing, and now we have been here for eight days." We introduced ourselves. I can still remember a man named Messerschmidt, a couple of Party officials whose names I have forgotten, and a couple of ordinary people. One of them, a technician, told me his story: One night when he returned home from work his wife received him as usual, except that night she had some American cigarettes and coffee. She explained that a girlfriend of hers had visited her with an American soldier. This aroused the man's suspicion. The next day he saw an American radio set in the corner of his living room. In a fit of anger he threw the set out of the window. Thereupon he had been arrested and brought here on a charge of damaging Allied property.

Contrary to precedent, I was indeed led out of that basement room after the lunch break. I found myself opposite a chief petty officer who seemed friendly and offered me some tea and cigarettes. The whole matter was about the code word "Rainbow," which the German naval broadcasting service had sent out after the surrender documents had been signed. The code word had resulted in the scuttling of most of Germany's remaining naval units. When the order was cancelled a short while later, much of the destruction had already occurred. The radio order violated the conditions of the capitulation. I was asked on whose authority "Rainbow" had been issued. With a clear conscience I answered that I did not know. But they would not believe me. "We will keep you here until your memory comes back!" I replied: "At the time I was not in Germany. We never received the order. As you know, the boats based in Norway were not destroyed." Then the petty officer requested that I give him my pay-book. I happened to have it with me. He leafed through it, probably to check where I had been posted at various times. At the back of the book was a little flap that I had used for small documents but now contained only a few postage stamps. The chief petty officer, evidently a philatelist, took great interest in the stamps, especially the 6-pfennig stamp of the Wehrmacht set that shows a U-boat commander operating

the periscope. He asked me: "Who is this officer?" I said: "That's me!" He replied: "No, that's impossible." "Why don't you take a closer look?" He looked at me for some time, then back at the stamp, and finally agreed: "Indeed, you are right."

This gave me my chance. I asked him, as if I did not know already, "Are you a stamp collector?" When he answered in the affirmative I said: "I'll give you the stamp as a gift." Since I suspected that he would decline the offer, I told him a little story: The picture on which the stamp is based came originally from a newsreel that a war correspondent had made while embarked on my boat during a war patrol. This newsreel was shown all over Germany. One day I received a letter from a young lady containing the original photograph. The latter shows me with my arms draped over the controls of the boat's periscope during a submerged attack. In pencil the young lady had written on the back of the picture: "I would like to be your periscope." "You see," I told my interrogator, "that was an offer. I did not take her up on it—something I later regretted. Perhaps she really was as charming as the words she had written. I really think you should accept my offer." He laughed, pocketed the stamp, and asked me where I would like to be taken. "To the train station," I replied. "I am sure my wife is anxious to see me." He had a car drive up, took me to the entrance door, and waved good-bye to me as his driver took me to the station.

In Celle we were once visited by two British naval officers. Both wore navy duffle-coats on top of their uniforms and apparently looked very sharp, judging by the reaction of the ladies in the house. They introduced themselves as Lieutenant Blake and Lieutenant Commander Beaverbrook. We had no snacks or drinks to offer. Blake produced a package of tea and my wife prepared several cups for us. After these preliminaries they stated their business.

First they wanted to know whether I had any contacts to the Russians. I could answer this question in the negative. Then they said they were interested in establishing contact with me and other former U-boat commanders to learn some details about the submarine service they were particularly interested in. In the course of our conversation I realized that they already knew much about our tactical procedures and our weaponry. For this reason and out of the conviction that I should do anything to strengthen the West, I did not hesitate to engage in detailed talks with them. They also were interested in keeping in touch with me. In those days first steps were taken to improve relations between the western Allies and the West Germans. As always it was easiest to start such a process with the military.

The two naval officers took their leave under the curious glances of the other inhabitants of the house. Afterwards we were bombarded with questions but remained reserved. At any rate, this visit by the British naval officers had the unexpected consequence of raising our standing with the owner of the house. When my wife invited him for cake and coffee on some occasion not long afterwards, he at last and generously agreed to have our rooms linked up to the central heating system of the house, which in the meantime had been repaired.

After a few months Blake returned. This time he was alone and seemed more confident than before. He again brought some tea, and we enjoyed a long conversation. He invited us to come to Hamburg and participate in a meeting between British naval officers and German U-boat officers. Before he left, he said: "If they give you any trouble at the university, don't hesitate to call me." I had to think of the despicable Education Officer and kept Blake's offer in mind. After six weeks Blake showed up as scheduled and took us in his jeep to Hamburg. For the first time in a long while I was allowed to do the driving myself, and I enjoyed the trip tremendously. In the British officer casino in Hamburg a large banquet had been prepared. The British were represented by officers and scientists, while our delegation consisted primarily of former U-boat commanders, among them Ali Cremer. This happened in late 1946. Here the first talks were held about the possible rearmament of West Germany, long before the politicians got into the act.

After this meeting we saw Blake a few more times. Then we lost touch. Years later I happened to read a newspaper article about George Blake, master spy, who had worked for the Russians against the British. He had been sentenced to the maximum term allowed under the law and incarcerated in a London jail, from which he later managed to escape under dramatic circumstances.

These bizarre experiences interrupted my studies only briefly. Otherwise, the School of Architecture was notorious for its spectacular parties. We celebrated them in our workrooms, all of them appropriately decorated according to the party's theme. Certainly, prospective architects had to be good at this sort of thing! The workrooms were literally transformed into places conducive to a most festive atmosphere.

Architects had the reputation of enjoying a somewhat closer relationship with Eros than the more reserved engineers and scientists, and this affinity became prominently visible in the themes and decorations we selected for our parties. The latter acted as real magnets for all kinds of students at a time when things looked so depressed politically and economically. I still recall our very first such party. We held it in the fall of 1946 in an old stable for horses because our workrooms had not yet been made available for such a purpose. The party's theme: "Yearning for Greece." My wife had draped me in a white bedsheet. As master poet, a laurel wreath draped around my temples and with golden sandals on my feet, I strolled through the crowd. Various groups of students rested and partied in the stalls that had formerly held the horses. We had put sawdust on the concrete floor so that we could dance more safely. Everyone brought his own drinks; we provided the music. In the midst of all the misery around us it was the most memorable party we ever celebrated in those days. After a long and exciting night we fell into our beds, happy but tired. When we woke up, our pillow cases had turned black from all the sawdust.

Once a few fellow students and I took time off from our studies for a vacation near Berchtesgaden. On that occasion we also went to the Obersalzberg, and I told the others what I had experienced there as the guest of the Bormanns. One of those present later misstated this entirely harmless story and used it against me when my position as a scientific assistant at the university was at stake.

Late in 1949 I passed my *Diplomexamen* with high honors. After several unsuccessful attempts to set myself up professionally, I applied to become a scientific assistant to Professor Graubner. The position hinged on a complicated system of hearings and voting that involved not only the other professors and their assistants but also the council of university employees, which at the time had communist leanings and was made up predominantly of lower-ranking academic personnel.

One day I was asked to see the acting president of the university. While waiting outside his office I met the scientific assistant of another professor who said hello to me in a somewhat distant manner. I should explain that there existed strong rivalries among some professors at the School of Architecture. These rivalries could become very bitter and determined, leading at times to trumped-up charges and rumors designed to bring down an adversary.

Professor Graubner had once prepared some plans for city construction projects for a local Nazi district leader. He had never joined the Party, but this temporary cooperation was enough to get him into trouble. Graubner, a native of the Baltic provinces, was used to standing up for his rights. He literally barricaded himself in his offices and left them only to give lectures and seminars, and to eat. He had to be able to rely totally on the people who worked for him. Apparently he had confidence in me and proposed me as his assistant. That is when the intrigues against me began. Their chief instigator happened to be the assistant of the rival professor and president of the council of university employees who had greeted me so coldly outside the university president's office.

We were both ushered in to see the president. The latter gave my accuser the opportunity to state his case against me. There were four major charges: (1) I had been a friend of Reich Leader Martin Bormann; (2) I had made anti-Semitic remarks; (3) I had said that all sailors are drinkers and had thus insulted the seafaring profession; and (4) I was a friend of

Pascual Jordan, whose publications reportedly had made him a close supporter of Hitler. The man added that my military background in connection with these troubling political entanglements would induce him as a member of the council of university employees to vote against my candidacy.

The university president listened to all this very calmly, then let my accuser go and asked me to stay. He said the whole matter was very unsettling for him, especially the way in which I had been attacked. It did not take me long to find out how and where the charges had originated. Obviously there had been a Judas in our group in Berchtesgaden. The last charge had been supplied by my accuser's wife, who as a lower assistant had been helping with my blueprints. We once had a conversation in which I told her about my meeting with Jordan and how impressed I had been by his insights. She considered him a charlatan. She also suggested that the university president harbored an aversion against Jordan. Both had been rivals from the time of their school days. Now she apparently assumed that labelling me anti-Semitic would have a profound effect on the university president because his wife was Jewish and he had lost his job during the Nazi era. Everything had been put together in a most clever and perfidious manner, but it failed to achieve the expected success.

At the conclusion of our talk the president hinted he would put no obstacles in my path. I also received unexpected support from the lower ranks of the council of university employees, the cleaning ladies. When asked whether they had anything against me they said no. But not only they spoke up on my behalf, I also received the unanimous endorsement of the university senate, which made the decisive difference. This way I joined Professor Graubner's staff as his scientific assistant on January 1, 1950.

In 1576, after five long years in the dungeons of the Inquisition, the Spanish mystic and lyricist Luis de Léon, professor of theology at the University of Salamanca, stood ready to give his first lecture since his arrest. The room was filled to capacity, everyone eager to hear how he would address his students whom he had not seen in five years. He took a look at his audience and then began: *"Dicebamus hesterna die . . ."* (As we mentioned yesterday . . .). I now sensed something of this composure in me. I wanted to forget the victories and the defeats, and I envied those who managed to do just that. I wanted to be carried along by the great currents of our culture as I had experienced them before the years of terror and as they could be revisited now. At the same time I felt a certain uneasiness about this attitude of self-possession.

In my search for historical parallels and how they had been captured by artists, I discovered Rodin, whose sculpture *The Citizens of Calais* masterfully expresses the notion of unconditional surrender. We could empathize with the fate of these human beings who in 1347, after years of heroic resistance, utterly exhausted and feeling the noose tightening around their necks, were forced to give themselves up to the enemy. In his work Rodin has erected a monument to all those who, after passing through phases of hubris, collapse, unspeakable suffering, and tragic entanglements, had to endure despair without hope. Our complete military and political defeat was reflected in the justice system that the winners of the war imposed on the vanquished and in the dismemberment of the Reich into occupation zones.

Under the pressure of these events we retreated at first into a kind of self-defense position. The totalitarian regime had created through its ideology a system of thought categories that kept on functioning for a while even after the collapse of the government. What made this ideology so powerful was that it had pervaded everything without opposition or alternative—the corporative organizations, the schools and universities, and the media. Those who abandoned the old categories and reoriented themselves too quickly or for opportunistic reasons were viewed with suspicion. But we found ourselves moving along in a gray zone, without clear guideposts, without an audience, full of doubts about the events around us, neither believing in our own system of justice nor accepting that of the others.

Not until I took up the study of architecture with its links to art and the humanities did the old categories lose their power and became once again overshadowed by the values that had informed our culture over the millennia. We students lived on this Island of the Blessed in splendid isolation, as it were, away from the political questions of the day until we learned about the mass executions behind the front lines and the genocide against the Jews, no longer as mere rumors but confirmed by eyewitness accounts and pictures. This added a moral dimension to our defeat that went deeper than all apprehensions after our military surrender. It depresses us until this day. Nothing can drag my generation from beneath the shadows that the crimes of the National Socialist regime have spread over us. I still hold this conviction very deeply as I write these words in 1990. Several years in the United States and fourteen years of travels in South America, Southeast Asia, and India have allowed me as a soldier, businessman, or tourist to notice how this shadow still hangs over Germans who left their country for a new beginning elsewhere. I have looked at documents and listened to eyewitnesses. There is no doubt in my mind.

A friend of mine, a physician, witnessed the following scene in a makeshift hospital for critically wounded soldiers toward the end of the war. One of the men, close to death, requests a private talk with the doctor. He rejects the offices of a priest. He makes it known that he has never belonged to the Church throughout his life and does not require the consolation of such an institution. He needs to speak to a human being. The talk with the doctor turns into a confession.

The man had been an ordinary policeman. After a while his superiors had attached him to a special unit. One day, he was asked along with others to attend a closed meeting where, under the seal of strictest confidentiality, they were told of the extent and methods of the Nazi genocide program against the Jews. The gist of the information was virtually identical with an address SS Leader Heinrich Himmler gave before an audience of Party notables in Posen on October 6, 1943. Himmler spoke immediately after Field Marshal Milch, Grand Admiral Dönitz, and Reich Minister Speer had briefed the same audience about the current military and armament situation. Here are excerpts from Himmler's speech:

> Allow me to take up in this context and in this close-knit circle of Party comrades a question that most of you have come to take for granted but that has become the most pressing problem of my life, the Jewish question. Today you give no thought to the matter and are relieved that in your district there are no more Jews. All Germans with few exceptions are also aware that we would hardly be able to sustain ourselves through the current aerial bombardments and through a possible fourth, fifth, or sixth year of war if we still had this poisonous plague in our people's body. Gentlemen, it is easy to say: "The Jews must be exterminated." For those of us who must carry out this demand it is the hardest and most difficult task one can imagine. Some of you will say, "Well, of course, they are all Jews," or "They are only Jews." It is not that easy. You cannot imagine how many petitions I have received, Party comrades not excluded, that state that naturally all Jews are pigs but that so-and-so is a decent Jew who should be left alone. I dare declare that based on the number of petitions and opinions in Germany there must be more decent Jews in Germany than their overall share of the population. In other words, we have in Germany so many millions of people who want to protect their one, famous, decent Jew that their number is greater than the number of Jews altogether. I only mention this subject here because you probably know from your own district and your own experience with respectable and decent National Socialists that each of them knows at least one decent Jew.
>
> I ask you never to talk about what you are hearing today in this room. We must address another question: What about women and children? In this case I have decided to find a perfectly clear solution.
>
> I did not feel entitled to exterminate the men—that is, to execute them or to have them killed—in order to nurture our nemesis in the form of their sons and grandsons. I had to make the toughest decision of all, namely, to have this entire people disappear from the earth. For the organization that had to carry out this operation it was the toughest assignment they have mastered to date. And the challenge has been met without our men and

their leaders suffering mental or spiritual damage. There was a danger that this might happen. The path between the two existing possibilities, namely, either to become too cruel and heartless and to cease respecting human life, or to go crazy and suffer a nervous collapse—the path between this Scylla and Charybdis is terribly narrow.

Himmler and his gang knew how to reach and stir the emotions, the instincts, and the irritability of unstable, authority-revering men. A general lack of logical thinking and historical awareness furthered this process. The inability to make precise judgments robbed them of the capacity to distinguish between truth and lies, between political necessities and outright crimes.

The closed meeting for the members of the special unit that the dying man had attended set in motion a machinery of death, itself a piece of an isolated system without contact to the rest of society. Under no circumstances was news about the horror that was planned here and later carried out to reach the outside world. Emerging doubts or pangs of conscience were countered by constant indoctrination and the relegation of problems to an inner circle of the initiated. These special units—there were six of them, each 120 men strong—operated behind the front lines. The men lacked nothing to numb their senses—alcohol, coffee, tea, the best food. Musical and cabaret entertainment were organized in such a way as to make any contact with the performers impossible. The main task of the units was to round up and liquidate Poles, Russians, and Jews, all of whom had been declared fair game through the so-called Martial Law Decree. The murders were carried out in different ways. Crowded together in meeting halls, factories, and even churches, the unfortunate were killed by means of machine-gun fire and hand grenades. Then the next group, the same procedure, until the buildings were full of dead. In the end the buildings were set on fire. It also happened that the victims had to dig their own mass graves and were then shot dead in the pits. Others then put a layer of earth and lime over the dead and even those who were still alive.

The man who confided in the doctor on his deathbed had managed to escape from the psycho-terror of his unit when the eastern front collapsed. Even then, while military defeat loomed all around, he had briefly been assigned to a concentration camp to help out with the busy gas chambers. The man knew that he would have to die one way or another. He saw the defeat of his people as an act of retributive justice, the righting of a wrong to which he himself had contributed. He died the next day.

From my meetings and talks with political extremists and fanatics I am prepared to draw the following conclusions. For adherents of a political ideology the end justifies the means. Many National Socialists and communists were ready to throw their received moral obligations overboard in pursuit of a political goal of whose validity they had become convinced. They stood ready to lie, to steal, to kill, to liquidate hundreds of thousands of human beings who stood in their path. For these people the principles of Christian morality were empty abstractions, obsolete prejudices of a despised bourgeois world.

Has it always been this way? Has the course of history always been accompanied and marked by violence? Has the end always justified the means? There can be no doubt that history has not been, at bottom, a "humane" process. Instead, it thrived on the use of force and violence. There are endless examples—Greece, Rome, the Persians, Alexander the Great, Genghis Khan, Napoleon, Hitler, Khomeini. Christianity has claimed more human lives in its religious wars, witch-hunts, the Inquisition, and its role in the colonization of non-European continents than both World Wars taken together. Power and the use of force have always lain close together.

One is tempted to conclude under these circumstances that power should be executed by the best. But who are the best? Who knows the proper balance between power and spirit, between order and chaos, between the demands of the state and individual freedoms and liberties? A look at history, especially religious and intellectual history, suggests that every anthropological group requires absolute moral standards as the basis of its existence in order to survive. On my many travels I have become acquainted with the different customs and ethical traditions of many cultures. They appear to have many similarities. Everywhere in the world you will discover that courage, generosity, justice, and honesty are basic positive values no matter how unique the society in question may otherwise be. By contrast, treason, cowardice, malice, sexual licentiousness, and cruelty are despised the world over.

Due to the regime's monopoly over information and the terror of the totalitarian state, we only learned after the war the full extent to which a criminal political leadership had perverted basic values of our existence and in many areas abandoned them altogether. It might have been possible to exploit certain weaknesses of the system to modify our otherwise uniform picture of the events. But even here the regime came prepared. It cleverly exploited the frequently false propaganda of the other side to further obscure the truth, just as had been the case in World War I. A thorough and correct analysis of all rumors, to sort the genuine from the manufactured news, became very difficult. In addition, the National Socialist system was very good at manipulating the fundamental traditional values of western civilization for its own purposes. Only truly independent minds were equipped to recognize such perversion of thought and word.

One thing that disturbs me profoundly is that many people today still express themselves in the language and diction popular in the Nazi era. I am appalled about the customary vocabulary one encounters in certain newspapers and books, or in the speeches given in some veterans' organizations, all under the protective mantle of the right of freedom of expression. Perhaps these are remnants of fossilized types who will die out with the passage of time. But I am worried when I receive letters from young people who express themselves in the language of yesterday.

We must be watchful and recognize that to sharpen the consciousness of mankind requires a permanent effort. To do so it is helpful to revisit again and again the experiences that can be drawn from the course of history and one's own life. Weigh your words! Take on a limited function in life, but carry it out in a conscientious manner! These lessons seem crucial to me.

From time to time my past has caught up with me. One day I was informed that the various certificates accompanying my military decorations, some signed by Hitler himself, and other such memorabilia had been found. Obviously I was interested in these historical documents because they constituted a part of my life. Their story mirrors the confusion of those days.

My parents had deposited the documents with the city administration in Hanover. When the last Nazi district leader took off in a hurry to seek refuge in the Harz Mountains before the advancing Allied armies, he took the documents with him in a safe deposit box. Since then I had considered the items as gone forever. Not long afterwards the leader of a Hitler Youth detachment that had just been dissolved at the end of the war found an abandoned truck along a country road in the Lüneburg Heath south of Hamburg. It carried the marking, "District Hanover." Since the man himself had once worked for the city of Hanover, he examined the truck's trailer and saw a safe deposit box that had been partially broken into. One drawer, however, was jammed and he opened it by force. In it he discovered my certificates and my ceremonial dagger. The man decided to ask his sister to safeguard the items while he himself went to be processed in a demobilization camp.

To hide and protect the items was easier said than done. It was well known in the family's hometown that the son had been a Hitler Youth leader and that his sister had occupied a prominent position in the National Socialist youth organization for girls. Not surprisingly, the house was subject to frequent searches and the family was the victim of reprisals, especially after the gates of a nearby concentration camp had been opened. Even though carrying or concealing a weapon could be punished by death, the man's sister customarily carried the dagger hidden under her dress, just in case she needed to defend herself against bodily harm. The certificates rested in a closet underneath some children's toys.

Once, British authorities decided to search the house from the attic to the basement. In the process they also began to dismantle the closet in question until they found a number of tin soldiers. They started playing with them and became so engrossed that they never completed their search.

To make a long story short, despite a number of close calls the family managed to hang on to the documents and the dagger. When matters quieted down politically they resisted selling the items to Allied collectors who would have paid them good money at a time when their family suffered financial hardship. One day they invited me to their house behind the dike along the River Stör, which flows into the Elbe. Both brother and sister were there, along with lots of children, to extend a cordial welcome to me. The house resembled a museum. Painted ceilings, beautiful old doors, and rustic cabinets testified to the culture and taste of these people.

After a speech that was as kind as it was solemn, they handed me the documents and decorations while sharing with me the adventurous story of their odyssey. Suddenly everything came back to me: the sea, my men, the boat. I told them all about my life as a U-boat commander. Images I had already given up as lost forever now reappeared. But it was as if I was looking into a blind mirror, for the images were hazy and faint, without clarity or luster.

We parted company late that night. A short while later I sent the sister a golden ornamental clock from my mother's inheritance from the early nineteenth century. It meant much to me, but it was little compared to what I had received on that evening. I am not talking about the documents and decorations. I mean the satisfaction that even in the darkest of times there are people of character and courage, and also among those who are marked by our political past.

FREELANCE ARCHITECT

My association with Professor Graubner was a most rewarding one, especially after we entered into a partnership in January 1953. He was a gifted artist with an uncanny sensitivity for proportion and detail. He had first drawn attention to himself when he planned and designed the Horticultural Exhibition in Stuttgart. A disciple of Professors Bonatz and Schmitthenner, he stood in a tradition of architects who preferred naturally occurring building materials such as freestone and wood. As far as principles of construction are concerned, we thought in terms of the industrial age, used steel and concrete, and did not reject artificial building materials such as plastics. We did not close our minds to the Bauhaus school of architectural design, which had advocated the equal importance of technology, function, and form. Whenever we had to decide between the two latter criteria, we favored form over function.

In 1919 the architect Walter Gropius founded his Bauhaus to prevent the enslavement of mankind by the machine. Gropius wanted to guard against a kind of mechanical anarchy, especially with respect to interior design and the industrial mass production of household items. He desired to remove the drawbacks of the machine without sacrificing its advantages. The result was humanized housing and industrial design.

I examined an example of such a humanized housing project in Osnabrück from an economic point of view. We planned and built a settlement of townhouses, using locally produced concrete supports and wall segments side by side with machine-produced wooden elements imported from Sweden. The houses were set in a park environment. After they had been completed and the families moved in, we carefully evaluated their living qualities compared to other kinds of housing.

We collaborated with Professor Janssen in the area of industrial design to bring about an optimal union of function and form, for instance in the case of mass-produced articles of daily use like street lights, chairs, and parking meters. The Bauhaus taught the equality of all art forms with regard to architecture. The basic idea was that designing is neither an exclusively intellectual nor an entirely material activity, but simply an integral component of the essence of a civilized society. This view replaced the notion of art for art's sake of an earlier epoch. When designing a theater, for example, we cooperated closely with scientists and technicians who were experts in acoustics, statics, stage directing, air conditioning, and the like, while also consulting our fellow art forms of painting and sculpting.

Gropius and his collaborators such as Mies van der Rohe, Moholy-Nagy, Klee, Kandinsky, and others were not only the last major innovators in the field of architecture and design but they also have given us a lasting philosophy of construction. It was not the founders of the Bauhaus but their less distinguished descendants who concluded a pact with the economic establishment and have since covered and cluttered the earth with mindless boxes of glass and steel. This liaison required its sacrifices and compromises, as in all cases of illegitimate love affairs. But the big cities are not the only victims of this arrangement. Whole regions, including some of the most beautiful of all, have been ruined in the name of profit and so-called consumer friendliness.

Architecture has since fled into a fancy world of self-delusion. "Postmodernity" has become a catch-all word devoid of any substantive meaning. Everything architecture has to offer is being indiscriminately combined if it pleases the consumer: the glitter of the rich and mighty; the mysteries of religious buildings; the pastoral simplicity of the primitive; and even what may be picturesque about misery. There are architects who copy slums. In the end there can be no architecture worth its name without some tension between the creative power of the artist and reality, which in turn is dominated by individual human beings and their cosmos.

While still a scientific assistant at the School of Architecture at Hanover in 1952, I had participated in a design competition for two new schools in Celle. Late in the evening of the day when the commission in charge was supposed to announce the winning entries, someone knocked on our door. My wife opened the door and in came Professor Zinsser, under whom I had passed my final exams. He said: "I have come to tell you that you have won both competitions. I was so happy for you that I wanted to bring you the good news personally." I was so surprised that at first I did not know what to say, but I was almost ready to hug him in gratitude. After all, this was my first open success and perhaps the beginning of a career. Winning first prize in both competitions meant a reward of 1,000 deutschmarks for each, in those days a heavenly gift. As expected, the usual intrigues did not take long to surface. The local, older architects with their good connections to city hall succeeded in having the contest annulled and repeated. This time competition was by invitation only, and that meant the end of my chances.

One night at a party, a far from sober fellow architect raised his glass and directed the following toast at me: "Congratulations on winning that contest with the help of Graubner." Friends restrained me. I was enraged because I had entered the competition without Graubner's knowledge, fearing that he would not like it if I took on extra business outside my regular duties. I decided to write that other architect a letter quoting Iago from Act III of Shakespeare's *Othello:*

> Who steals my purse, steals trash, 'tis something, nothing,
> 'Twas mine, 'tis his, and has been slave to thousands:
> But he that filches from me my good name
> Robs me of that which not enriches him,
> And makes me poor indeed.

What did Graubner and I design and build after we became partners? I do not wish to go into the details of our struggle for contracts and the hard work involved in our daily routine, spending our mornings at the construction site, afternoons at the drafting board, evenings and nights at the contests. Nor do I want to dwell on arguments with presumptuous and insolent patrons. That is a part of any freelance business. In the end we were judged by our achievements.

In Bochum we built the theater and an administrative building for the Ruhrstickstoff Aktiengesellschaft (AG); in Hanover the headquarters of the Preussag and the Salzdetfurt AG, as well as an elementary school; in Herten the administrative building for a mining company; in Greven (Westphalia) a textile plant for Schründer and Cramer; in Hildesheim the suburb along the Michaelisstrasse, a bank building on the market square, and an annex to the city hall. In Aachen we redesigned the area between the cathedral and the city hall.

But our real love and specialty was the building of theaters. There are two considerations that govern the design of every modern theater: to be able to see and listen to the activities on the stage equally well from every seat in the audience. As far as acoustics is concerned, one must distinguish between spatial acoustics—the influence of the shape of the room on acoustic characteristics—and constructional acoustics—the impact of building materials used in the interior design of the theater. Most important is the shape of the auditorium. It must be right from the beginning, while there is always the possibility of making decorative modifications. Visual quality is dependent on seating arrangement as well as distance, angle, and general perspective of the viewer in relation to the stage. In addition, and especially since the days of Max Reinhardt, theaters must allow for the most intimate communication between actors and audience. This relationship is crucial for the success of theatrical productions. It also means that the play can be projected directly into the audience by designing the stage and ramp accordingly. As we saw it, the key problem of building theaters is to allow for a reasonable variability of the border region between stage and auditorium. The proper design of the proscenium absorbed our special attention, first in Bochum, later in Mülheim and Lünen, and finally in the case of the National Theater in Munich.

The National Theater became the ultimate challenge. The city authorities favored a design that incorporated as much as possible the neoclassical core of the building, a notion that to us looked dangerously close to a mere restoration. The traditional five tiers had to be retained at all cost; the outward appearance of the structure was not to be changed; and much emphasis was placed on regaining the former festive atmosphere that had graced the interior of the building.

The theater had been built based on a design by Carl von Fischer. After the fire of 1823 it had been rebuilt by the Hildesheim architect Leo von Klenze. Klenze had not slavishly followed Fischer's original plans but had incorporated additional ideas consistent with the artistic currents of the late neoclassical era. We argued that we, too, should be given such limited artistic license in order to leave our personal, unique handprint on our work. We solved the problem of retaining the five tiers while affording equal visibility from all seats by developing a balcony system that focused without compromise on the center of the stage.

After we had won the competition and the contract we had to face much criticism, not only from the state authorities but also from the influential Bavarian Castle Administration and the Munich Theater Circle. The latter, we had to admit, had made major financial contributions to the project. It was at that point that I retired from our architectural partnership. In the end Graubner compromised on virtually all of our design principles, with the result that the National Theater in Munich today is once again a tiered theater in the classical sense that no longer meets the demands of equality in visibility and audibility. Our once highly praised design became another neo-neoclassical building.

Klenze's classicism grew organically from the intellectual and artistic currents of his time. Graubner's neoclassical details are pure decoration, already a hint of post-modernity. The central box, for example, no longer accommodates a king and his entourage and with its flanking caryatids seems bombastic. The same holds true for the huge columns supporting the proscenium boxes. The tent-like ceiling and the chandelier have remained true to our design. After all, the colors gold, ivory, and red can never spoil a theater.

Those years as a freelance architect followed different coordinates than my years as a soldier. While my military career had been dominated by political ideals and submission to *raison d'état*, my years as a student and architect brought me intellectual diversity within the framework of political pluralism, limited at first, but steadily expanding. Architecture means a struggle for the optimal form, a struggle within oneself, with the members of one's team, and with the organizational, economic, and social factors that influence architects from without. Most problems are solved through compromises without giving up essential principles of design. The work of architects is characterized by teamwork and a readiness to compromise. A U-boat commander experiences what has been called loneliness of command. He is bound to a hierarchically organized command structure, but on the spot he makes all crucial decisions.

While I was engaged in freelance architectural work I became a member of the Association of German Architects after a board of experienced architects declared me qualified upon study of my designs and publications. I also joined the Association of Architects and Engineers. Otherwise, I became active in a group of people with intellectual and artistic leanings. We met in the restaurant "Wein-Wolf" in memory of the poet Gottfried Benn who had once been there thinking profoundly about art. Indeed, he wrote an essay about the subject entitled *"Weinhaus Wolf."* Here I became acquainted with Professors Wickop and Zinsser; the landscape designer Professor Hübotter; the pianist Dahlgrün; Ploog, the editor in chief of the *Hannoversche Zeitung;* Alfred Toepfer; and others. We talked about the latest currents in art, about justified and unjustified reviews, about modern music, about the death penalty—in short, about a vast variety of subjects that were of interest to us and the broader public. Here I left the ivory tower into which I had retreated for years.

The Navy, too, made contact with me. The Navy League asked me to investigate rumors that Prien, the famous U-boat commander, had been killed in a concentration camp instead of losing his life on the high seas. Reportedly the rumor was spread by a former Luftwaffe lieutenant. I arranged a meeting with the man and learned that he had indeed been in a concentration camp but had never met Prien there, nor had he ever said anything about him. I also asked how he had ended up in a concentration camp. He told me that one day he and fellow officers had been drinking in the officer casino. Next to its entrance were two busts, to the left one of Hermann Göring, the head of the Luftwaffe, and to the right one of Hitler. As the officer left the room he had jokingly placed his cap on Hitler's likeness and said in a loud voice, "It certainly does not look too bad on a corporal." This remark was overheard and reported, and the officer was sent to the concentration camp on a charge of *lèse-majesté*.

Knowing of my career as an architect, the Navy League also requested my participation in the interior design of the Naval Memorial at Laboe. It had been built based on plans submitted by Professor Munzer after World War I. Since members of the Navy League had arranged for the financing of the project, the organization was in charge of its upkeep. After World War II the building had been looted by Allied soldiers and partially damaged. The plans for the renovation included the desire that the fallen of World War II be likewise honored. This called for new ideas, new designs. The Navy League asked Professor Munzer to take charge of the project, while I was to be his assistant. As it turned out, Munzer and I got along splendidly; we agreed on all crucial issues at our first meeting and without the slightest sign of differences spoke with one voice. The trouble was that the leadership of the Navy League, its majority comprised of men without artistic background or interests, failed to understand our suggestions. I succeeded in redesigning the exhibition hall and won the Navy League over to the idea of having the painter Richard Schreiber contribute two sgraffito works for the occasion. Then I went to Washington and left Professor Munzer to wrangle with the Navy League. The following letter shows what the controversy was about:

Dear Professor Munzer:
   Your recent letter recalled for me the brief time of our collaboration in redesigning the Naval Memorial. Our common work proves that in questions of design there are no fundamental differences of opinion among men who, based on their creative disposition and professional background, are alone entitled to address and decide questions of art. I gather from your letter that you continue to struggle to keep the structure free from all unqualified additions and kitsch. Sadly, I can offer only words of encouragement to back you up in this matter.
   It is true that the memorial was financed by the Navy League, but it belongs to the entire German nation. There are only few structures that can

make such a claim. And from this claim grows the obligation to redesign this memorial based on the finest artistic quality so that it can express to the entire people the honor that is being bestowed on its fallen soldiers. The rival designs that you sent along neither meet this obligation nor do they come close to fulfilling the self-evident demand to balance the external size of the structure with a corresponding interior design. The quality of your work and your personal reputation demand that you withstand efforts to alter your designs under all circumstances and with all possible consequences.

I would be grateful to you if you could keep me informed as to the outcome of your intervention, and I wish you energy and steadfastness so that this matter may be resolved to your satisfaction.

Cordially yours,
Erich Topp

Here are some specific objections of mine to the two designs favored by the Navy League:

Both designs emphasize mass and material. The possible rejoinder that this material served as a cover for the men is only partially valid. For example, among the mentioned vessels some lost not a single member of their crews, in other cases parts of the crew were saved, others became total losses. On this panel they are grouped together indiscriminately. Our modern fascination with statistics should not be extended to graves. Only military historians must know that we lost 199 U-boats in World War I and 752 in World War II. The boundary of eternity is not indicated by the placement of grave markers. It is rather a metaphysical, irrational borderline that is located in the realm of the spiritual and should only be symbolized by artists of genius.

Already in the entrance hall it should become clear that the men sacrificed themselves for an idea and that they were sacrificed on the altar of political power. The materials used in that room should touch the subconsciousness of the visitors in such a way as to make them sense the loyalty, suffering, and horror of the fallen. As far as the inscription is concerned: The oath was sworn to the Kaiser in World War I and to Hitler in World War II. It is simply wrong to say: "True to their oath, they gave their lives for our people." Considering the misuse of the oath in the Third Reich and its devaluation in the consciousness of our population, one is well advised to find simpler formulas. By all means we should avoid pathetic phrases. That also holds true for the expression, "As the law demanded." This sentence takes us back to classical Sparta where the law had a moral foundation and was not abused by heartless cynics to carry out their own criminal designs, as happened in the Third Reich.

Years later I was reminded of this earlier controversy when there was a deep debate over the design of the Vietnam War Memorial in Washington. The American nation wavered between two conflicting views, namely, between the patriotic certainty of having done the right thing, and the traumatic experience of having become entangled in something that was wrong. I was reminded of my contributions to the interior design of the Naval Memorial in Laboe and the struggle that I lost to the traditionalists. I did not succeed in engaging an artist who would create inside the memorial's tower a visual requiem for the dead. Instead of such an artistic expression it was decided to build a mock-up of the Battle of Jutland. In this way the memory of the dead was overshadowed by the representation of a clash of battleships.

In Washington, too, the fight was not only about taste and style but also about sensitive artistic expression that would present through metaphors and symbolism the inevitability of human suffering. A female student at Yale University, her family of Chinese background, won the design competition. Her project is of simple dignity and devoid of empty rhetoric. It consists of two walls of black granite, one 248 feet and the other 33 feet long, that meet like two wings in an acute angle. Together they seem to embrace a soft hill before their ends taper off into the distance. The granite walls contain no words of dedication, only the names of the more than 57,000 men who died or remain missing in Vietnam. This monument is no political confession. It does not take sides and justifies nothing. It is a requiem for the fallen, a quiet and simple list of the dead for the living to contemplate.

Traditionalists took issue with the design because it lacked the sense of heroism and patriotism that every war memorial was supposed to convey. How similar the arguments! They had in mind a monument like the one near the bridge over the Potomac commemorating the fallen of World War II. It shows how a group of infantry soldiers raise the American flag over Iwo Jima—incidentally, a scene posed for a photographer.

In the end a Solomonic decision was reached. The design of the Chinese student was carried out. Not far from it, but causing no visual interference with the wall of the dead, a sculpture showing three watchful infantry soldiers was erected—one white, one black, the third an American Indian. Next to it stands a tall flagpole.

On October 1, 1956, having served the ten-year sentence imposed on him at the Nuremberg Tribunal for the "chief war criminals," Grand Admiral Dönitz was released from his prison in Spandau. One of his first visits as a free man was to our house in Hanover. He stayed overnight. We had long conversations. He was eager for information and orientation after those long years of isolation in Spandau. We decided to have lunch in a restaurant. Dönitz enjoyed being among the public. With a loud voice he invited his wife to join in our conversation. Soon the diners at the other tables and the waiters knew who our guest was. When we left they lined up at the exit, for everyone wanted to see Dönitz. He proudly walked through the crowd. Briefly he hesitated and took a long glance at a pretty young woman. When his wife urged him to keep going, he said: "Don't be so pushy. I have not seen anything like this in eleven years." The pain of his incarceration broke through one more time.

He asked me how he should act now that he was a free man again. It was a reasonable question after his long isolation from social and political developments. I gave him this advice: "Take a long time to assess the situation in which you find yourself. You will be swarmed by journalists who are out to get a sensational story. Make as few public statements as possible. Such an attitude will earn you respect from those who are critical of you." A half year later he had been persuaded by a publisher to write his memoirs, which came out under the title, *10 Jahre und 20 Tage.* They were later complemented by two more books, *Mein wechselvolles Leben,* and *Antworten auf 40 Fragen.* All three are attempts to justify his actions. The meetings in my house and later at his retirement seat of Aumühle showed that Dönitz, too, had returned home.

But while for us coming home brought with it a time of soul-searching, of self-assessment, and a return to peace and truth, Dönitz would continue to give the impression of a desperately stiff and inflexible mindset. He had returned, but he still lived in the world he had left ten years before. I had to think of Lot's wife looking back and turning into a pillar of salt.

You cannot fathom a human soul. Undoubtedly the idea of National Socialism captured Dönitz. He was intoxicated by the military successes to whose glamor he contributed himself and that blurred his vision. All that is human. Then the shadows lengthened with the declining military successes, the defeats, and finally the catastrophe. He saw these shadows as if they were ghosts that could be exorcised. His personal life was ascetic and full of suffering. There can be no doubt his U-boat men's drama of life and death affected him deeply, as did the loss of his two sons. In our many meetings and conversations I have never succeeded in finding out from his casually expressed sentiments what really went on underneath the surface of his mind and in his soul.

Grand Admiral Dönitz's apologists hold that he was an unpolitical officer, but I am not convinced and here my criticism sets in. His unconditional commitment to Hitler, his decrees and speeches that reflect National Socialist ideology and utterances of its chief spokesmen—all this induces me to reject this assessment. As Commander-in-Chief of the Navy he enjoyed, as do most flag officers, access to a high level of information. So much we know today from the talks he gave; so much we can deduce from his presence at meetings where, for example, SS Leader Himmler openly described his strategy of liquidation against Poles, Russians, and Jews. From my own experience as a flag officer, albeit under a

different regime with freedom of opinion, I learned that official information was but a small part of all the information I ultimately had access to
from other sources as well. I conclude from this experience that Dönitz
knew more than he ever admitted.

Quite independent of the preceding considerations one must demand
from men in the highest positions of leadership political responsibility
for what they did and failed to do. In vain the world waited for a "final
word" from Dönitz that could have been seen as a kind of confession of
his entanglements with a criminally tainted political regime. Many expected that he, as we, would feel the need to admit to a moral defeat.
However, I do not think it wise to speculate which kind of belief, thinking, or conviction enabled Dönitz to span the abyss of infamy of which
he must have been aware. Not unlike Hamlet, he seemed to say that no
one could penetrate the heart of his secret. He knew of the mass executions behind the front lines, that expression of a monstrous contempt for
the value of human life. His reaction: "It is not my business to get involved in matters that lie in the realm of the political leadership." This
comes very close to a passive toleration of the insane crimes and stands
in sharp contrast to the traditions and basic principles that for generations had formed and informed a soldier's world.

One day, I believe it was in late 1956, I received a telephone call from
Heinrich Schwich. As a war correspondent he had accompanied us on a
war patrol. During a surface attack against a convoy he spoke his dramatic account directly into a tape recorder. He remained calm and collected when a tanker filled with gasoline blew up spectacularly some 800
yards away. The heat was murderous and I sent all nonessential personnel to take cover below. Schwich simply kept on reporting, even when
our boat became an obvious target before the burning horizon and destroyers began firing at us.

By the end of the war Schwich had become the chief commentator for
Radio Berlin. When the Russians approached he defended the station
with a handful of soldiers. He was captured and spent six years in East
German prisons. Bodily a wreck but unbroken in spirit, he was finally
released and made it to the West. Schwich drew my attention to the
book, *Haie und kleine Fische* (Sharks and Little Fish) by Wolfgang Ott,
who had been a naval officer. The plot dealt with two of man's basic
themes and experiences since creation, love and death, set against the
backdrop of the war. Whether all the details of life on the minesweeper,
in occupied France, or on the U-boat matched wartime reality, only those
who were actually there may be able to judge. How genuinely Ott caught
our sense of shock and upheaval, and what made the book truly a work
of confession for our generation, only those whose life has been changed
by the war can sense.

The book annoyed and scandalized many of its readers. But any provocation of this kind also illuminates a complex situation. People who do not know that pornography can be stimulating for some and despicable for others will feel scandalized. As will those who fail to realize that obscenity is a stylistic means of expression to portray the shocking as truly appalling—and not only since the days of James Joyce, Norman Mailer, and Henry Miller. People will likewise feel provoked by the jargon of a French prostitute, or express outrage when some officers are depicted as naked, with their deficiencies exposed. Readers who judge in this fashion will miss the true meaning of the book, will fail to discover the courage to act independently or the readiness to suspect basic human traits behind every mask. Such readers will never understand the grim irony vis-à-vis those for whom obedience is a higher virtue than freedom of thought.

I endorsed the book, wrote a review of it, and later worked as a technical consultant when it was made into a movie. The studios were in Bendesdorf near Hamburg. The director was Frank Wisbar. During the war he had been a German officer. Later he emigrated to the United States and directed a number of well-known films, among them *Nasser Asphalt*. He had a wonderful personality and was fascinated by this project. The film architect, likewise a genius in his field, recreated in full detail the central control room as well as the decks and bunks of a Type VIIc boat. While the film was being shot, the central control room was flooded with a huge amount of water. A bearded actor played the role of the chief engineer. When he emerged completely drenched after one of the scenes, he said to my wife: "No ten horses could have dragged me onto a real U-boat." We all stayed in a farmhouse. The film crew and the actors were an open-minded, funny group. We enjoyed many interesting talks, about ordinary subjects and some not so ordinary, depending on the situation, but always invigorating.

To take up the cause of Buchheim's book, *Das Boot* (The Boat), was of special concern to me. He masterfully captured in a literary sense the reality of U-boat warfare as I myself had experienced it. His subsequent books, *U-Bootkrieg, Die U-Bootfahrer,* and *Zu Tode gesiegt,* also helped make Germans comprehend at last the deadly struggle and defeat of the U-boats and their crews. It was a perhaps unintended but nevertheless positive by-product that both the book and the movie version of *Das Boot* corrected many stereotypes about German soldiers. I wrote to Buchheim:

> It is remarkable to me what your book depicts as the "reality" of the U-boat war after 30 years. I mean by this a higher reality that derives from the ambiguity of our existence and from the unfathomable depth of our individual experiences. This reality speaks to us in images that have undergone

changes over the years so that our eyes can no longer see the original impressions. It is this that has fascinated me about the book. Many must have had experiences like those described by you. But it requires a special *clef* to give them a form that captures all nuances and currents, all inner and outer upheavals.

Buchheim is one of the few who never stray from their path. He hates compromises. He will not deviate one inch from what he has experienced as the truth. He carries the world he described so well inside himself. It was predictable that those who do not carry a world inside themselves and who only drift along on pieces of wreckage furnished by their memory, compensated for such a deficit by reacting with furious aggression. Since I took Buchheim's side from my dual experience as a U-boat commander and as an artistically creative individual, I became the target of a portion of these attacks in all their narrow-mindedness and pitifulness. Well, all of that is now past me, but Buchheim's work has stood the test of time. It has been translated into all major languages and reached several million readers.

A member of the German Embassy in Washington has told me that the movie version of *Das Boot*, even more so than the book itself, has done much to undo traditional stereotypes held about Germans in the United States. Indeed, it was awarded an "Oscar." My engagement for Ott and Buchheim in letters, talks, and publications brought a flood of reactions. They covered the entire spectrum from outrage ("No, it did not happen this way!") to lack of understanding ("How could you as an old U-boat man help those creatures foul your own nest?!"). I witnessed public protest actions against the books ranging from a collective boycott of bookstores to demonstrations against the publishing house. All this encouraged me even more to make my position unambiguously clear. As a creatively active individual I reject categorically any collective judgment with respect to artistic matters. Collective judgments are manipulated judgments. They shake the very foundations of our civilization, our right to form our own opinion. Our recent past is full of examples of such manipulated judgments. It forced a number of our greatest artists, painters, and thinkers to leave their country either by force or voluntarily because their life was threatened or they could no longer make a living under the prevailing circumstances. Every creatively active person is most sensitive when this subtle atmosphere of freedom and tolerance from which all real art and culture sprouts is endangered.

In the participants of the last war, the books rekindle the memory of all the infernal situations and horror that war visits upon man. They also bring back the images of men who kept on fighting amidst the collapse and the insanity of further bloodshed because such were their orders. As a member of the West German Navy I learn from these books that a sol-

dier is neither a caricature nor a potential murderer, but that he represents the whole scale of human and manly life with all its strengths,
weaknesses, and mistakes. These books could only have been written
and can only be understood before the backdrop of one of the mightiest
intellectual metamorphoses western civilization has ever gone through.
In our century something has been set in motion that in an incredibly
short time has transformed the traditional foundations and notions
about man's very existence and his environment. The work of Einstein,
Heisenberg, and Freud, to name only a few, contributed in the field of
science to revolutions whose intellectual impact has been and remains
explosive. A few creatively gifted minds are trying to map out paths
through this incredibly broadened field of manifold experiences with respect to nature and the human existence. I find it self-evident that the
means of expression and presentation must be broadened accordingly.

WEST GERMAN NAVY

Many friends and acquaintances found it difficult to understand why I
gave up my successful career as an architect to rejoin the Navy. It was no
easy step for me, and I took it only after careful calculation of advantages
and disadvantages.

When we built the Mercatorhalle in Duisburg I came into close contact
with the city administration. At the time they were looking for a new director of public construction for the city. My name came up. I was interested in the position for two reasons. My partnership with Graubner
had begun to run into problems, and we agreed that we would end it as
soon as conditions allowed. Another reason was that by taking this influential post in the middle of the Ruhr District we were likely to get to
build more projects in a region that was rapidly expanding economically.

And then there were my contacts with the new West German Navy.
Several officers working in the personnel section had let me know that
the Navy desired my return to active duty. My starting position would
likely be a military-political assignment with NATO in Washington. It
was no easy decision for me. My friend Klahn, the painter, told me, "Let
your heart decide for you." I replied: "My heart is where I can feel the
breath of the world." He looked at me as if he was about to declare that
this must be another of my illusions. But then he said: "Well, I see you
have made up your mind." I went to Washington, and from the moment
I arrived there I knew that I would not regret my decision. But the six
months before I could take up my assignment in the United States were a
testing time of doubts and challenges for me.

What was the West German Navy like in 1958; how did I experience it?

Diary:

January 15, 1958

Arrival at the "Red Castle by the Sea," the naval academy, or Marineschule, in Flensburg-Mürwik. How my perspective has changed over the years! After working as an independent architect I sense the atmosphere of a monastery, little light and air. Artistically insignificant decorations from the fin de siècle era, narrative wall paintings, pithy sayings. We are shown to our rooms. The bedroom has six bunks; we share bathroom and shower.

Official welcome. Nothing of importance. In the evening: "Gentlemen, the Admiral!" *Flottillenadmiral* Hubert von Wangenheim—narrow lips, protruding chin, a big, bent nose, had been a farmer after the war. Each of us gives a brief summary of his life. An incredible mosaic. Every profession is represented, from a top industrial manager to a former member of the Foreign Legion: grocers, millers, gardeners, sales representatives of all kinds, a deputy mayor.

Topics of conversation: Modern artists are only interested in making money, mainly charlatans. It is useless for me to join the discussion. Other subjects: via South Africa to the question of racism. Strong words about the white man's claim to supremacy. The danger of mixing the races is being emotionally demonstrated: "Would you allow your daughter to marry a Negro?" That is the end of the argument; everything stays on the surface; nothing profound.

At midnight we bring out three cheers to honor someone's birthday. The cheers sound shallow, hang stale in the room. How full and genuine they sounded fifteen years ago. Of course we have to empty our glasses in one gulp; that's the tradition. We sit by the fireplace until 1:30 A.M. Would anyone care for another glass of beer? Well, that means one more for everyone. There is no direct pressure to conform, but if you exclude yourself you become an outsider in no time.

We get up at 7 A.M. We have to shine our shoes ourselves and also make the bed. Breakfast at 7:30 A.M. At 8 A.M. our work routine begins. A petty officer of the administrative branch tells us about the new regulations, about compensation for being separated from our families, about reclaiming travel costs, and so forth. Such things should be handled quietly and quickly, not last four hours. One in our group mentions he has seen officers with the rank of major behind typewriters. The motto of West Germany's armed forces seems to be: Everyone must lend a hand. The style of subalterns has triumphed everywhere.

At 12:30 P.M. we receive our new uniforms. Poor fabrics, small selection. One cannot do anything about it. I feel as if I was in a panopticon, looking in from the outside through dirty little windows. The millers, gardeners, and sales people are being put in uniform. But no uniform can disguise what differences lie beneath the identical caps. This is no elite that is being fitted out here.

In the evening a meeting with my Crew classmate Heinz Kühnle. We talk about the new type of naval officer without the division of the corps according to specialization. Each officer should be exposed to as many different fields as possible. That will bring out his talents. Midshipmen will have to learn how to be a welder, an electronic technician, how to do things at a work bench. I think it is a good idea.

Admiral von Wangenheim makes a clear statement about the abortive plot to kill Hitler on July 20, 1944:

Those who demand from me that I respect the decision of the men of the 20th of July must be prepared that I respect the decision of the others who fought on to the end. The question of superior insight is necessarily linked to one's information level which would open up the possibility of criticism and acts of resistance. The problem of resistance remains an acute one for us Germans as long as Germans live unfree on the other side of the border. I respect the dead of the 20th of July; I reserve judgment about the men who now claim to be members of that resistance.

March 8, 1958

Took a walk along Flensburg Bay. Pleasant and quiet. Looking out over the sea helps, too. My wife called that Duisburg has raised additional questions. I must add that by that time I had not yet decided for good whether to return to active duty. While I did participate in this orientation course, I kept the option open of remaining a civilian. Hamlet: "Thus conscience does make cowards of us all, and thus the native hue of resolution is sicklied o'er with the pale cast of thought."

March 13, 1958

My first day at sea aboard a French-built submarine chaser. We provide cover and escort for the U-boat *Hecht*. It would be no exaggeration to state that nothing works on this ship except for the sonar and radar equipment. A rubber dinghy transfers me to the U-boat. The boat and its commanding officer trained under me in the last phase of the war. It's the old odors, the old atmosphere, but everything even more cramped than I recalled it from the war. The officers are rather resigned and reserved; nobody quite knows what lies ahead, what all this will lead to. But the enlisted men are first-rate.

March 17, 1958

We tour Cuxhaven Naval Base. Paperpushers and bureaucrats have a field day here, very little efficiency. The signal station is badly improvised, the quarters no different from the old barracks. The arsenal reveals a hodge-podge of obsolete weaponry from formerly American, Turkish, French, and Italian stocks.

Where there is nothing to do people create assignments and projects artificially. Every officer seeks to justify his area of responsibility to manifest himself by appearing to work extra hard. Only a third of the old pier for ocean liners is usable, the rest in need of repair. The oil pier can only service minesweepers with their relatively shallow draft. No possibility for larger vessels to moor. The contract with British Petroleum was concluded by superior authorities in Koblenz without knowledge of the local situation. Tank trucks must make twelve round trips from their depot at Grooden to ensure adequate reserves. The base is supposed to function as a supply point for all kinds of naval units. It is a small beginning. Every morning the only available bus takes the security guards to the base. All this reveals not only a deliberately slow start but also mutual mistrust between the various naval commands, bureaucratic gridlock, and tolerance of mediocre human performance.

Exercise *"Lion Bleu."* We get a briefing about the strategic situation. Lots of abbreviations that make little sense to me. Once again everyone is eager to justify his own existence here. These are adults at play, and they take themselves very seriously as they let their units of minesweepers, corvettes, and supply ships of 600 tons steam along at 6.3 knots while a nuclear exchange is under way. Gannet and Seahawk aircraft fly eye-level reconnaissance at an altitude of 300 feet, then come back to rearm as fighters and bombers. The supervisor of the exercise, *Flottillenadmiral* Karl-Adolf Zenker, sums up the purpose of all this: to defend the "Wet Triangle" of the German Bight once the new destroyers and PT boats are operational. I was struck by the notion how completely the lessons of the last war appeared to have been forgotten and how quickly innovations in weaponry will eradicate even these remaining ideas of traditional naval warfare.

March 24, 1958
Training Depot Glückstadt. The installations look comparatively modern. Introductory presentation by Commander Herbert Schultze. As volunteers the basic attitude of the soldiers is positive. But there is also disappointment over broken promises. They do not get shipboard commands; they sit around in shore-based units instead. People talk openly about these matters and the economic reasons for signing up. Some of the lieutenants and lieutenant commanders have little prospect of being promoted. Therefore they act like typical bureaucrats, never doing more than is minimally necessary. They know all about soldiers' rights but look away when it comes to their obligations.

March 25, 1958
We tour the entire compound—swimming pool, exercise rooms, the gymnasium, dining hall, the kitchen. Everything appears quite generous. From the first floor windows you can see the Elbe River. On the other side the parade ground. Formal exercises, saluting, handling rifles—just as in the old days. Nobody is being pushed to the limit.

While listening in on a presentation about nuclear, biological and chemical weapons, which is being taught here no differently than a rifle drill, one of the men asks me about my collaboration in making the movie *Sharks and Little Fish*. The questions make clear that the men are quite critical of the old-school training methods. I feel it will require much intuition to find the right way to treat these men.

In the afternoon we are off to Neustadt Naval Base. It is exciting to revisit the old U-Boat Training Command with its beautiful grounds right on the water's edge, the familiar officer casino where we had celebrated many a merry party with Endrass and other Crew comrades.

March 28, 1958
We are guests of the Technical Naval School. Its commanding officer, Captain Hans Looschen, has organized the place analogous to the staff of the former U-Boat High Command. Every day there is a comprehensive briefing involving all departments so they know what is going on elsewhere. But here, too, the same complaints. No clear concepts; nobody is prepared to assume ultimate responsibility for the construction schedule. For example, the PT boat program undergoes changes all the time. All weaponry and instruments such as sonar are

among the items still to be decided upon. It is a tedious, hesitant process to get clearance through the central procurement office. Those who want to push ahead wear themselves out. Verbatim: "And that in our command where we do not even have to deal with ordinary pencil-pushers."

March 29, 1958

Baltic Training Squadron, consisting of *Eider, Trave,* two refurbished Canadian corvettes, and six formerly British coastal minesweepers. Young, fresh commanding officers who enjoy their privilege of holding a shipboard command, albeit on ancient vessels. Here you do not sense problems caused by the slow procurement system. Delays in promotion are compensated by other factors such as visits abroad and the enthusiasm of the youthful crews. The vessels themselves are on the verge of falling apart, held together only by their coats of paint. You can penetrate the wooden hulls easily with the tip of a knife; the diesels have about had it because of a lack of spare parts and are being kept alive by mechanics who must possess a touch of genius. Yet everywhere you feel eagerness and commitment on part of the men.

March 31, 1958

We are guests of the Personnel Training Command. Captain Heiko Fenn, a fine, sober-minded officer, briefs us about the training levels of enlisted personnel. He believes development up to the rank of chief petty officer functions well and organically, but there is little prospect of further advancement beyond that point. There is the possibility that the best and brightest will be taken over into the regular officer corps.

April 1, 1958

We are at the Naval Arsenal in Kiel. Its director, Herr Ludwig, went to Pakistan after the war to organize a shipyard in Karachi. He is a friend of Karl Fischer at the Defense Ministry in Bonn. This assures close cooperation between him and the procurement office. Here the bureaucratic juggernaut is being circumvented because Fischer has direct access to the defense minister. Dr. Fischer thinks the United States considers us primarily as a scientific reservoir. For this and other reasons the focus of our efforts should be on research and development. The arsenal is generously designed with an eye toward future expansion and possible use for civilian purposes.

Summary of the Orientation Course:

In all the commands we visited we met three distinct types of officers: (1) older officers, mostly junior captains and full captains, who regard their return to active duty as a mere transition period before retirement; (2) officers of the middle ranks, lieutenant commanders and commanders, men with wartime experience, well-rounded and self-made men in the interim, men who now desire a predictable career and sometimes are genuinely eager to make lasting contributions to the service; and (3) younger officers, mainly lieutenants, who have great expectations for the future.

We also had a talk with the Fleet Commander, Admiral Rolf Johannesson. I asked him whether the Navy was likely to regain its former position. His reply:

1. Parliament, the Chancellor, and the President consider the Bundeswehr a necessary evil, and do not mind saying so. The state does not protect its own child. A child that is only tolerated but not loved will develop differently than a child that is blessed with parental love. The present situation is likely to produce complexes that will retard a healthy development of the armed forces.

2. Widespread conformism undermines creative and constructive thinking. For most there exists only one strategic situation. Alternative views are not being considered. This system can become dangerous considering the far from brilliant qualities of most men in leadership positions. Valuable ideas are being swept under the carpet. As a result mediocrity reigns supreme.

3. The top brass of the Navy has no frontline experience. That has negative consequences in the areas of strategy, tactics, and training.

Throughout the orientation course I had many depressing experiences, but here and there I also saw promising beginnings. I met several officers who towered above the rest, men with whom it would be possible to build up the Navy properly. I learned to appreciate the importance of NATO, and after a long inner struggle I decided in favor of reactivation despite all the difficulties and mediocrity I had witnessed. I knew I would exchange the generosity and freedom of my life as a freelancer for something I had little control over, for instance petty administrative details. I became part of a bureaucratic ladder whose rungs were occupied by men less qualified by performance than by seniority. The nonconformist outlook I had won through my artistic work was likely to earn me criticism and hostility, but also friendship with like-minded officers. All this was clear to me from the beginning. I decided in favor of the Navy and thus in favor of Washington as my first assignment.

Early in 1959, after our move to Washington, I received a letter from Dr. Wulf Müller in Celle, an old acquaintance of mine. His views not only showed me that my decision to go to Washington had been the right one but also demonstrated how many of my opinions he shared, even if he arrived at them from a different perspective:

We understand, of course, that the turmoil of changing careers and residences did not allow for long farewell ceremonies. All the more we appreciate that even while enjoying the beaches of the Gulf of Mexico you managed to drop a few lines to an old friend back home.

Naturally we envy you for the change of scenery and the move that now, thank God, is finally completed. Despite the many novel impressions, you are likely to remain in touch with our concerns over here. The great controversy over Berlin makes clear that the division of that city and of Germany has brought about something that Mr. Weinstein in today's *Frankfurter Zeitung* calls a split consciousness affecting all Germans no matter where they may live. You will probably agree with me that the timing of bringing up this question now is not particularly advantageous for us.

No one sees a satisfying solution anywhere, and many fear that the American public will lose interest in the problem one of these days. Then the temptation will increase to either sweep the German Question under the carpet or to solve it by force. Being a world power means carrying a heavy burden. The history of ancient Rome makes clear that the Roman citizens had no particular plans to dominate the world, in fact they did not understand at first the responsibilities that grew from their own successes. These responsibilities descended upon the shoulders of the ruling people gradually and were not fully appreciated for quite some time. Our German problem acts as a brake for those who exercise power today. If they get involved in it at all, they are unlikely to do so out of affection for us.

It is a bad feeling to be dependent on others. Perhaps a future generation will be kinder to those who started World War II in order to introduce to the world a third superpower in violation of so many human and divine laws. But even then we will be accused of having chosen mediocre leaders, men whose hubris grew in proportion to the dangers they found themselves in and who brought about deliberately what every reasonable human being would seek to avoid. Now we have to bear the consequences. We have had a lot of luck and are proud of our so-called economic miracle. The hectic preoccupation with economic reconstruction may in part have been an escape from the helplessness and insecurity that we all felt over the question whether it is still appropriate in our times to think in terms of fatherland and a common destiny for our people. Those who nevertheless ponder such problems end up torn and perplexed. If you are an optimist you may console yourself with the hope that in the course of human affairs divine punishments have often been challenges from which grew renewed strength and a new sense of responsibility.

Anyone who wants to do something for the future and freedom of our children must constantly adjust his thinking and learn to adapt. I congratulate you on having the courage to throw your bourgeois baggage behind you, not to return to old symbols and old comrades, but to be among those who reach out to new shores.

Diary:

On July 22, 1958, I landed at New York's Idlewild airport and set foot on American soil for the first time. New York—a city that has pushed individualism to its limits, ego magnification and utter helplessness. A city radiant with intellectual and artistic activity, but also weighed down by social tensions and terrible crimes. A city pulsing with life and creating loneliness on the edge of existence. A city that attracted me like a magnet and then repulsed me after a short time. Only much later would I get to know and love the place.

Two days later, arrival in Washington. Mighty thunderstorms. Captain Friedrich Kemnade, whom I am scheduled to replace, and his lively, charming wife Britta await me at the airport. A most cordial introduction into an alien environment.

The next day I report to my immediate superior, General Hans-Georg von Tempelhoff. A pleasant, open personality. My colleagues here are Army Lieutenant Colonel Wilhelm Thomas—bright, critical, aggressive—and Luftwaffe Lieutenant Colonel Adalbert Tägtmeyer. The latter appears very helpful. After the war he worked as a miner, which has left an imprint on him. I served on the staff that represented Germany in the Military Committee of NATO.

That night the Kemnades take us to a gigantic, open amphitheater, Cater Baron, in Rock Creek Park. Huge crowds; I guess about 20,000 people altogether. Unexpectedly good acoustics, but rather poor and formal from an architectural standpoint. The problem of parking is made easier by discipline and consideration for others. The musical program is an odd cross section of the American soul, a mixture of gospel music, musical comics, solo performances, both serious and humorous, prayers, and Christmas carols. The whole presentation moves somewhere between sentiment, kitsch, and irony, but somehow it is a celebration of life and joy. What a difference to Beethoven's "Ode to Joy." Here one senses next to the clever and psychologically experienced business manager the easily impressed naiveté of the masses. This crowd is like any other, amorphous but ready to be shaped. It is open to the joys of life and art.

The following encounters are spotlights, pieces of the mosaic of the Washington atmosphere that brought color into our life:

A conversation with Mr. Archibald of the Foreign Office. He thinks Washington's cultural scene is relatively insignificant when compared to Philadelphia or New York City. Its main attraction seems to be the cocktail parties. Constitution Hall is run by a reactionary board of directors; the black singer Anderson was not allowed to perform there. Instead, Mrs. Roosevelt arranged an outdoor concert for her. Even though racial discrimination has been outlawed, it remains an undisguised social phenomenon. A black Nobel Prize recipient was barred from joining a white tennis club in New York. India's ambassador in Washington and his family wanted to go swimming in Chesapeake Bay. They were not allowed to use the beach reserved for whites. A hotel in Atlanta refused to give a room to the economics minister of a black African country. [These observations were made in 1958.] The social integration of blacks is likely to cause a wave of unrest. Still, Mr. Archibald believes that American pragmatism will solve the problems in the long run.

A talk with Admiral Denny of the Royal Navy. He mentions how difficult it is to coordinate fourteen different opinions under the auspices of the Standing Group, NATO's military executive, without endangering military effectiveness.

My first meeting with the Chief of Staff, Colonel Gernot Nagel, whom I am slated to replace. Very conventional, little substance. He represents a group of officers preoccupied with external appearances like playing tennis and talking about vacations and parties. They bathe in the luster of their wartime experiences and stand shakily before the backdrop of another war. All they can do is to dissect as neatly as possible the military options.

We take a walk to the White House, to the Washington Memorial, and to the Capitol. It was quite an enterprise considering the distances involved, the traffic, and the complete lack of sidewalks. When we got home we were exhausted.

On February 19, 1959, the Member of the German Bundestag, Vice Admiral (ret.) Hellmuth Heye, wrote me as follows:

> You will receive a telephone call from the Member of the Bundestag Baron zu Guttenberg. His father was a naval officer belonging to Crew 1912. He is one of our younger representatives, but clearly destined to become a future political leader. His family has money and real estate in Franconia (Castles Guttenberg and Deidesheim). He is a bright intellectual with fine political instinct. Has a charming wife, liberal-Catholic, many children. It would be mutually beneficial if you could advise him during his stay, for instance suggest whom he should contact. He would like to meet Allan Dulles. Perhaps you or Hermsdorf could make the arrangements. Dulles should be interested in talking to him. Guttenberg has been invited to stay in the United States for six weeks. His English is excellent.

From this initial contact grew a friendship among two politically like-minded men. On several occasions the Guttenbergs were our guests in Washington. We exchanged experiences from our respective areas of responsibility. Thanks to my growing familiarity with the political situation in the Atlantic Alliance and in the United States, I was able to pass on to Guttenberg much information he was interested in. Our contacts, by correspondence and otherwise, remained frequent until Guttenberg became Parliamentary State Secretary under Chancellor Kiesinger and too busy politically to keep up the pace of our earlier exchanges. In July 1968 he let me know of the seriousness of his illness.

Guttenberg stood solidly in the tradition of Christianity and of the values of western civilization. Educated by Jesuits, he grew up in an environment that taught him to guard against intolerance and tyranny. When he was taken prisoner by the Allies in 1944 he worked dedicatedly against Hitler. This line of thinking would characterize him all the way to his last great speech before the German parliament in May 1970 when he was already marked by his fatal illness.

He admonished, he warned, he provoked. He was a fighter who was not afraid to confront his colleagues in parliament, the media, and the public. His adversaries treated his public speeches with spite and hatred. Being a baron whose family had lived in its home castle for 800 years and who had served in the "feudal" 17th Cavalry Regiment in

Bamberg, Guttenberg suffered much malice as a representative of the people. His noble family background brought out the cheapest prejudices against him. In 1965, during a debate at the Free University in West Berlin, he was openly ridiculed for demanding as the primary goal of German policy freedom for all Germans and an end to the totalitarian regime in East Germany. He was yelled at and noisily interrupted when he referred to the part of the world that did enjoy freedom and democracy and when he characterized the Federal Republic of Germany as a free and sovereign state.

Such disappointments accompanied his political life to the very end. Even during his last great speech before parliament, when he was visibly close to death, a fellow representative derided him by suggesting, "Let's give him the benefit of extenuating circumstances." Guttenberg replied that he had lost yet another illusion. He believed that politics must rest on a strong moral foundation. He stuck to his principles without regard for ideologies. He had suffered under the lawless tyranny of the National Socialist regime and knew what he was talking about when he would tolerate no compromises over the question of free self-determination.

He was not a nationalist; he was a patriot. He drew the inner strength for his independent stance from his faith in God, from his familiarity with the currents of freedom that have pulsed through our history, and from his personal experiences under a dictatorship. The principles he represented could not be measured with the yardstick of politics as usual; they had different dimensions. He had great hopes for democracy. He thought Herbert Wehner to be the strongest representative of the Social Democrats and developed friendly relations with him. It was Guttenberg whose long negotiations with Wehner paved the way for the Great Coalition between the Christian Democrats and the Social Democrats.

On December 18, 1962, he wrote me:

> Thank you so much for your letter indicating that the common initiative of Minister Lücke, Mr. Wehner, and myself has made headlines even in the United States. You probably have also learned what kind of consequences I had to face in my own party about this matter. At the moment I am quite busy defending myself against my own "colleagues."

Incidentally, the "consequences" Guttenberg refers to concern a reprimand he earned from his own party, the Bavarian Christian Socialist Union, for having followed Chancellor Adenauer's request to discuss the possibilities of a political coalition with the Social Democrats. His own party boss, Franz-Josef Strauss, had not been informed of the matter.

Guttenberg was not without illusions. The "representative of the nation," as he was sometimes called, nevertheless arranged the deal with the representative of International Socialism. With it he laid the basis for the subsequent treaties with the East, treaties whose substance he opposed because in his eyes they undermined West Germany's integration into the West. In Guttenberg's view, Soviet intentions always covered a broad spectrum. One of its principles, expressed in various disguises, was the desire to control all of Europe. Soviet political and military measures depended on strategic considerations, changing tactical conditions, and efforts to exploit real or suspected weaknesses of the West. Western politicians, according to Guttenberg, had to remain aware of these guidelines of Soviet policy. Crucial for him was the solidarity of all Germans, in the East and the West, as well as solidarity among the political parties. Without it there could be no future for the German people, neither as a nation nor as an integrated component of the European Community. He stood in the forefront of forging this solidarity, but he found only few followers in his own party and even fewer among the political opposition.

One evening Guttenberg, Captain Edward Wegener, the German naval attaché in Washington, and I had a long talk about morale and motivation among our soldiers and also about how to get the public to embrace the basic values of our constitution more enthusiastically. The immediate occasion for our conversation was a visit of three young officers of the German destroyer Z 5 whose ship was then in Norfolk and who had been guests in our house. During that meeting I had made several disturbing observations. The officers (1) displayed a lack of tolerance for the views of others, toward their host country, and for the American way of life; (2) expressed a yearning for great, over-arching ideals while seeing their own life and environment in nihilistic terms; and (3) displayed a lack of historical knowledge that led to an inability to see the great intellectual currents of the past and to place the events of recent history into that wider context.

I must admit that human greatness has become a somewhat relative term and is being measured today by different criteria than in the past, something that has done damage to the image of the great men of yesterday. Psychoanalysis enables us to examine aspects of individuals and situations that did remain obscure before. New findings are not being swept under the carpet but are openly debated. This is the situation in which young men must function today. Only those who have the proper mental and intellectual background and are open to the influences of the world around them will be able to experience the exciting diversity of life's phenomena.

I asked Guttenberg and Wegener what kind of mental and intellectual guidance our young officers receive. How far do we assist them in finding their own stand on major issues? Where are ideals still strong enough that they have an impact on the life and thinking of our young officers? Wegener, who had been in the United States for some time, noted that the intellectual insecurity of the officers had only partially to do with the lost war and the discontinuity of German history. All nations, even the American people, witnessed the phenomenon to some degree. He also thought we should engage the citizen in uniform more directly in the values he is supposed to defend. A soldier must be imbued with these values and committed to them emotionally before there can be a true willingness to stand up for them. This commitment is, after all, one of the three pillars on which the strategic concept of the West is based.

Wegener suggested we should model our officer schools on universities and stress academic subjects more prominently. At the very least there should be contacts between the various institutions, faculty exchanges, and the like. Officer candidates would be required to take survey courses as part of a *studium generale* but also be given the opportunity to do research in a specific field like history, technology, physics, or international law. For this reason more qualified faculty should be hired, libraries enlarged, and curricula expanded beyond the present narrow subjects. The officer should see his area of specialization whenever possible as part of the broader historical, cultural, economic, social, and political context. Wegener's ideas, by the way, were expressed long before the creation of Germany's universities for military personnel.

Guttenberg disagreed. He wished we were right and that indeed there was a chance to persuade individuals through rational means to stand up for a common cause. He feared, however, that such an attitude did not reflect man's true nature. Emotional forces, he argued, are always stronger than anything else, certainly stronger than the force of reason. He believed that one must also try to mobilize the people's emotional resources. That required the reawakening of prime symbols, of archetypes and ideals that the entire people could understand instinctively and follow in its quest for motivation.

Wegener got a little restless in his chair. As a rationalist he seemed uneasy about this appeal to archetypes. In his opinion the time had come to throw out emotions growing from the subconscious, such as love of country, and to replace them with knowledge about historical contexts and the analysis of political necessities. For him, instincts and irrational motivations should be controlled by rational insight based on careful studies. Our profession demanded a solid historical background as much as a watchful eye for the specific problems of our time. Our defense is not the mere defense of territory but makes sense only if we commit ourselves to our common values, for the future existence and welfare of our people.

I repeated my question: Will we have soldiers who are prepared to defend the freedom of their people with their lives? In short, is it possible to teach bravery?

I had followed with great interest the theoretical and philosophical propositions of my guests. In my experience proper motivation to fight is relatively easy to achieve and should not be a major problem in a war. Bravery, I am convinced, grows directly from the experience of solidarity, of comradeship. The fighting spirit of a U-boat or a company of soldiers stems from the knowledge of mutual dependence, of mutual loyalty, from one's responsibility for a comrade, and, not least, from the will to survive. It was the immediacy of these concerns that made the difference. Less crucial, but not unimportant, were such values as defending one's country, the fatherland, duty, and the service oath. We should not assume that things have changed dramatically in this respect. We still see people risking their own lives to save others. We recall images of miners underground rescuing their buddies without much concern for their own safety and survival. Only a few individuals ever manage to raise the values of our western civilization to the level of a personal experience that is both exciting and worth defending. As for the masses, we will have to rely on more elementary forces such as the experience of solidarity and comradeship.

A few extracts from my extensive correspondence with Baron von Guttenberg can show better than a retrospective summary what moved and concerned us in those days, often matters that are still or again in the news.

I had prepared an analysis for Guttenberg about changes in the application of military power and about the importance of naval power for NATO. He wrote back on August 31, 1963:

Dear Captain:
  Many thanks for your letter of August 8. The theses you presented could easily become the skeleton for an entire book. I only fear that you do not now have the time to write that book, however beneficial it would be.
  Since I do not have the time at the moment to discuss in detail every one of your important suggestions, allow me to agree with you that the problems of modern military power seem like a late justification for Karl Marx in the sense that apparently quantity has been transformed into quality and the very nature of military power has thus been changed as well. This calls for a revision of Clausewitz. Recently Pierre Gallois made the following interesting comment to me: "Clausewitz had written that the purpose of war is the destruction of the enemy's army to take over his territory and possessions. Today it seems the other way around. The purpose of nuclear war appears to be the destruction of the enemy's territory and possessions, which also means the defeat of the enemy's army."
  I, too, have the impression that the "conspiracy" I suggested to you in the past is becoming more and more desirable. The global political scene

seems almost more ominous than our domestic one. While the clear and always well-understood policies of Adenauer's government are now giving way to the unprincipled improvisations of Chancellor Erhard's coalition, the Americans and the English seem to come to an arrangement with the Soviets for which we have to pay. For this reason a hard core must be formed inside the Christian Democratic Party and in parliament. Would you be interested? I think we should get together and talk about this matter in more detail. Could you possibly meet me in Bonn in early October? Please let me know. The second week in October would be best for me.

We met in Bonn. He suggested I should become a member of the Christian Democratic Party and seek election to the West German Bundestag by way of one of the "state lists" without the need to fight local opposition. It was a tempting proposal, but given my experiences in the past as well as in the present, I felt I could do more for the Navy if I remained on active duty. This, as it turned out, was an illusion. The Navy let me go at the age of fifty-five. But more about that later.

On October 2, 1963, Guttenberg wrote:

Dear Captain:
The Soviet Union needs a "rest" but otherwise continues unchanged its revolutionary and expansionist intentions. Moscow's only reason for pursuing a policy of détente is that the Kremlin leaders face difficulties and see themselves forced to pull back their stakes temporarily. As Professor Löwenthal suggests, this Soviet dilemma is primarily a result of the West's successful resistance in the cases of Berlin and Cuba. The other interpretation, namely, that Khrushchev wants to avoid trouble with the West in order to deal with Mao, appears hardly convincing to me. The Chinese "comrades" do not yet marshal an arsenal impressive enough to put real pressure on the superpower Soviet Union. The true significance of the breach between Moscow and Peking lies rather in the long-range consequences of an unbridgeable schism. This schism challenges and partially ends the "legitimacy" that allowed the communist world to present itself as a kind of "union of those who have seen the light."
The key question the West must answer now is how to treat an adversary who obviously is in trouble and as a result offers us détente. While searching for an answer to this question I see the danger that the Soviets will achieve under the pretense of détente what threats could not bring about in the past: the legal consolidation of the division of Germany and the collapse of the Atlantic Alliance. This is not just a theoretical possibility. The danger is real and pressing because even today we can see that the Soviets know how to improve their situation when they are down, while the West seems incapable of capitalizing on the failures of the enemy.
If we assume for a moment that the military clauses of the Moscow Treaty restore the balance between East and West, the scales are clearly loaded in favor of the Eastern side if we analyze the treaty's political as-

pects. We should remember that Khrushchev had good reason to thank the American and English delegations publicly for having accepted the proposals presented by the Soviet government. Ulbricht's participation as a player in this deal means undoubtedly added recognition for the so-called Second German State and represents a significant Western concession to the Soviets with regard to Germany's future. The treaty's history and conclusion demonstrate the evident intention of the Anglo-Saxon negotiators not to sacrifice the desired reduction of tensions through a partial ban on nuclear testing by interfering with Moscow's ploy of bringing the "GDR" into the global political arena. For me this part of the treaty is a limited success for the Soviet policy of détente.

It seems paramount to me to warn against the continuation of a policy whose first step this Moscow Treaty represents. We failed to take our stand with regard to the most crucial point, namely, how to respond to an enemy that has fallen on hard times. Instead of asking the East to pay a price for the breathing space it needs, we actually reward them for their troubles. Instead of insisting on progress in the questions of Berlin and German reunification, we allow détente to become a concession to the East and weaken our traditional resolve not to elevate Ulbricht to a player on the international political scene. I am saddened by the fact that the joining of a Soviet policy of détente and Washington's "peace strategy" brings for Germany no more than the perpetuation of the status quo. We see here the possible beginning of a situation where we mistake the Soviet Union's "desire for détente" for a genuine change in its attitude when in reality there is no changed political will, only a temporary dilemma.

Even if the Moscow Treaty as a first concrete step toward détente does not result in any modifications in the military relations between East and West, the clauses dealing with military arrangements nevertheless deserve analysis from a political point of view. There can be no question that the treaty reinforces the common intention of the main nuclear powers to keep membership in that exclusive "atomic club" limited. Without getting into the self-evident argument that one should limit the unchecked proliferation of nuclear weapons to other countries, one can still raise the question whether there is no alternative between an exclusive group of nuclear powers and unlimited proliferation. For instance, arming European NATO partners in collaboration with the United States with nuclear weapons seems to me a greater contribution to the maintenance of world peace than, say, San Marino's declaration that it will refrain from testing atomic devices.

These considerations make clear what consequences the limitation of membership in the nuclear club to the *beati possidentes* of the present moment are likely and perhaps intended: The bipolar power situation in the world today will remain untouched as long as the United States and the Soviet Union maintain their nuclear hegemony within their respective military alliances. It goes without saying that the Soviets, given the nature of their regime, will not share their nuclear monopoly with their satellites. We cannot deny that the situation is different in the West. The petrification of the present arrangements with regard to nuclear power, implicitly agreed to in the treaty, should be measured with a different yardstick.

Furthermore, I think it worth considering that this first effort by the two superpowers to cement a bipolar world balance has in actuality already failed. Red China will not give up its nuclear arsenal, and France is determined to develop its *"force de frappe"* further, as the French Defense Minister Messmer indicated the other day. In this sense the Moscow Treaty does not bring us the end to the Cold War, but likely the end of the bipolar structure of the world under which we have lived so far.

We Germans must decide whether we want to support or retard the creation of an additional power center. In my opinion we should work decisively in the direction of an Atlantic partnership, which in turn presupposes a strong and united Europe as a true partner of the United States. A Europe that is militarily entirely dependent on the United States is likely to begin to question its own sense of security the more the two superpowers become mutually indestructible and begin to come to partial military arrangements among themselves with regard to nuclear weapons. If this development continues, a weak and detached Europe is destined to end up in the wake of the only atomic superpower on European soil, the Soviet Union.

For all these reasons I support de Gaulle's refusal to become a signatory to the Moscow Treaty. Apparently in efforts to create additional power centers a certain race has begun between Western Europe and China. Only a strong and united Europe at the side of the United States can induce the Soviets to end the Cold War in Europe in time and for good before a stronger China would force the United States to conclude a fake peace with the Russians so that the latter could deal with the Asiatic threat. Red China is determined to become such a power center, but it lacks for the time being the necessary industrial and technological resources. Europe has such a capacity but it lacks the necessary determination.

The proposed "Discussion about an all-German Peace Treaty" seems to be based on a point of view that does not regard Western Europe as united. For the concept of a West European power center would necessarily require two conditions: one, that conventional détente must lead to changes in the territorial claims of the Soviet Union in Eastern Europe; and two, that an all-German peace treaty is only feasible as a result of a fundamentally changed situation involving the entire European continent. Such a transformation appears only possible if the Soviet Union and the United States are prepared to accept Europe as a powerful negotiating partner.

One cannot apply history directly to present-day problems because history never repeats itself. But one can expand one's insights, which in turn allows us to comprehend what is needed to solve the problems of the day—for instance now, after 1989, as breathtaking developments are in the making. But especially in this situation one should recall Bismarck's basic principles of government, which included the idea that political strategy requires patience and restraint, and that it is crucial to act decisively when the time is right. "True wisdom comes from the realization that, while you can set your clocks ahead, time does not run faster as a result; moreover, a preparedness to stand by while a situation is developing is a precondition of successful policy."

On December 28, 1966, I wrote to Guttenberg, who, with the formation of the so-called Great Coalition between the Christian Democrats and the Social Democrats, had become State Secretary in the Chancellor's Office:

Dear Baron:
   Along with our best wishes for the New Year I would like to include the hope that with the adoption of a good part of your political views by the new cabinet you will be honored accordingly and be allowed to share more political responsibility.
   We view the political developments with considerable ambivalence. One could say that the West has won the Cold War to a certain extent. But now the West seems to feel so free from threats that it not only endangers its unity but also puts its very security at risk. The ministerial meeting in Paris brought us the spectacle of euphoria over détente at the same time that the Soviets announced a 7 percent increase in their defense budget. The West has not figured out what to do with its really quite limited victory, how to get from coexistence to peace and how to go from a divided to a united Europe. In the past it was easier to accept a divided Germany in a divided Europe than a divided Germany in a more or less unified Europe.
   One thing is certain: the Soviet Union has not capitulated and has not given up East Germany. There can be no German reunification without the consent of the Kremlin. But to bring that about we need to create a favorable constellation, which in turn depends on patience and long-range planning. Military concessions will bring no results, even though we may be forced to make them anyway, given our financial situation.
   In conclusion, one could say that the Warsaw Pact has strengthened its military potential and that we should pay more attention to military realities than to political intentions, which can always be changed or disguised. Even a certain political calm cannot hide these facts. To the contrary, I could imagine that the East tries to imbue the West with a false sense of security and to rob us of crucial insights into the true situation.
   Indeed, this lack of insight appears to have reached new heights. For years now the West has been lacking political guidelines behind our military and strategic considerations. As a result the military planners of the United States, France, Britain, and the Federal Republic are badly divided. The mistrust of the politicians in West Germany has made the Bundeswehr into an instrument that could potentially be much more effective. For years we have been arguing over the question how to maximize the Bundeswehr's potential. Our answer to that question has been ignored for years. Only the Luftwaffe has taken the opportunity to press its demands when Generals Trettner and Panitzki resigned. Basically, we want to trans-

fer the experiences of modern business management to the military sector. Our leadership arrangements are too divided and complex to deal effectively with the necessities that grow from the mission of the military, from the external threat, from long-term planning, and from technological innovation.

For instance, the Inspector of the Navy has only limited influence over recruitment, training, and treatment of the Navy's personnel. For his shipbuilding program he depends on technical advice from experts over whom he has no formal control. He has to tolerate technological design and development projects in which he is not interested. These flaws in the organization of the Defense Ministry cannot be overcome even if everyone collaborates loyally. The highest echelons in the leadership of the Bundeswehr should not be organized in such a way that each department is responsible in its particular area of specialization for the entire military and that all coordination is done at the highest level. I would prefer a system that retains an integrated top-level organization but gives greater independence to the various branches of the armed forces, that is, a stronger congruity of assignments and responsibility in all areas of specialization. That is how it is done in the Anglo-Saxon countries and also in France because it makes sense. We believe this is the only way to achieve efficiency and cooperation, credibility for our readiness to defend ourselves, and effective operations if war breaks out. The highest leadership must remain unburdened so that it can deal with the truly decisive questions and can rely on well-functioning branches of the armed forces that are marked by the freedom to lead, to decide, and to carry responsibility.

If we want to justify our enormous defense budget and if the military is to become an effective instrument in the hands of the government, it seems paramount to me that we address the question of a reorganization of the Defense Ministry.

These ideas, pushed for years by the Luftwaffe and the Navy, were finally adopted under Helmut Schmidt in 1970. The *Inspekteure,* or Inspectors, of the three branches of the military became true military superiors of the soldiers under their command and answered directly to the defense minister in matters of personnel, materiel, budget, and infrastructure. With the help of systems and project specialists they gained immediate influence inside the ministry, especially with regard to research, development, testing, and procurement.

Late in July 1968, Guttenberg sent me these grave lines:

Dear Admiral:

I enjoyed your kind letter. Many thanks for it. Sadly I have a piece of bad news for you. After lots of German doctors lied to me for years about my true state of health, American specialists have finally diagnosed the problem. They believe I am suffering from a serious and progressive nervous

disorder for which modern medicine has no cure. All in all, this is not nice
and rather depressing, but man has to digest what he is being fed.

Best regards, also to your wife.

Sincerely yours,
Karl Theodor Guttenberg

The news of his serious illness and of his death in October 1972 did not
surprise those who knew him, but it still touched many of his friends
profoundly. He conquered death by the conviction that he could not escape it. Upright, incorruptible in attitudes and character, again and again
he forced his tired body to return to the political arena to guard against
any lapses in the question of German unity and to defend the foundations of our common state in freedom and justice. Since he knew that he
had only a few more years to live, he grew stronger in his convictions.
He proved that actions speak louder than words, but also that a politi-
cian has to stand behind his words. He said what he thought, and he did
not give up even when he knew himself abandoned.

Marked by his serious illness, Baron von Guttenberg gave his last long
speech before the German parliament on May 27, 1970. It has moved me
much, and here are some excerpts:

> We Germans, all Germans, have the right to be free and to determine our
> own destiny. This has been, is today, and must remain the hard core and
> the inalienable goal of all concrete German policy where and as long as this
> policy is carried on by democrats.
>
> For my friends and for myself I want to emphasize strongly and in all
> seriousness, but sadly also out of concern, that we who carry responsibil-
> ity for our country are not prepared to respect or acknowledge so-called re-
> alities if they are based on injustice. And allow me to add this question: Is
> there one among us who would declare in all seriousness that a wrong be-
> comes acceptable simply because it has been around for years or even dec-
> ades? I ask everyone in this body to ask yourself this question, and
> especially the Social Democrats who as a party deserve the honor to have
> contributed thousands of martyrs under Hitler's regime: Would anyone to-
> day be ready to make his peace with Hitler after having held out for thirty-
> seven years? My answer is No. And for the same reason we cannot accept a
> new injustice on German soil. I take the courage and the liberty to appeal
> to our conscience and to remind us that even those who think with a good
> conscience that they act in the interest of peace can be subject to dangerous
> miscalculations. And such miscalculations become most serious if one as-
> sumes one can counter a militant, totalitarian ideology with that kind of
> value-free, plain pragmatism that is otherwise quite appropriate for deal-
> ings among democrats. . . .
>
> Democracy in Germany has gone under once before because the Ger-
> mans were caught in a spiritual and moral confusion, because the line that
> divides a democratic state based on liberty and justice from a totalitarian

regime of criminals was swept away. I have reason to warn that this line could once again be violated, and this time by democrats. I do not even need our constitution; I need only my conscience to tell me that I as a member of this body carry responsibility for my entire people, and in particular for those who are condemned to live in silence. Nobody can deliver us, the freely elected representatives of the German people, from the duty to care for the destiny of our entire people. And furthermore: Is there one among us who would take issue with my contention that the love of freedom of the people in East Germany is in any sense less than that of the Czechs and Slovaks who in the spring of 1968 touched the conscience of the world?

The "representative of the nation" made clear something that is as valid today as it was in 1970. He spoke with an energy, conviction, and clarity that would encourage others, even though it was he who deserved the most to be encouraged. Even when staring death in the face he held up a bright torch. This torch was lit once more when on November 9, 1989, the members of the German parliament rose and sang in unison the national anthem as word arrived that the Berlin Wall would be torn down and East Germans were free to move once more. On that day it became clear that Germany was much more than the sum of economic forces. It contained an archaic consciousness of values and identities that transcended all daily concerns.

I had to think of Guttenberg's argument in our discussion about the motivation of soldiers: "We must bring back to life the archetypes that are sleeping in the soul of our people." On that day it was proven that the idea and reality of Germany as our fatherland was rooted in the collective archaic consciousness of the German people, not as a sudden option of the politics of our times but as a sign of ancient common ties and slowly grown ligaments.

More "Spotlights" from Washington:

September 5, 1958
National Press Club: During lunch a presentation by "Skipper" Anderson, who commanded the *Nautilus* during her voyage underneath the ice cap of the North Pole. No new details, but the atmosphere was interesting. Here they celebrated a national hero. And the hero presented himself as very informal and genuine. Even if the results of the *Nautilus* expedition appear minimal, one should join the American nation and its navy in their joy over setting this record, particularly after the many blows the American consciousness had to suffer over the past months.

I had to think of the audacious *Nautilus* adventure of the Australian Arctic explorer Sir Hubert Wilkins. In 1931 he tried to prove, with the help of an old submarine as well as fantastic gadgets such as ice-drilling equipment and underwater sensors to locate the bottom side of floes, that permanent weather stations on the pack ice could be supplied by submarines. Wilkins, a researcher who wanted to broaden mankind's horizons, failed because his project could not be realized with existing technology. Thirty years later, on a nuclear submarine independent of external air supply, Anderson became the first man to sail beneath the polar ice cap. I congratulated Commander Anderson on his successful mission.

September 9, 1958

Another visit to SACLANT (Supreme Allied Commander, Atlantic). Talked to Captain Morante, the Italian liaison officer. When World War II broke out he happened to be in China in charge of an Italian merchantman. He scuttled his vessel, blocking the ship channel of the Yangtse River. For this action he and his family were hauled off to a Japanese concentration camp. He was not released until 1946. He told me in so many words, which I had trouble believing: "Vessels carrying war materiel from the United States to Russia were not attacked by the Japanese on the basis of a secret treaty with the Americans, who diverted to Japan the equivalent of one third of the shipped items in other important commodities such as oil."

October 12, 1958

The entire family makes a trip to the Skyline Caverns. Beautiful autumn weather. In one of the caverns we could admire a so-called natural wonder rendered utterly into kitsch by colorful illuminations. The high point came when a stalactite in a human-like shape was transformed into a stylized madonna and presented to the audience to the sounds of "Ave Maria" played on a scratchy record player. That, too, is America.

We visited Harpers Ferry, a place of national significance. It once was the site of a munitions plant, and it was here that the Civil War began. We have some personal ties to the place as well. Several relatives of my wife are buried in the cemetery at Harpers Ferry. Her grandfather's uncle had emigrated to Virginia, and we found the tombstones with the names of our ancestors.

March 24, 1959

Lunch in the cafeteria of the Capitol with Mr. Rivers, a Congressman from Charleston, South Carolina, and friend of the Navy, and Undersecretary Dewey Short. Comradely atmosphere. Afterwards a tour of the Capitol, including the memorial hall where each state is represented by sculptures of two of its most prolific personalities. Artistically the sculptures had little appeal. Mr. Rivers was quite unhappy with the French. He saw them as a weak element in the NATO alliance according to the saying that a chain is only as strong as its weakest link. After all, logistical resupply of the troops in Europe is supposed to be channelled through French ports. Presently there is a big struggle over how to balance the budget and how high defense expenditures should be. But this is nothing new, of course. Plutarch tells us of similar problems some 1,800 years ago. Perseus, King of Macedonia, accumulated an immense treasure to be used for his defense against Roman attacks. But he was so tight-fisted that his mercenary soldiers deserted. Perseus became Rome's wealthiest prisoner. I think we can learn something from his fate.

Another peek into the American soul. The Department of Defense published this news release on June 23, 1959: "Space monkey 'Baker' will be honored by the American Society for the Prevention of Cruelty to Animals. Its president, William Rockefeller, will personally preside over the ceremony."

April 6, 1959
The great ceremony to celebrate the tenth anniversary of the founding of NATO took place in Norfolk under the auspices of SACLANT. First the "Honor of the Flag" with Paul Henri Spaak, Josef Luns, and the members of the Council. Later, lunch in the staff officers' mess. Then the big parade. Later, a party aboard the Canadian warship *Bonaventure.* Finally, a dinner party given by Vice Admiral Cooper, Commander Anti-Submarine Defense Force, and Vice Admiral Thatch, Commander Anti-Submarine Warfare Carrier Group. Germany was represented by Gebhardt von Walther, our ambassador to Mexico; Wilhelm Grewe, our ambassador to the United States; Franz Krapf, also from our embassy in Washington; and our consul in Norfolk, Herr Weiss.

During the day we also had a chance to tour the *Nautilus.* It was the first time that a nuclear-powered submarine was being shown, and not only to the officers but also to their wives. I shall never forget how Mrs. Krapf—very lively, charming, nine months pregnant—tried to descend through the very narrow hatch and the vertical companionways into the boat's interior in her elegant shoes with their two-inch high heels. Below her, American sailors stood by to catch her in case she lost her balance. "There is lightening," we used to say in the old days whenever a lady showed some of her underwear. Fortunately, Mrs. Krapf made it safely into the boat. When I offered to be her guide through the vessel, she asked me: "Captain, have you ever been on a U-boat?" With a clear conscience I could answer her question in the affirmative.

The military ceremonies of that day were tied in with the local Azalea Festival, so named after the hundreds of many-colored flowers that beautified a local park. Inside the park was an artificial pond and next to it stands that could accommodate thousands of spectators. On the other side of the pond, on a little hill and under bright skies, the coronation ceremony of the Azalea Queen and her court was under way. The contestants were young ladies supplied by the embassies or military missions of the various NATO countries. On that day our daughter Maren represented the Federal Republic of Germany. The jury gave first place to the daughter of Lyndon Johnson, the Vice President of the United States. This decision seemed to confirm the leadership claim of the United States as much as the sense of tradition inherent in the American nation.

Lyndon Johnson sat one row ahead of us as an especially honored guest. Before the ceremonies started he strolled leisurely through the groups of assembled NATO representatives and also greeted their wives. When he got to my wife he asked her how she liked her stay in the United States. She mentioned among other things that our other daughter had just married an American. This led to a

longer conversation about our extended family, some of whom lived in Austin,
Texas. One of them happened to be Louis Southerland, President of the Association of American Architects. Johnson cut in: "He is my neighbor. Please say hello
to Uncle Louis." Ever since that conversation, which many others overheard, my
wife has been called "Johnson Baby."

April 15, 1959

A visit to Norfolk by the German Defense Minister, Franz-Josef Strauss. I accompanied him to SACLANT. During the flight he was busy catching up on various press reports and dealing with matters of public relations. Five minutes
before we were scheduled to land in Norfolk he asked me to brief him about the
situation at SACLANT. That seemed a rather short preparation to me. After we
arrived he had a meeting with Admiral Wright. Afterwards he gave a press conference in which he stressed a number of points very well.

Later that evening in Washington we officers met at the house of Wolf Dietrich
von Schleinitz, the military attaché, to have an informal talk with our defense
minister. For about ten minutes I had the opportunity to discuss with him the
structure of the Baltic Command and the question of strategic mobility. Then
things got heated when Strauss accused Krapf that his visit had not been properly prepared. He compared his own impressions to reports about the visit by
Willy Brandt, then mayor of West Berlin, who had come to the United States a
short while before and whose activities had been very well planned. Strauss became very aggressive indeed. Since it is known that he did not hesitate to speak
his mind, one word led to another. Krapf responded to the accusation in a correct
and factual manner while Strauss remained emotional, egged on by his entourage who always took his side. Finally a general stood up and told Strauss: "Herr
Minister, these Byzantine arrangements surrounding you make me sick." He
then turned around and left the room. Unfortunately, in all the sound and fury
of the ongoing discussion between the two contestants and their respective
cliques, this example of living one's convictions went unnoticed.

April 20 to May 10, 1959

On vacation in Mexico. I had to think of my midshipman cruise on the *Karlsruhe* and our trip from Acapulco to Mexico City, where I had stayed with the Kügelgens. I phoned Mrs. von Kügelgen upon our arrival. She immediately recalled
those days and invited us to visit her.

Her husband, who had been a medical doctor, had died following a riding accident. She herself struck us as a ruling duchess with her tall, elegant appearance
and her white hair. Still a center of Mexican society at the time, she told us of her
family's fate during and after the war. Then she introduced us to an architect by
the name of von Wutenau, formerly in the German diplomatic service and a consul in New Orleans. He had quarrelled with the Nazis, resigned from the foreign
service, and gone to Mexico. At first, based on a superficial training in archaeology, he had found work in conserving old art objects and had taught himself the
basic principles of architecture. When we met him he had risen to be one of Mexico City's leading architects, building the most magnificent houses in the old colonial style for the well-to-do. His outward appearance was very modest, almost

grotesque. His car was held together by a piece of rope even though he could easily afford a more comfortable lifestyle given his considerable income. Fascinated by the ancient civilization of the Aztecs, he had participated in numerous excavations, especially on the west coast, and owned exquisite ceramic sculptures that were once part of the Aztec culture.

He showed us a treasure of some 300 so-called *Idolos*, small heads sculpted from clay that had likely been used as votive gifts at the sacrificial sites. He saw in them traces of all human races. Since the finds came from a period about 1,000 years prior to the colonial era, he was advocating a theory of convergence under which Mexico in earlier times had been a melting pot of many different races. He believed, for example, that already in those early times whites, Indonesians, Indians, Chinese, and even Negroid people had lived on Mexican soil. Listening to him was exciting, especially since he had the gift to project his own fascination with that theory onto others. His views, which he also presented to the public, have never been accepted by the scientific community.

On a trip to Guernavaca with its famous frescoes by Rivera and its tropical character, we passed through Taxco, a city centered around old silver mines. Built picturesquely against the backdrop of a mountain, the city survives today as a main attraction for American tourists, condescendingly called gringos, even though they are crucial to Mexico's economy. In Taxco we met Wutenau again, this time as the owner and inhabitant of the so-called Humboldt House, an old patrician building where Alexander von Humboldt had lived for a while and where today are stored pictures and manuscripts by him.

About a year later we made a second trip to Mexico. We spent two weeks in the old Aztec resort town of Ixtapa with its radioactive thermal baths. It was a funny feeling to look across the dark fluid at the talking heads of the other bathers, among them many Jews from Mexico City. At first they kept their distance from us. Later, when they realized that we did not match their stereotypes of "Nazi Germans," we got along quite well, and from those encounters developed our friendship with Sari Brimmer.

Sari Brimmer was born in Vienna, had lost a part of her family, and had built up a new life for herself in Mexico. She had a daughter, Gaby, who had been paralyzed through cerebral palsy since she was two years old. In the beginning Gaby could neither talk nor move. Everything was done to improve the child's prospects under the given circumstances. Thanks to the life-long devotion of a local Indian girl, and after attending specialized schools, she managed after a while to understand five different languages. She learned to type on a custom-built typewriter by using her toes, the only parts of her body she could move. Thus she could communicate with others from her wheelchair. She was an individual of high intelligence, great beauty, and remarkable charisma.

Sari Brimmer had heard of good homes for the handicapped in Switzerland, in England, and in West Germany that would accept such children and provide well for them. I thereupon contacted an architect with whom I had once worked in Hanover and who belonged to the anthroposophical movement. I asked him whether he could recommend a suitable place. He responded immediately, and I informed Mrs. Brimmer accordingly. This is what she wrote back:

> I am driving out to the camp that specializes in spastic children and is directed by Mrs. Sahlmann, a German pediatrician. Over the course of twenty-one years these people have put together a whole village. You can reserve a place for your adolescent children by contributing to a trust fund. My sister, Dr. Betty Modley, will come with me because I am not sure that I am emotionally strong enough to handle the encounter.
>
> Later I will be flying to Israel—the land of my fathers—as I have been taught. I fear daily about the continued existence of this piece of earth that was and remains a refuge for the persecuted and desperate among my people. Well, we will stick to it because it was the basis of our existence to remind our children again and again to respect their fellow human beings as a guarantee for peace. That is the only way for me, the way of the mother. Won't you agree, Frau Ilse?

In 1988 we were reminded once more of Sari Brimmer. The movie, *Gaby,* showed the fate of her daughter who in the meantime has developed so far that she writes newspaper columns and books. She even wrote the script for the film about her life. The movie, an artistic masterpiece, chronicles her handicapped life in all its details and brings out her passionate yearning for a normal life that she will never enjoy. When Helen Keller, who as a blind person had written a number of world-famous books, was once asked what she thought about death, she said: "I will walk through a tall gate—and I will be able to see." I wish Gaby Brimmer has faith in a similar vision.

Besides enjoying these fleeting encounters and experiences in Washington I also endeavored, given my access to all kinds of information, to explore the surface and background of American political life and to convey my impressions to those in Germany who seemed interested in knowing about them.

Most of my activities had to do with military matters. Political decisions are dependent on the mentality of the people who make them. Americans are a mixture of many races; their mentality flows from many sources. It is complex, difficult to define, and America's political experience therefore is not without contradictions. I will try carefully to describe and explain this complex fabric of philosophical, historical, and traditional factors.

Their frontier experience gave Americans a clear sense for the real. Their pragmatism is perhaps best expressed in the saying, "Truth is what works." The roots of this attitude may lie in Calvin's puritanism, but it is a secularized, enlightened version of it. Truth defined as success presupposes experimenting, keeping statistics, methods of ascertaining public opinion, and an imperturbable faith in freedom and democracy. This philosophy has resulted in great accomplishments, not least the equality of all before the law regardless of race or national origin. Social barriers have been torn down and a common "American way of life" has taken over. Democracy seems to have something doctrinaire about it. Americans apply the principles and liberties spelled out in their constitution not only to themselves but assume that their social and political experiences should and can work just as well for other societies without bothering to analyze whether such a wholesale transfer is justified or desirable. The God-given conviction, the manifest destiny for the American people to spread out westward across the continent, found its climax on August 29, 1959, when Hawaii joined the union as its fiftieth state. America offers a place to live for everyone, opportunities for everyone, chances to succeed to everyone. Something of the nineteenth-century belief in "God's own country" I could still sense when I became familiar with the land and its people between 1958 and 1962.

I experienced this uniquely American way of doing things when the Standing Group invited us staff officers of the national representatives to visit the Strategic Air Command (SAC), the North American Air Defense Command (NORAD), the Air Force Academy, and also one of SAC's air bases. At the Air Force Academy, "Truth is what works" meant the selection and training of a group of young men to become a part of a precisely functioning mechanism within the pluralism of a rich democratic society with the goal of molding it into a reliable instrument of American policy. Set against the majestic scenery of Colorado's snow-covered mountains, the buildings of the academy betray their function in their very architectural design: constructive, matter-of-fact, no luxurious decorations, no sentimentality, no idyllic illusions.

Every year some 712 freshmen begin their four-year course of instruction. In their first year the young cadets move around on the double; in the mess hall they sit on the edge of their seats. The daily routine is hard, but the drill does not discriminate. These young men learn that discipline and asceticism will one day enable them to act as an elite. This feeling of belonging to an elite is underscored by the finest instructional resources. The library's periodicals section contains some 100 different journals, 50 daily U.S. newspapers and 26 international papers, among them from Germany the *Frankfurter Allgemeine Zeitung* and *Die Welt*. There are excellent facilities for social activities, including an auditorium that seats 3,000 people, its acoustics so well designed that there is no need for loudspeakers. No more than twelve men belong to a group, supervised by the best instructors. The well-lit and comfortably furnished rooms are each shared by two men. The library contains some 200,000 volumes.

The huge dining hall can accommodate 3,000 cadets simultaneously, another remarkable demonstration of the desire to foster a sense of equality. Should one of the cadets fall ill, he can follow his lessons from his room by way of closed-circuit television and an intercom. There are no opportunities for a private life outside the compound, say in cabarets or bars. All social life occurs in the same clean and bright rooms of the academy. One of the academy's objectives is "to develop in its cadets the highest form of discipline—that self-discipline which enables a man to see his responsibilities and to carry them out without compulsion."

The tasks these cadets would later have to take care of were demonstrated to us at SAC, at NORAD, and at Whiteman Air Force Base. The mission of SAC is clear, "to conduct strategic air warfare on a global basis, to deter war. Should deterrence fail, S.A.C.'s objectives then become to destroy the aggressor's will and capability to wage war." To achieve these objectives at all times, SAC has at its disposal some 1,500 B 47s; 500 B 52s; several B 58s; a sizable air refueling capacity; and missiles. Brigadier General Huglin demonstrated for us how SAC maintained constant communications among all its bases and also with the President of the United States no matter where he might be at any given moment. We were very impressed by the huge Operational Control Center. It functions with the assurance of a mathematical formula. Here are no hypotheses, no principles; just the maxim, "Truth is what works."

NORAD is in charge of air defenses in cooperation with Canada. It is a joint command. The system of powerful radar stations, the DEW Line, and the CAN Forward Scatter Line cover all of North America and extend westward to the Aleutians and eastward to the Azores. Four or five aircraft are constantly airborne; elsewhere the Navy operates radar pickets. If the stations pick up a target that is identified as hostile, the latter is attacked and destroyed. The process goes through four phases: detection, identification, attack, destroy. All attacks are carried out locally but are initiated and controlled centrally. Given modern technologies, especially early warning signs, the North American continent is barely large enough to react in time to an attack.

The last link in the chain was our visit to SAC's Whiteman Air Force Base. Here precise planning and solid training combine to make decisive action possible. Eight days of highest alert are followed by routine training for the balance of the month. During the eight days everyone is in a state of readiness, and each alarm is a full alarm. Only when the aircraft is airborne does the pilot learn through code words how far the mission is to be carried out. Wherever the crew happens to be, it must be ready at a moment's notice. Cars stand by to take the men to their planes on a specially marked road. The aircraft are ready to go; the first one is moving down the runway eight minutes after the alarm is sounded. As if on a parade ground, the remaining planes follow with amazing precision. This is the pinnacle of what can be achieved in terms of organization while always keeping in mind that no one is perfect.

All talks about NATO's strategic concept, not excluding those held during our tour of SAC, necessarily focused on the subject of our nuclear potential and its credibility in terms of effective deterrence. In this sense deterrence is not threatening the other side with a war that one is neither willing nor able to wage oneself. Rather, deterrence means the defender's ability to force a potential aggressor into a kind of war that he cannot or will not wage because either his own losses are likely to be unacceptable or his chances for victory too small. Thus, deterrence boils down to a mixture of known facts, clever misinformation, and the psychological preconditioning of the adversary. Together these factors are designed to impress a potential aggressor and to reassure one's own side.

As long as the strategy of deterrence is in place, it is impossible to put one's own cards on the table in order not to lose the game from the beginning. There is no public announcement of possible scenarios, just as it was unthinkable in the past that one of the parties involved would make its operational plans known to the enemy. One is led to believe that many of the theories published on both sides today are merely designed to keep the enemy guessing. Any discussion about security questions and disarmament must take into account the potential enemy's psychological response. Ever since NATO was founded, and as numerous publications make clear, there have been many different opinions about our desirable strategy. While this kind of shadow-boxing is likely to continue, we should be mindful of the fact that at the present time our security depends in the last analysis on the functioning of a chain of risks that extends from the front lines to the nerve center of the alliance at the Strategic Air Command in the United States.

In my eyes the Berlin Crisis of 1961 proved how this chain of risks functioned in practice. Already in November 1958 Khrushchev had initiated this crisis over Berlin in a speech given in the Sports Palace in Moscow. The speech was followed up by an official note in which the Soviet Union denied the western Allies their continued right to occupy Berlin and demanded their withdrawal from the city in an ultimatum. The Soviets threatened to transfer their occupation rights to the East German government and thereby forced the West to adopt one of three alternatives: to cave in to the Soviet demand; to resist it by force; or to negotiate with the as yet unrecognized East German state. The city of Berlin, the catalyst for all hopes of a reunified Germany, was to become an independent political unit—which, given geopolitical necessities, would sooner or later end up as Moscow's satellite.

The Geneva conference of the foreign ministers of the four Allied powers in May 1959 exhausted itself in propaganda speeches on both sides. This formal conference was followed by secret meetings among the four powers about the future of Berlin, initiatives that spanned the spectrum from compromises on part of the West to attempts at blackmail, such as threats to close the land approaches to the city, on part of the Soviets. The talks oscillated between definite dead ends and a feverish search for a practical solution, for suspending the meetings would have led to a dangerous confrontation.

We in Washington assessed the situation as follows: The formerly united front of the NATO members had virtually collapsed. As always in situations like this one, everybody talked about the need to take a firm and united stand. But only the Americans let it be known that they were ready to block the Danish straits and to mine the Dardanelles should the Soviets decide to deny us access to Berlin. The Americans were the only ones ready to defend the rights of the West "without giving an inch," as Eisenhower said. This we should never forget.

In contrast to the firm determination of the U.S. government, the U.S. press brought up the proposal to place Berlin under the control of the United Nations to meet the Soviet pressure. As one paper wrote, "Out of this nettle danger, we pluck the flower, safety." Backed by the federal government, the German Social Democratic member of parliament Fritz Erler rejected this suggestion with two arguments: (1) The fate of Berlin would be subject to unpredictable majority votes in the United Nations, where especially neutral countries were likely to change their mind frequently; and (2) Such a solution was likely to put the question of German reunification on the back burner as far as world opinion was concerned. What saved the situation in the end was Khrushchev's visit to the United States. This U.S.-Soviet summit meeting stressed the equal ranking of the two superpowers and paved the way for a reconvened conference in Geneva to work out a compromise.

Once, in a discussion with Guttenberg and Dr. Swidbert Schnippenkötter of the political section of the embassy, the Berlin Crisis became our central topic. Guttenberg was convinced that the Soviets were intent on using Berlin as an excuse to perpetuate the division of Germany. For the Russians and their satellites, a reunited Germany, possibly even occupying a leading position in Western Europe, was the ultimate nightmare. Thus, Khrushchev's attempt to solve the Berlin problem in an aggressive fashion was psychologically motivated and contrasted with the actions of the western powers.

Schnippenkötter feared with some justification that a blockade of Berlin would not only harm political activity in the city but endanger the very idea and mission of the city itself. Berlin had to remain an oasis of freedom from which, in many different ways, rays of hope reached out to East Germany and the other Russian satellites. It was a place that offered temporary asylum to the victims of repression and tyranny whose plight touched the conscience of mankind.

Guttenberg was optimistic and suggested that in the face of the open Soviet threats the West must be ready to harden its stance politically and increase its strength militarily. Whether there would be enough time to hold on to all presently occupied positions remained to be seen. Guttenberg thought that Khrushchev had achieved two goals by challenging the West: the desired summit meeting with Eisenhower; and the de facto recognition of the status quo in Europe as it had emerged after the war.

Against these notions Schnippenkötter advanced the analysis of the political section of the embassy. For him the Americans had few illusions about the meeting. There was nothing that suggested in any way a revision of existing policies. The first priority of the United States was national security. None of those in positions of authority expected a change in policy from anyone. The only positive thing about the visit was the expectation that such a meeting might contribute to improved mutual understanding and gain more respect for and from the other side. This analysis assumed that neither side was interested in developments that could lead to an irreparable loss of prestige. The dangers that such a meeting could open up were well understood. Schnippenkötter concluded that the true test of statesmanship is to remain watchful while at the same time trying to reduce tensions with the other side.

Guttenberg then spoke about the impact of the Berlin Crisis on the West German public. He argued that the West Germans were quite aware that Berlin had become the playball of superpower interests on which Bonn could exert little influence. The tension between the power blocs was very complex in nature, and the media did not help by presenting the issue in an either simplified, distorted, or exaggerated manner. Many developments were being discussed in a sensationalist tone. Guttenberg agreed with us that the superpowers in their statements did not only play to the politicians on both sides but also tried to influence public opinion. For the citizens of West Germany this meant living daily with danger and the threat of war. One could label this passively as the Cold War or actively as psychological warfare. Living under such tensions and suspense is likely to wear you out. Politically, the permanent crisis over Berlin no longer engaged the average citizen on a daily basis. Therefore it was paramount to remind the German nation again and again of the importance of Berlin as a living symbol and to demand the reunification of the country.

Guttenberg's credo: Only the reunification of a free Germany can ultimately solve the situation of Berlin. To keep up this demand is crucial for realistic reasons even if the Soviet Union refuses to talk about the issue. It is in the interest of the West to maintain Berlin's present status until a final solution is worked out. The East has announced its intention to change this status gradually in its favor. All negotiations have failed so far because the two standpoints are absolutely incompatible. The West must succeed in convincing the East that it will not be able to achieve its offensive goals. Only through such a step can we lay the foundation for real negotiations. Only then the Soviet Union will understand that a so-called interim solution would entail not a modification of Berlin's status but a major change.

French President de Gaulle, whose past policies made him look anything but an "appeaser," reached conclusions in 1959 that still pass inspection some thirty years later:

1. We must work for détente as before, put an end to all actions and speeches designed to provoke the other side, increase trade and cultural exchanges, and encourage tourist exchanges.
2. We must continue to pursue balanced disarmament, especially with regard to strategic weapons, to alleviate the pressure on mankind and the temptation to bring about total destruction.
3. East and West should cooperate in providing aid for the underdeveloped areas of the world as well as work together in the great projects of science and technology on whose results man's future depends.

On September 15, 1959, Khrushchev arrives at Andrews Air Force Base for an eleven-day visit of the United States. Bright sunshine, strong security measures, and precautions. The crowds are curious but remain reserved. A few hesitant shouts of "welcome" only after the motorcade has passed. Eisenhower is seated in the car between the Khrushchevs. Khrushchev seems somber, serious. Mrs. Khrushchev is more the mother type, occasionally waving to the spectators. In his speech at the airport Khrushchev talks much about peace. He emphasizes Russia's leading role in the sciences and mentions the first rocket that has landed on the moon. "The weight of the moon has increased in comparison to the Earth." Those words likely contained a genuinely felt realization.

How did Americans react to Khrushchev's visit? "The man who came to teach and not to learn." Khrushchev has completely misunderstood the western mentality. The West remains calm; Khrushchev shouts everything from the rooftops. The West desires moderate progress; "Khrushchev is going for the millennium." The West wishes to restrict the arms race; Khrushchev wants to sweep the entire problem aside with a kind of Christmas card pacifism. He does not like to discuss those things over which he has some control, such as mutual inspection of military facilities, Laos, Tibet, and so on. The things that no one can manage he wants to do at once. It is truly astonishing that he wants to cooperate with the Americans on the moon but not on earth. He does not mince words when it comes to making his point of view clear. He is a symbol of his country, full of vitality, self-possessed, resolute, proud, eager to discuss matters. In the end he has done us all a favor by visiting the United States. He has drawn the line. Personal contacts are no substitute for policy. The visit has brought the Allies of the United States back to reality.

On September 21, the talk between Khrushchev and U.S. labor union leaders ended with total disagreement. Walter Reuther, the leader of the United Automobile Workers, made it clear to Khrushchev that the unions oppose communism: "We do not believe in any form of dictatorship. We like our own system with its guaranteed freedoms." In the discussions Khrushchev came across as amiable as long as he talked about matters of little consequence. But he could become quite insulting when he insisted on being correct about details. For example, a discussion about self-determination had to be broken off because Khrushchev became too enraged. Reuther commented on his meetings:

> Mikoyan was easier to talk to because he was able to listen to the arguments of the other side and address them in a calm manner without giving up for a moment his communist convictions. With Khrushchev it was easy to exchange superficial platitudes; once you say something profound or provocative, he will become excited and insulting. A dangerous, emotional man.

In August 1960 I had a meeting with a Mr. Hermsdorf of the Central Intelligence Agency (CIA). He offered details about the U 2 planes and the shooting down of Gary Powers over the Soviet Union, which Khrushchev had exploited for propaganda purposes at the summit conference. This aircraft is made from wood and plastic, has long wings, no catapult seat, and no landing gear. It is difficult to be picked up by radar and carries eight different cameras whose combination of lenses can even detect camouflaged targets. The flights have been carried out for years but are dependent on favorable weather conditions. Other intelligence targets, particularly ports, are being investigated by one-man midget submarines. Both the flights and the submarine operations have brought casualties. I was surprised that the CIA admitted it had difficulties getting recruits for such missions. The American soldier has much patriotic motivation, but he is not the kamikaze type. The open admission that such flights have been undertaken for years and will be continued seems to suggest that U.S. policy has hardened again.

Hermsdorf, the CIA man, has done much for the United States, especially in Central America. He also performed valuable services in connection with the founding of the Federal Republic of Germany by being very helpful to certain politicians at the time who have risen to influential positions today. He has been awarded the German Federal Order of Merit.

Hermsdorf died in early November 1960 of cancer. Dr. Georg Federer, our Consul General in New York City, Erich Strätling of the German Embassy, and my wife and I were present at Hermsdorf's funeral. It was an impressive ceremony at Arlington National Cemetery, which is reserved for Americans who have earned the gratitude of their nation. It was a wet, foggy morning. After the memorial service in the chapel the coffin was draped in the American flag and drawn on a gun carriage to the gravesite. Two marines folded the flag according to an ancient ritual and handed it to Mrs. Hermsdorf. Barely visible through the fog, a bugler on a nearby hill played taps, a tune made famous by the film, *From Here to Eternity*. Finally, three salvoes were fired by a squad of marines. A very impressive, unforgettable moment of farewell.

While the pressure on Berlin continued through 1961 and 1962—the East began to erect the Berlin Wall in August 1961 without much reaction from the West—the crisis over Cuba came to a head. One must interpret the Cuban Missile Crisis as a symbol of changing perceptions in the application of military force. Military power is as effective as always, but the aspects of its application have undergone a transformation. Clausewitz defined war as the "continuation of politics with the help of other means." For him, war amounted to the ultimate but also legitimate means of imposing a decision upon another state of the international system. Today all efforts on the part of the superpowers to enforce political decisions by military means have become questionable.

This has been so for all practical purposes since the Korean War. General MacArthur was kept from practicing on the battlefield what he and generations of other military leaders before him had learned at their service academies, namely, to break the military power of the enemy by all means and to end the conflict as quickly as possible with minimal loss of life.

The causes behind this change in the exercise of military power are easily understood:

1. In contrast to earlier times, even a limited shift in power can have global repercussions (e.g., Afghanistan, Iraq, Iran).

2. In the nuclear age superior weapons guarantee neither the survival of the attacker nor that of the defender. A limitation and selection of appropriate means must be made by the political leadership.

3. The international balance of power has changed. Instead of a balance between several powers we have today latent tensions between two dominant superpowers as well as the presence of a great number of emancipated young nations that exploit these tensions. They often in-

terpret the principles of international law in an arbitrary fashion. The lack of constraint among these new nations when it comes to the use of military force must be compensated for by circumspect and cautious behavior on the part of the superpowers.

4. Social stratification, man himself, and his manipulation by the means of mass information and propaganda undergo constant transformations whose speed outpaces the ability of regulating institutions to adapt to this process.

5. The fast pace of technological development has led in certain areas to doubts as to the objectives of innovation.

To solve certain problems—for example, the test ban on nuclear weapons in the atmosphere, in space, or underneath the oceans—presupposed the application of new technological procedures in order to be able to verify and control compliance with treaties. All these societal and technological changes suggest that power can only be exercised in a responsible manner if it is proportional in scope to the challenge it seeks to meet. This means in particular:

1. The variety of challenges must be matched by a broad spectrum of possible solutions within the range of political, economic, and military options; the most drastic solution of all being the forever incalculable risk of using nuclear weapons.

2. Today's immense quantity and quality of military weapons, as well as the increased possibility of them being misused, requires careful political control over their application.

3. The transformation in the exercise of military power leads on both sides to tacitly accepted attempts to limit the exercise of force by drawing political and military borderlines that are being recognized by both sides. First attempts at political limitation were the disengagement plans that would have created militarily weakened zones. So far they have remained mere plans. An example of military limitation is the idea of so-called sanctuaries, protected zones that are not absolutely safe from enemy action but are tacitly recognized by both sides on the basis of threats and counterthreats that create an uneasy balance. In the Gulf War between Iraq and Iran, U.S. warships with the assistance of British and French units protected international sea-lanes against attacks by Iran. These vessels remained more or less unmolested because both sides recognized the advantages of such a sanctuary with all its implied limitations.

4. One can say in the broadest sense that war as a means of solving differences between the great powers has lost much of its former significance and that force can only be applied in a limited way. Blaise Pascal once wrote: "Justice without power is helpless. Power without justice is tyranny. Therefore we must strive to harmonize power and justice with each other to make what is just strong and what is strong just."

The Cuban Missile Crisis is an excellent case to demonstrate this shift in the exercise of power.

I had an extended correspondence about the origins and course of the Cuban Missile Crisis with Colonel Dr. Friedrich Beermann, who stayed on in Washington after I assumed my next assignment. I became a witness to the beginning of the crisis with a high level of information when I participated in the Amphibious Warfare Course for Senior Officers from September 10 until December 7, 1962, in San Diego. One must remember that after Castro's revolution and the transformation of the island into a socialist state, Cubans in exile had staged a liberation attempt in April 1961, the Bay of Pigs affair. This action had been funded by the Americans, had been planned by the CIA, and had been carried out with President Kennedy's consent. The operation failed largely because Kennedy refused to commit U.S. forces.

In April 1962 the United States launched Exercise Landphibex off the coast of North Carolina and in the Caribbean. Some 40,000 marines took part along with the aircraft carrier *Forrestal*. The exercise culminated in a simulated amphibious landing on a U.S. island in the Caribbean. It was meant as a warning to Cuba and the Soviets. Cuba had become increasingly dependent on the Soviet Union and begun to expand its military potential well beyond any legitimate need for self-defense. The Americans monitored this build-up carefully. U 2 spy planes photographed the entire island from an altitude of some 60,000 feet. The planes carried the latest in photographic equipment. The pictures were so accurate and advanced in resolution that you could read on them the headlines of a newspaper.

Early in 1962 it was learned that several thousand Soviet military advisors worked on the island, that MIG jets had been delivered to the Cuban air force, and that an air defense system was being installed with Soviet assistance. In the meantime, the Pentagon and the CIA discovered a so-called missile gap in the U.S. defenses. There had been a heated discussion about this subject during the most recent presidential election. The new President Kennedy was determined to close the missile gap as part of a nuclear expansion program. For months this subject made headlines in the American media.

The CIA claimed to have evidence that the Soviets were likely to respond by installing medium-range missiles on Cuba because in their estimation there was no missile gap and the U.S. expansion program shifted the strategic balance to the advantage of the Americans. The U.S. government warned the Soviets in writing against such a step, which would trigger the gravest consequences. To beef up his warning Kennedy gained congressional approval to call up 150,000 military reservists if necessary—a limited military demonstration.

By mid-October 1962, aerial photographs proved beyond doubt that

Kennedy's warning had not been heeded. The Soviets had begun building launch sites on Cuba for medium-range missiles. The U.S. government reacted by forming a crisis management team and decreed that all crucial information and possible actions be kept strictly secret for the time being. In a meeting with the Soviet Foreign Minister, Kennedy brought up the subject of medium-range missiles on Cuba and their possible consequences, but he left Gromyko in the dark as to the full extent of his information.

The crisis management team worked out three alternative lines of action: aerial bombardments, an invasion, or a blockade. All preparations were carried out in such a way as to be likely to find the support of U.S. allies at a later point. The three alternatives led to appropriate military preparations. Squadrons of fighter-bombers and air defense units were transferred to Florida to carry out possible air strikes. For the invasion options, the U.S. Navy concentrated amphibious and fleet units in the Caribbean, ostensibly for an exercise that had been planned independently of the present crisis. And for the third alternative, a blockade, fleet units stood by in naval bases close to Cuba. In all three options one had to take into consideration that Khrushchev might overreact, perhaps even launch a preventive nuclear strike. To guard against this possibility strategic bombers were kept airborne around the clock and all other SAC units placed on fifteen-minute readiness alert.

When Kennedy accepted the risk of a nuclear exchange, he said openly: "In their efforts to defend their vital interests, nuclear powers must avoid at all cost a situation in which the enemy has to choose between a humiliating retreat and nuclear war." By building up his chain of risks in a consistent manner to the point of threatening to use his nuclear arsenal, Kennedy not only reassured the uneasy peoples of Central and South America but above all gained credibility with the Soviets, as could be seen from some of Khrushchev's reactions.

The political, military, and legal deliberations lasted only a few days. Then the government decided in favor of a blockade, which could be escalated depending on the response of the other side. Since a blockade constituted an act of war under international law, it was appropriately camouflaged as a "defensive quarantine." This nomenclature made it easier to gain the support of the Allies through diplomatic channels. The legal justification for the U.S. step was drawn from the charter of the Organization of American States (OAS), whose members come exclusively from the western hemisphere. Any involvement of the United Nations was deliberately shunned because it might have enabled the Soviets to adopt certain countermeasures in waters controlled by them. Kennedy's diplomatic finesse gained him the support of the OAS nations. In the last phase of the preparations, just before his feverishly awaited public announcement, Kennedy worked out all essential details, dispatched special envoys to the various NATO member states, and briefed his cabinet and the Congress. One hour before his speech, Kennedy called in the Soviet ambassador.

Given America's obsession with unlimited freedom of the press and the journalists' fierce competition for sensational stories, it is almost a miracle that such an important and extensive political, military, and diplomatic operation could be kept secret until the moment of Kennedy's speech. Some tricks along with the deliberate dissemination of misinformation created some confusion. In the end, when some of the details were beginning to seep through, a patriotic appeal to the leading publishers achieved the intended result. That, too, should not remain unmentioned.

Simultaneous with his step to announce his decision to the public, Kennedy undertook additional measures. Dean Acheson informed the European NATO countries and had personal visits with President de Gaulle and Chancellor Adenauer. The United States introduced a resolution in the Security Council of the United Nations to ban the further construction of Soviet missile bases on Cuba and to have the already installed facilities removed. Likewise, the leadership of the OAS approved the measures of the U.S. government. The U.S. ambassadors to Guinea and Senegal in Africa intervened in those countries in order to revoke Moscow's landing rights there for flights to Cuba. All these measures worked so well that the Soviets found themselves faced by a united front. In order not to humiliate Khrushchev, Kennedy offered at the same time to cooperate with the Soviets once the crisis had been cleared up.

A retrospective analysis of the crisis reveals a number of miscalculations as well. We know today that there was no missile gap when Kennedy took over. The accelerated nuclear expansion program was also based on a misinterpretation. The Soviets underestimated the U.S. resolve not to tolerate nuclear weapons in Cuba under any circumstances. But these mutual miscalculations led to measures and countermeasures in the political, military, and diplomatic arena that were in line with the respective challenges. The "quarantine" with its limited time frame and geographical coverage and with its selected use of military force gave the Soviets time to sort out their options and possible consequences.

But above all was the realization that in pursuit of one's country's vital interests one should never place the enemy in the dilemma of having to choose between humiliation and full-scale war. The conflict could be localized by limiting the means of military force and by taking advantage of political and diplomatic options. International solidarity prevented the export of the conflict to other regions. There was no new crisis over Berlin; the U.S. missile bases in Turkey were not attacked. The confrontation of the two highly armed nuclear powers was restricted to the use of conventional forces in pursuit of their respective political objectives.

The Cuban Missile Crisis also demonstrated the importance of sea power, again under the perspective of the changed application of military force in modern times. The strategy of the free world is intimately linked to the problem of being able to move without restriction across the oceans and through the air. Naval superiority in the Atlantic is as crucial as our control of the air space above it. The Atlantic Ocean is and will remain the core of our western alliance.

In both World Wars the Atlantic and its peripheral waters played an important role. NATO could not function, indeed could never have come about, without the option of reinforcing and resupplying military forces in Europe, of building and securing bases overseas, of being able to freely exchange raw materials and manufactured goods. In southeastern Europe, Greece and Turkey could never have been joined to the alliance without the reassurance that other NATO countries controlled the Mediterranean and rendered it a safe supply route. The same applies to Norway and Denmark in northern Europe. Their future, along with that of Germany and England, would be seriously threatened if the Allied navies could not control and defend the North Sea and the North Atlantic. To secure the freedom of the seas is a vital necessity if the free world wants to reach its national and international goals. To gain and to maintain supremacy at sea is a precondition for survival in case of a major conflict.

The Cuban Missile Crisis underscored the role of sea power in the context of a dangerous struggle between the two nuclear powers. The use of U.S., British, and French fleet units during the Iran-Iraq War assured the flow of oil to the western world. In the future the members of NATO will have to rely on sea power just as they have in the past. A true partnership between North America and Western Europe requires that the vital sea lanes of the Atlantic remain open under all circumstances.

In October 1961 our time in Washington came to an end. Ambassador Grewe thanked me for my work and saw our departure as a human loss. *"Toujours on perd, toujours on gagne."* Dr. Hans-Georg Wieck of the embassy's political section, with whom we had closely collaborated, gave us a farewell dinner. Later I saw him again in Bonn in the planning division of the Ministry of Defense. As our ambassador to NATO and as head of the Federal Intelligence Service he would become known to the public.

Our last evening in Washington, somewhat improvised, was spent at the Strätlings, their other guests being Seymour Bolten from the CIA, Jim O'Donnel from the State Department, Dr. Dalma of the *Münchener Merkur,* and the Bavarian State Secretary Franz Heubl. Bolten argued that the Germans must try to understand the U.S. situation with its unique political legacies and inevitabilities. On the other hand, the Americans should make a greater effort to understand that the Germans are one people divided by the Iron Curtain. We Germans should trust the Americans. They are communism's natural enemy and consequently our natural ally. To act in panic betrays defects in political leadership. Such actions bring back old notions of Germany playing one side out against the other, as at Rapallo, and lead to instability. In both nations subgroups exist with strong prejudices. Only strong political leadership based on a realistic assessment of the world situation can reduce these prejudices over time.

Since then there have been several times of tension between the United States and the Federal Republic. They prove how little people have learned from the past and how futile our efforts have been in changing the old misconceptions.

On November 18, all our friends are there to see us off. They even sing *"Muss i denn zum Städtele hinaus"* for us. Then we take the train, parlor class, to Stamford, and from there on to Darien to say goodbye to our now "American" daughter Ingrid. Two more days with the Walters in Upper Montclair.

Professor Helmuth Walter is one of the great men of German science. I knew him from World War II when he had designed and built the motors for the V1 and V2 rockets as well as the so-called Walter propulsion system for U-boats. A man of true genius, he had been cashiered by the British after the war and eventually ended up in the United States. I met him again for the first time in Washington when we were both guests of the German naval attaché. At the time Walter worked for the Worthington Corporation in New Jersey. From that point on we renewed our friendship through visits and correspondence even after I had gone back to Germany. I sat on the board of directors of his firm in Kiel, which Walter had built up from scratch after the war. He constructed a stationary prototype of his Walter propulsion engine for the Federal Defense Ministry. Unfortunately the Navy decided against using this system, which is independent of external air intake, when it built its new generation of U-boats.

One of the two remaining evenings we spent at the Metropolitan Opera. They performed *Tosca*, an unforgettable experience. The last evening we decided to go to the Apollo Theater in Harlem. Our friend Conny Beckmann had recommended the place and spoken enthusiastically about the velvet-skinned, brown Negro women who danced at that theater. We took a taxi to get there. The driver spoke German. He had visited Germany and fallen in love with it. His brother, a dentist, had married a German. When my wife asked him whether he, too, would like to marry a German girl, he replied that as a cab driver his chances would be fairly slim.

Inside the Apollo Theater we were the only whites. Everyone else was black. The presentations, the audience—everything reflected the black mentality, and that at a noise level ten times higher than what our ears were used to. Wild movements and gestures, and outcries that made us fear for our lives. During one of the wildest scenes we spied Professor Walter at the lighted entrance. Relieved, we allowed him to escort us out of the room. Mrs. Walter only shook her head and said they and their friends would never have even thought of entering this witches' cauldron. Well, in those days it was still possible; nowadays you would risk your life.

On November 21 we left New York for Europe under bright, sunny skies. Shortly before our departure I wrote to a friend of mine:

> I find it wrong to blame the Americans whenever the slightest thing goes wrong for the West. They are and have been our most faithful allies and have done much for us in the past. I must think of the Berlin Air Lift of 1948, of our high standard of living, and not least of the fact that during the recent crisis over Berlin the Americans were the only ones to respond with an effective military build-up in order to improve their negotiating position vis-à-vis the Russians.

On both sides one encounters people who are interested in undermining the good relations between the United States and Germany. Again and again they fire ideological broadsides against U.S. capitalism, against interventionism, and against the American economic system even though it has created a gross national product greater than that of West Germany, Japan, and the Soviet Union combined. After living in the United States for four years, I am prepared to say that "intellectual" anti-Americanism, although dangerous, has so far not succeeded in threatening the Atlantic Alliance. I hope this bridge across the Atlantic will continue to withstand such quarrels in the future.

Chief of Staff, Fleet Command, October 1963 to October 1965

The Fleet Commander was Vice Admiral Heinrich Gerlach, an extraordinarily sensitive, almost nervous man of high intelligence. Thanks to his unconventional measures, especially in matters of personnel and training schedules, we were able to get the modernization of the fleet under way. In our view combat conditions had undergone such changes that the Navy would find it difficult or be altogether unable to fulfill its mission with traditional means, particularly in view of the enemy's numerical superiority. Until well into World War II the human eye had been the most important and often the only sensor aboard a vessel to spot the enemy. Twenty years later modern devices like radar, sonar, active and passive sensors, electronic countermeasures (ECM), and infrared supply such a wealth of data that the human brain is not equipped to process it reliably and satisfactorily in the short period of time before a decision must be made.

Our first basic problem therefore required that we master this massive flow of information to gain a picture of the tactical situation and to assess it accordingly. The second basic problem was how to respond to fast modern missiles of considerable range that gave us only a brief time to initiate countermeasures. The answer to these changed conditions on the battlefield lay in the introduction of electronic data processing. It would support and accelerate the following aspects of military leadership: situation analysis; situation assessment; decision making; and command and control. While it was relatively easy to improve the data processing capacity and response time of individual vessels, the next step had to be to expand these capabilities at the level of the entire combat force in order to enable the force commander to meet his leadership responsibilities properly.

The Link 11 System connected individual fleet units through automatic data exchange and created a complete picture of the local situation, thus making its assessment easier. In addition the system allowed for the immediate transmission of command decisions with regard to fire control and target selection. It became the basis for a quick, coordinated, and economical response by the combat units in question. In order to meet the three demands of improved data processing capability, reduced response time, and automatic data linkage, we created the shipboard systems SATIR for our guided missile destroyers; AGIS for the PT boats of the 143 class; and PALIS for the PT boats of the 148 class as well as for the *Hamburg* class destroyers.

To integrate the Fleet Command into the system and to allow for the coordination of measures at the highest level, the Fleet Headquarters had to be tied into the process. Its coordinating and command function required direct linkage to various other echelons such as air defense, the coastal radar organization, Telecommunications Unit 70, the Navy's logistics control center, the various NATO commands, the naval air force, and other fleet units. Above all it was crucial to provide the political leadership without delay with a picture of the situation, something that is especially crucial in times of international tensions and also in the exercise of maritime control measures.

Next to these basic challenges I found it important to imbue my staff with a better esprit de corps. One vehicle was to hold regular briefings, conferences, and talks with the officers, meetings that were also open to the civilian officials on our staff. My main goal was to avoid an atmosphere of "splendid isolation" in which nothing but the Navy mattered. Instead, I wanted the political and social questions of our days to be included in our deliberations.

For example, the assassination attempt against Hitler on July 20, 1944, with its problems relating to obedience, duty, and conscience, was one of the subjects we discussed in our meetings. I believe that this day cannot be compared to other national memorial days such as those that commemorate the founding of the Second Reich, the defeat of France in the Franco-Prussian War, the Battle of Jutland—all days that in the past provided outlets for patriotic fervor. July 20 is a very different day for us. It is a day for contemplation, a day for painful memories; a kind of national day of mourning that stands for difficult and dark times, for times of shame and humiliation; a day that brought a ray of hope and today allows us to breathe a little easier.

July 20 also reminds us of the long chain of failed revolutions in the past century of German history. If for 200 years now the history of France is being marked by a series of generally successful and progressive revolutions, German history over this span shows a long chain of abortive or at the very least unfortunate revolutions: 1848; 1918; 1933; July 20, 1944; and June 17, 1953. So far only the peaceful "November Revolution" of 1989 has set a different tone.

In 1848 the political forces of nationalism and liberalism, so strong elsewhere in Europe, failed to win the upper hand. Occasioned by problems in the fleet, the Revolution of 1918 was directed against the war and the monarchy. But it was burdened with the stigma of the military defeat and the fact that it seemed to exploit a national emergency. Its leaders, the moderate Social Democrats, trusted neither the "Red" sailors nor the socialist working class and found themselves before long driven into a compromise with the forces of the old regime, in particular the military, in order to ward off attacks from the far left. It is not surprising that the day of this revolution, November 9, was never celebrated during the Weimar Republic.

Hitler's so-called National Revolution of January 30, 1933, was tainted from the beginning by terrorism. There was genuine social change, but political hubris very quickly brought on war, military collapse, physical destruction, and through criminal actions of the regime the greatest moral defeat ever in the history of the German people.

July 20 was an uprising of the national conscience against this regime's crimes and injustice. The plan miscarried and it became impossible to avert the ultimate catastrophe. Nevertheless, July 20 like the revolutionary days of 1848 belongs to those events that we can be proud of and that did not prove futile if we allow for a longer historical perspective. July 20 is and remains a day of great and lasting significance in that it was a manifesto for justice and freedom. It bolstered the reputation of the German people after the events of the Third Reich and after the collective and unjust accusation that the Germans had been lax in their resistance against Hitler's regime of terror.

By now many years have passed. Most of us no longer carry within ourselves an intimate picture of the events of those days. But there are still witnesses who, coming from different points of view, tell us about that day. Usually they can be divided into two groups. The first has char-

acterized July 20 from the beginning as an uprising of the national conscience against a regime of crime and terror. By contrast, we who were
fighting the enemy at the front and knew relatively little about events
back home condemned July 20 as a stab in the back of the fighting soldiers, as collaboration with the enemy, as high treason, and as a breach
of our service oath. Today we have gained distance to those events and
can judge them without passion, soberly. But what had really happened?

After five years of war and struggle for our very existence, an assassination attempt was launched against the Führer. The men responsible
were a group of military officers who had sometimes close, sometimes
looser contacts to labor leaders, politicians, and representatives of the
Catholic and Lutheran Churches. What had brought these people together? It was the totalitarian claim of the regime toward its citizens, a
claim that disregarded all religious and moral obligations on part of the
state. The conscience of a nation rose against this claim, represented by
the few who knew and were determined to resist.

An extraordinarily clever leadership had managed to convince the entire nation that it found itself in a struggle for survival against capitalism,
against Jewish bankers, against Bolshevism, and against enslavement by
other European nations. By employing a confusing combination of
truths and lies, Nazi propaganda easily overpowered the average citizen.
Today we know that we were the aggressors against the Czechs, the
Poles, and the Russians; that we murdered millions of Jews; that thousands of political dissidents were killed; and that we drove great, progressive minds in the sciences and in art into exile.

An oath sworn on a person who disregards all ethical rules has its limitations under these extraordinary circumstances. But only a few were
able to stop obeying; only a few had the information required to see the
breadth and depth of the problem and the inner strength to nullify an
oath that Hitler himself had broken from the very beginning.

History provides many instances of seemingly inescapable and tragic
entanglements. Those who have the strength to cut through the Knot of
Gordium at the risk of their lives must remain outside our considerations
at this point. But even among the resistance there were failures. It would
take matters too far to expose each member of the resistance to a close
psychological analysis. Certainly, their privileged upbringing and their
environment motivated their actions, but that renders the latter no less
noble. For in the end it is actions that speak the loudest, especially if they
are undertaken from the strength of inner faith and conviction.

From my own experiences abroad, from the uncounted discussions I
have had with those who were persecuted and driven out of Germany, I
believe I can judge what the deed of July 20, 1944, means. The men of
the resistance brought Germany the first credit after the war in the eyes

of the world. Through their deaths they atoned for the terrible crimes that Hitler inflicted upon the German people and all his victims. I believe this will remain the lasting significance of this day.

One day we had a fascinating discussion about the meaning of tradition. Among those present were Dr. Warner, a teacher who was more of a philosopher; Dr. Besch, a theologian who had become a teacher; Vice Admiral Gerlach; and myself. My notes taken during our discussion still occupy me today.

Man is nothing without the knowledge, experiences, abilities, and insights that our forebears have been passing on to us from generation to generation and that we must adapt to our present context. This uniquely human characteristic we call tradition. Tradition transcends the life span of an individual and touches on all aspects of our social order: ethics and morality; religion and justice; culture and symbols. Taken literally, tradition refers to that which has been passed down from our ancestors, but as we use the term today it also points to the future in the sense that traditional forms can be filled with new meaning. Wherever such a reevaluation process does not occur, tradition degenerates into a mechanical, self-justifying habit that mistrusts any form of innovation and becomes stuck in certain permanent relationships as far as religion, society, and history are concerned.

Tradition is tied to intellectual and spiritual currents. I raised the question to what extent it is linked to metaphysics as well. Surprisingly liberal for a theologian, Dr. Besch suggested that the rebellion against metaphysics reaches far back into the past. Already the Greeks, notably Xenophanes, tried to liberate logos from mythos. As a result of the Renaissance and the Enlightenment we can discover similar tendencies in the work of Hegel and Marx. To install a metaphysical superstructure above our body of traditions is not a necessary requirement, but it has been done often in the past. There are examples in our history where absolute atheists promoted traditional western values such as duty, justice, freedom, and humanitarianism. Dr. Besch had Frederick the Great in mind.

I tried next to place the basic values of our tradition into the center of our discussion. For my generation faith, loyalty, courage, honor, and fatherland stood out as such basic values and commitments. Whole generations have lived with a combination of these values, sometimes leading to mirages and self-delusions. Myths grew up around them. Then came Darwin. He supplied the fighting hordes with scientific justifications for their actions—struggle for existence, selection of the fittest. Hegel and Nietzsche furnished the philosophical background. German idealism made war the "father of all things." Dr. Warner reminded us that Heraclitus's dictum is often misinterpreted because it is not to be taken literally. Rather it is a metaphor for the struggle of rival forces that constitutes the nature of the human existence.

Gerlach added that the basic values as described by me did not only affect my generation but rather the history, legends, and myths of more than 2,000 years of western civilization. Their strongest representative is the hero. The encyclopedia defines a "hero" as "a warrior of extraordinary bravery whose deeds and fate separate him from the rest and make him a model for many." I had to think of Gottfried Benn's observation about "the lost illusions about the glory of the hero and the myth of power" and how already Cervantes in *Don Quixote* had satirized the role of the hero in a changed world. But I also was reminded of the men in totalitarian states who stood up for justice and freedom and who maintained their stand until the bitter end despite physical and mental torture. Were they not heroes, too? I remembered the U-boat commander who removed a portrait of Hitler from his boat's wardroom with the words, "We are not in the habit of worshipping idols." He criticized the regime, did not believe in the final victory, but did his duty nonetheless. Denounced by his executive officer, he was arrested, tried, and executed for "undermining the fighting spirit of the military." I saw the women in the bombed cities who fought for the lives of their children between their workplace and the air raid shelters and lost this struggle. Were they not heroes?

We all agreed that a modern soldier's chief task is to prevent war through his very existence, even if he must be trained to use nuclear weapons as a last resort. His relationship to the word "hero" evidently differs from that of a traditional "warrior of extraordinary bravery." Every generation faces anew the challenge of analyzing and assessing the chain of traditional values that for centuries have determined our course of action and will matter in shaping our future. This is an inescapable task as long as each generation carries with it a sense of responsibility, creative energies, and the desire to improve state and society. The obligation to reevaluate traditions is particularly urgent after great catastrophes. The post-war generation cannot limit itself to setting new accents but must design a humanitarian order that can withstand the menace of totalitarian powers and Promethean forces.

Once more I asked the question: Which basic values should we retain? We were unanimous in the view that the central virtues that had always informed a soldier's life are as valid as ever: intelligence, courage, justice, moderation. Gerlach listed intelligence first because it defined the goals and contents of the other virtues. Courage, for example, presupposes that I know whether my courage makes any sense. The past war produced many situations in which the traditional limits of decisions and of bravery were stretched, quite apart from the question whether the actions paid off or not.

The same holds true for justice. Did we always know what was just? Intelligence provides us with the ability to come to alternative conclusions. Every soldier and every member of the resistance movement made a decision for and against a particular course of action. Every individual must be able to determine for himself or herself what constitutes courage, justice, and moderation. Not everyone is equipped to do this; those who are carry an even greater burden of responsibility than the rest. To live up to these virtues is something I owe to myself. One can expect from me that I do so, to the extent they can be taught; but you can never command others to embrace such virtues under pain of punishment.

We also agreed that these basic virtues and their interpretations have changed little since the time of Aristotle and Thomas Aquinas. And yet it is our obligation to reassess them constantly against the backdrop of our changing world. Finally, I asked to what purposes the pursuit of these virtues should be tied. Is it enough to say that society should benefit from them, to further the *bonum commune?* Or would we still need some kind of metaphysical consideration? We came to the conclusion that in this case everyone would have to come up with his own answer.

Other nations enjoy the advantage of never finding their chain of traditions severed. On October 11, 1971, I was present when Japanese Emperor Hirohito visited Bonn. Japan, like Germany, is a conquered nation and is also burdened by many war crimes. For me, the Emperor personified Japan's traditions in the best sense of the word. In 1941 he listened to a presentation of Japan's top politicians and military leaders whose purpose was to gain the Tenno's consent for a declaration of war. His only reaction was to recite the words of an ancestor of his from a line of rulers that went back 2,000 years. It was a symbol of peace, words that stressed the importance of the sea as a link between countries and peoples. In 1946 Hirohito accepted before a U.S. military tribunal full responsibility for Japan's war guilt. There were no attempts at justifying what he had done. Here tradition, dignity, and form merged in an impressive combination. In contrast, Germany's top politicians of all stripes still try to make political hay out of confessions of guilt that lack any sense of historical dimensions.

My time as Chief of Staff at the Fleet Command was a time of contemplation and learning. In this period I gained many new insights from many different sources, even though my experience had to remain a limited one given the massive holdings of the archives and the work of historians who were busy assessing the available materials. But the insights opened a world for me in which I wanted to participate and articulate my viewpoints by way of correspondence, book reviews, and panel discussions. This attitude encouraged me to become a consultant for the Bavarian Broadcasting Service when it did a six-part television series about

"The German Soldier in World War II." The North German Broadcasting Service interviewed me for its documentary *"Gegen Engeland,"* which chronicled the Battle of the Atlantic. I also agreed to be interviewed by the American Broadcasting System for a U.S. television production.

Department Head for Planning; Deputy Inspector of the Navy; Navy Chief of Staff: November 1965 to December 1969

I took up my post at the Defense Ministry at a time of strong tensions between the planning staff for the entire armed forces and its counterpart in the Navy. The overall planning staff had issued a decree that characterized the Navy's role as follows: "Operations are to be limited to the western Baltic and those parts of the North Sea coastal waters that are under German jurisdiction. There is no need to build guided missile destroyers."

My first considerations and questions were these: Is our way of presenting our case adequate? Does the other side lack essential insight and information? Is it just another case of how to cut up the pie, given limited resources in the defense budget? Or are we poor salesmen when it comes to promoting our ideas? I reached the conclusion that we needed very careful planning by systematically using scientific methodology and operations research.

In dealing with our adversaries we had to develop a kind of fact-based rhetoric that was free of appeals to emotions and hypotheses and instead stressed reason, precision, insight into complex circumstances, the capacity for self-criticism, and a certain professional optimism. Here U.S., British, and French military policy supplied working models for us so that we did not have to start from scratch. My stint in Washington and my close connections to the Pentagon had familiarized me with the methods we needed to apply. In particular we had to deliver the proper ammunition to the political leaders of parliament so that they could present the concerns of the Navy with a high degree of credibility to the committees in charge of national security.

As far as Berlin was concerned, NATO had created so-called contingency plans that allowed for a range of political, economic, and military countermeasures in case of renewed challenges by the other side. These options included so-called maritime control measures. They ranged all the way from electronic interference with enemy communications, interrupting enemy ship traffic, and blocking of certain waterways, to the blockade of large areas of ocean space. Next to the obvious ability to defend one's own country the implementation of such measures in times of crises required warships equipped with the latest in naval and weapons technology.

For the next few months the emphasis of presentations and meetings rested on just that point, namely, to familiarize everyone engaged in top-level planning with the need for modernization and the reasons behind it. At the same time we demonstrated to outsiders how crucial modernization was for the Navy itself. We knew that the restructuring of the entire Bundeswehr would hit the Navy hard. We were prepared to accept budget cuts and modifications of many kinds, but to preserve the core of a modern navy, as our own planning staff had worked it out, remained a goal we would not give up. Everyone of us, down to the lowliest sailor, had to keep this goal in mind.

This goal kept us moving ahead, gave us inspiration when the going was tough, became the psychological basis for our personnel recruitment, and strengthened us in our daily work. It also gave us the backbone to stand up when we were challenged by others, for example the press, television, radio, members of parliament, friends in our own ranks, and representatives of the other branches of the military. In particular we tried to complete plans for the procurement of guided missile corvettes and present them to the defense committee. At the same time we lobbied individual members of parliament of all parties. By mid-1966 we reached the point that the acquisition from the United States of three guided missile destroyers of the *Adams* class became a distinct possibility, especially in the context of the "Offset Agreement" that tried to balance the cost of stationing U.S. troops in Germany by the purchase of American-made weaponry for the German military.

In a meeting with the defense minister on September 17 the revised building program for the Navy was approved: We would buy three guided missile destroyers from the United States and construct four guided missile corvettes in German shipyards. The minister in particular expressed his appreciation for the Navy's successful efforts to save money and personnel. It was predictable on the other hand that our agreement with the minister would face stiff opposition from the overall planning staff of the armed forces, as well as from the ministry's economic and budget departments.

On October 3, 1966, I became Deputy Inspector of the Navy, relieving Rear Admiral Hetz who took over as Fleet Commander. Among my first actions in my new post I sought the cooperation of my colleagues representing the Army and Luftwaffe, Major Generals Hubert Sonneck and Dr. Adolf Hempel, respectively. We arranged for a weekly conference to talk about all items before they would be passed on to the overall planning staff of the armed forces.

After the four guided missile corvettes had been approved by the defense minister and at last also by the top leadership of the armed forces, our attention shifted to aircraft with ECM (electronic countermeasures) capabilities and so-called Elint trawlers (electronic intelligence). Already during normal times, but especially in times of international tension, it was paramount to gather a broad spectrum of insights into a potential enemy's intentions. Such insights allowed our side to select from a correspondingly broader choice of instruments to control the situation. Conventional methods of gathering such information, for example spies, could do little for us under the circumstances. About 90 percent of our information came from electronic reconnaissance. Therefore it was important to strengthen our capabilities in this area. The Navy in particular could make a considerable contribution to this intelligence-gathering effort by operating in the open waters of the Baltic Sea even in times of peace and by employing electronic listening equipment at relatively short distances against East Germany, Poland, and the Soviet Union. This contribution made the Federal Navy an interesting and desirable partner in NATO's intelligence exchange.

During my term in office we had many foreign visitors, among them the Royal Navy's Admiral Clutterbuck, then Deputy Commander of SACLANT, and Admiral Bush from the Channel Command. A very important visit was that of the SACLANT Commander himself, U.S. Admiral Moorer. The talks we held with him about our responsibilities and capabilities were informative for both sides. Afterwards we gave a dinner reception for him at the Hotel Dreesen, an evening planned and arranged by the Inspector's aide-de-camp.

The whole affair came off as follows: The Inspector of the Navy, Vice Admiral Zenker, and I welcomed Admiral Moorer and his staff with a glass of champagne in the lobby of the hotel. This would have been fine had the lobby not also been used by the other guests of the hotel, who naturally cared little for us and our dealings. Then we retired to the second floor where two connecting rooms had been prepared for us. The long table and the chairs stood so close to the walls that the waiters had trouble serving the meal. First we had a soup. Then fried chicken as the main course, which in the United States seems to be reserved for the poor, and finally ice cream for dessert. Afterwards we returned to the same busy lobby where, once again in the company of the other hotel guests, we had a cup of coffee and a glass of brandy. Being familiar with the generous American standards of hospitality, I found this reception most embarrassing. I had to think of Admiral Johannesson's prediction that the Bundeswehr would remain an unloved stepchild of this state, and also of the red carpet treatment that foreign diplomats and politicians customarily received on their visits to Bonn.

The next day we were invited to the residence of the U.S. ambassador in Bonn, George McGhee. Here the table was laid with exquisite china; the various crystal glasses beautifully reflected the light of the burning candles; there were flower arrangements in the colors of the German flag; and the seating arrangements were such that the waiters had plenty of room to serve us.

After the dinner, as is usual, the gentlemen and the ladies split to do their own things. We men retired to the library for political talks. It was the time of the Great Coalition and the Vietnam War. U.S. President Johnson had expected more public support from his allies, especially from the Germans. This support had been withheld and the atmosphere between Washington and Bonn was rather chilled. When Washington and Moscow negotiated the nonproliferation treaty for nuclear weapons without consulting their respective allies, German Chancellor Kiesinger had spoken of a complicity among the superpowers—an unfortunate and inaccurate remark that had further cooled relations. McGhee argued that Kiesinger's comment was inaccurate because Johnson needed to have some successes in foreign affairs in order to improve his popularity at home, where he had come under fire because of Vietnam and race riots. The ambassador was very interested that evening in giving us a glimpse of America's problems, and he tried to create the impression that he was doing everything possible to overcome the misunderstandings on both sides and to improve relations between Washington and Bonn.

In the meantime the ladies had retired to the dressing room of the ambassador's wife. In the middle of the room stood a huge bird cage, painted white, very elegant in its rococo design. This cage was home to a big black bird from India with a huge beak. As soon as the ladies entered the room the bird burst out into the most ordinary of laughters and uttered in a croaking voice: "I like pretty girls, I like pretty girls!" This was followed by another burst of laughter. How long must it have taken the ambassador to train this bird until everything came out perfectly?! It certainly was highly entertaining.

By 1968 I was slated to become the next Deputy Chief of Staff for Planning and Operations at the Headquarters of NATO's AFNORTH (Allied Forces, Northern Europe) Command in Kolsas, Norway. My appointment had been agreed to and welcomed by SACEUR, the Supreme Allied Commander, Europe. On March 8, 1968, State Secretary Paul von Hase of our Foreign Office asked me to see him. He showed me a telegram he had just received from our ambassador in Oslo. The message stated that in the interest of good relations between Norway and Germany, and considering the impending big parliamentary debate over Norway's continued membership in NATO, it would be vital that my anticipated appointment caused no problems whatsoever for the Norwegians. Even if my appointment were not publicly announced, there could be no doubt that those in Norway opposed to NATO and to Germany would want to know everything about me and my career. He therefore asked that he be supplied with as exhaustive information about me as possible, information that would enable the Norwegians to judge whether and how far opponents of NATO would be able to find a personal pretense to torpedo my appointment. The director of the political section of the Norwegian Foreign Office had expressed his concern that my candidacy would be especially in jeopardy if I as a U-boat commander had sunk Norwegian warships or merchantmen during the war. The Norwegian official requested for his personal use a summary of my activities during the war, including the circumstances leading to my imprisonment in Norway, any actions that might have raised Norwegian animosities toward me, in particular the sinking of Norwegian ships, participation in the occupation of Norway, and possible incriminating publications.

The accompanying memorandum of the German ambassador in Norway, Richard Balken, stated that he considered the concerns the Norwegian official had put forth in the name of his government basically justified given the present political situation. He thought, however, that in certain details the Norwegians were carrying matters too far. The ambassador went on to describe the gathering domestic campaign in Norway against that country's continued membership in NATO. He seemed convinced that the opponents of NATO, lacking arguments of a political or military nature, would revive their campaign by appealing to latent anti-German sentiments in the country. It would be disadvantageous, therefore, for the Norwegian government as well as for the German embassy, if after my appointment matters came to light that could be exploited by the NATO opposition in Norway.

Our personnel department thereupon put together a document detailing "Topp's four points of contact with Norway." They were: (1) executive officer aboard *U 46* during the occupation of Narvik in the context of "Operation Weserübung;" (2) a stopover in Bergen to refuel *U 57*; (3) being taken prisoner in Norway at the end of the war; and (4) the sinking of four Norwegian merchant vessels.

The State Secretary expressed to me his view that, after reading my curriculum vitae and my file, the whole affair was personally embarrassing to him and that his evaluation of me had only gained as a result of getting to know more about me. After weighing all factors in this matter, however, he suggested that a quiet settlement of the problem would be in everyone's best interest. Raised in the tradition that *raison d'état* should outweigh any personal ambitions, I concurred with the State Secretary. This led first of all to a letter written by the Inspector General to the Commander-in-Chief of Allied Forces in Europe, General Lymen L. Lemnitzer:

Dear General Lemnitzer:
You were kind enough to agree to my suggestion of 12/4/67 to appoint Rear Admiral Erich Topp as Deputy Chief of Staff for Planning and Operations at the Headquarters of AFNORTH to replace Rear Admiral Erdmann.

> Today I must inform you that new considerations in connection with the modernization of the German Navy render it impossible for us to assign Rear Admiral Topp to that post. We find ourselves in this phase of modernization unable to forego Topp's collaboration and special experience. I trust you will understand why we would like to withdraw Topp's nomination. I shall present to you before long the name of another admiral to replace Rear Admiral Erdmann.

Second, a proper formula had to be found to avoid the impression that the minister lacked backbone. Third, efforts had to be made to ensure my personal integrity against possible attacks by the Norwegian communist press, which might be tempted to produce banner headlines reading, "Murderer of our sailors in high NATO position." Even if the sinking of four Norwegian vessels at night, out of British-escorted convoys and without knowledge of their nationality, was perfectly justified under international law, the press might nevertheless have exploited the incidents against me. By withdrawing my nomination we avoided a situation that could have played into the hands of the communists in Norway in connection with their campaign against their country's continued membership in NATO.

On October 10, 1968, when Admiral Fritz Guggenberger took over the command originally scheduled for me, General Lemnitzer is said to have remarked to the Norwegians: "I hereby send you an admiral who has sunk only British ships."

At about the same time we had the great debate about the naming of the three new guided missile destroyers. Three names had been suggested, each one representing a branch of the armed forces: *Admiral Lütjens* for the Navy; *Colonel Mölders* for the Luftwaffe; and *Colonel General von Fritsch* for the Army.

The press had already created some excitement about Lütjens, who had sent a well-known loyalty message to Hitler just before he went down with the *Bismarck*. In the case of the devout Catholic Mölders, his twelve kills as a pilot during the Spanish Civil War were conveniently played down. But the name Fritsch ended up in a public crossfire of different opinions. One side saw him as an Army leader independent of any entanglements with National Socialism, an outstanding personality with an exemplary character who had steadfastly fought against the mean defamations his adversary Himmler had brought against him, and who had heroically sought and found death at the head of his regiment during the Polish campaign outside Warsaw. On the other side there were irrefutably insulting remarks Fritsch had made privately about Reich President Ebert and the Social Democrats, as well as certain passages in a letter in which he expressed political opinions that had already been brought up in connection with the International Military Tribunal at Nuremberg after the war. Both sides never doubted Fritsch's personal integrity or leadership qualities. Because of Fritsch's remarks and the likely political protests ahead, the Navy suggested to the minister to name the destroyer *Rommel* instead. Rommel was at home and abroad a highly respected officer on account of his military successes and chivalric attitudes, a man who in the last phase of the war had joined the resistance movement and was known to have been forced by Hitler to commit suicide because of these connections.

Such controversies, no matter how insignificant they may appear to us today, were prone in those days to ignite painful discussions about proper respect for tradition in the armed forces and were symptoms of the inner difficulties the Bundeswehr had to overcome as long as its leadership had once served in the Wehrmacht. Similar problems remained in the Bundeswehr's outward representation, in defining its proper place in the state, and in improving its public image. Twelve years after its creation these matters were far from solved. I often had to think of Johannesson's dictum of the armed forces as a "necessary evil." No wonder the soldiers' self-image suffered under these circumstances. But the military leadership, too, contributed at times to the difficulties by not taking unambiguous stands in important matters and by not presenting outsiders with a clear profile.

One example to illustrate these difficulties was a conference for some 200 top-level military commanders that was held in Kassel in May 1968. This meeting made headlines when a group of demonstrators, some 100 high school and university students from Frankfurt, blocked off the entrances to the city hall where the conference took place and began shouting noisy anti-military slogans. To pass through the demonstrators was only possible under insulting and embarrassing circumstances. In order to be able to deliver their presentations to the assembled admirals and generals, the main speakers, State Secretary Rolf Lahr of the Foreign Office and Minister for Science and Development Gerhard Stoltenberg, had to be flown by helicopter to an inner courtyard of the compound. Despite this incident the Inspector General of the armed forces remarked that he did not notice a decline of authority. Along with a number of other officers, I had expected that the state or the city would use police to clear the entrances to the building or, if that was not done, that the conference be cancelled in protest. But others feared a police action would make headlines in the press, something our group thought could only improve the reputation of the armed forces. After all, is it not the obligation of the authorities under Article 1 of our Constitution to respect and protect the dignity of man? The Christian Democratic member of parliament, Hans Dichgans, wrote thereupon in a letter to Minister of Defense Gerhard Schröder: "I feel very much reminded of the Caudine Yoke [symbol of a humiliting defeat the Romans suffered at the hands of the

Samnites in 321 B.C.] If I consider the continuing decline in the exercise of authority in our state, I am gripped by deepest apprehensions."

Toward the end of my time as Deputy Inspector of the Navy I became indirectly involved in what would become known as the Grashey Affair. In March 1969 Major General Helmuth Grashey, then Deputy Inspector of the Army, gave a speech to a number of general staff officers at the Leadership Academy. His remarks were highly critical of the concept of "Inner Leadership" and of the parliament's special deputy for military matters. Grashey not only addressed specific instances of mishandled situations but criticized the very way the leadership system was designed.

Hearing of Grashey's speech, the Inspector General convened a meeting at which the Inspector of the Army, Lieutenant General Albert Schnez, the Inspector of the Luftwaffe, Lieutenant General Johannes Steinhoff, and I representing the Navy were present. General de Maizière began our talks with a brief summary of what had happened and tried to play down the incident. He called it a derailment and implied that the defense minister planned to issue a generous statement. Schnez basically agreed with Maizière. He knew Grashey as an intelligent officer who had spoken freely and openly without having given himself enough time to prepare his remarks properly.

For Steinhoff and myself, Grashey's speech went beyond the matter of a few ill-chosen words. We argued that a public statement by the military leadership should not give the impression of creating a process of solidarity. The speech was already being discussed in the public and was a cause for controversy. Therefore it was mandatory to take a clear stand to clarify the matter in the eyes of the public and to avoid mistrust among the citizens toward the military leaders, especially among the political opposition, which had agreed to the idea of the Bundeswehr only with reservations and had been critical of it in the past.

I emphasized that the principles of Inner Leadership were in line with the constitutionally mandated mission of the armed forces. This did not mean that they should not be adjusted if a changing Zeitgeist made modifications desirable. The leadership concept should not be allowed to become a matter of individual interpretation. The Bundeswehr as part of the executive branch is subject to parliamentary supervision. Such control also means that the Bundestag watches over the principles of Inner Leadership, which were designed to integrate the armed forces into our modern industrial society. If this process is successful, it contributes to the credibility of our strategy of deterrence. Steinhoff, too, demanded a clear statement. It was important for him to abandon the lie that grew from the discrepancy between stated goals and reality. For him, Grashey merely represented the tip of the iceberg.

I have discussed the conference in Kassel and the Grashey Affair in

some detail here to show that the top military leaders in their relationship to the public exercised a degree of caution and distance that we considered misplaced. Perhaps it had to do with the fact that the political
and military leadership shared the city of Bonn and were thus in close
and sometimes awkward contact. We believed we could do more for the
military if we showed a genuine profile, both in situations in which we
were attacked by the public and in response to our own mistakes.

Since I often had to fill in for the Inspector of the Navy, Vice Admiral
Gerd Jeschonnek, I developed a close relationship with General de
Maizière on several occasions. To deduce from the incidents discussed
here that he suffered from a lack of willpower to exercise authority would
be to gain a wrong picture of the man. De Maizière was undoubtedly the
right man at the right time in the right office to deal with the residual
mistrust many held out toward those who headed the armed forces. He
was a masterful pilot in difficult waters, using his high intelligence and
great experience to circumnavigate the obstacles in his path and always
stressing the primacy of civilian political control. It would be unfair to
measure his charisma among the soldiers by the few visits he made to
the small and, to him, unfamiliar Navy. His style and appearance were
exemplary. Neither his line of argumentation nor his choice of words
ever betrayed insecurity, even though he had to be careful in his words
and actions at a time when the self-image of the military and its relation
to the state underwent a remarkable transformation.

His greatest disappointment, it seems to me, was that he could not
push through the reorganization of the top echelons of the armed forces.
He wanted to strengthen the office of the Inspector General by exercising
immediate command control over all branches of the military. All three
branches—Army, Luftwaffe, and Navy—preferred the American solution of the Joint Chiefs of Staff. Here the Inspector General was more or
less a colleague and partner of the branch inspectors, little more than
first among equals. For us it was important that the inspectors exercised
direct military control over their branch of the armed forces. We in the
Navy were also concerned that we had a direct and decisive role to play
in the design, development, and construction of the vessels with which
we would have to fight without downplaying the legitimate concerns of
the civilian offices involved. While we agreed with the leadership staff of
the armed forces (Fü S) about reforms regarding weapons design, development, and procurement, we disagreed with de Maizière's plans for a
revamping of the entire military command structure. In our meetings we
deputy inspectors always coordinated our views to present a common
line of argument. I also had close contacts with the Inspector of the
Luftwaffe. We usually agreed on all crucial issues. When I left the Navy
in 1969 he said to me, "It looks as if your refusal to help reform Fü S has
cost you your career."

In 1967 an official trip to England allowed me to gain a close-up view of the British military leadership. Their self-image and inner strength seemed exemplary to me. The impressions I gathered confirmed that in the last war we faced a high quality opponent. Now we sat together in the same NATO boat, albeit at a friendly distance. The occasion for my trip was an invitation to participate in the Atlantic/Channel Symposium 1967 as well as an invitation to meet the Supreme Allied Commander, Atlantic, and the Allied Commander in Chief, Channel, at Lancaster House, St. James, London, on October 4. We had lunch in the Painted Hall, an old, venerable building, in the presence of Prince Philip, the Duke of Edinburgh.

In every respect my stay in England was an unforgettable, interesting series of events. In Greenwich I experienced the tradition of a world and sea power. Even in its afterglow the once mighty empire has its fascination. It has formed the English, given them both self-assurance and their sense of understatement. I met a number of the most outstanding representatives of this people and I returned home enriched through many valuable human contacts. Also impressive for me were the many cultural and historical attractions, such as the National Museum, Windsor, Eton, Winchester, Romsey Abbey, and all that with Captain E. G. Kray, our naval attaché in London, as our expert guide.

On August 6, 1969, Defense Minister Schröder, then vacationing on the island of Sylt, made the decision that as of October 1 Admiral Kühnle would take over my responsibilities as Deputy Inspector of the Navy and I would be without official assignment for the rest of the year. I decided to stay my course, fulfill my duties as usual, and suppress my own emotions. Outwardly I showed myself relaxed and accepted this exit in style, including the honor of receiving Germany's Great Order of Merit.

At the official retirement ceremony I made these points clear to the State Secretary:

1. I accept the decision not to send me to Norway because it is the right thing to do from a foreign policy point of view.
2. I consider myself the victim of political animosities abroad. Any other military establishment in the world would have compensated such a victim within its means in his own country. SACEUR will note with interest that the officer who was supposedly indispensable for the Navy is now being retired. The State Secretary replied: "You have done great things for the Navy as I already told you in connection with the Oslo affair. You have done much for the armed forces in general, but the constellation was not in your favor. Is it painful for you to take your leave?" I answered: "Real life always requires changes and adjustments, no matter how painful they may be." The State Secretary: "The Navy will have a tough time under Defense Minister Schmidt." My response: "The

Navy is used to fight." The State Secretary: "That reminds me of Mac-Arthur who, his troops surrounded by the Japanese in the Philippines, was ordered to return to Washington. As he left he set the signal, 'I shall return.' And return he did." Why did he tell me that? Did he somehow think I would make a comeback?

If I let my four years at the ministry pass in review, I must admit there were things I did not handle very well. On the other hand, I was clear in my mind that one can only play with the hand one has been dealt. I would also say that my time in Bonn brought me the satisfaction of realizing that our modernization program was now under way or at the very least well thought out.

Everyone approaches his assignment with certain experiences, with energy and enthusiasm. Then comes the realization that possibilities and limitations face each other in a rather stable relationship. Allow me to mention just two of these limitations: the small size of the Navy as one of three branches of the armed forces, and the organization of the ministry. I saw it as one of my obligations to maintain and defend the independence of the Navy as one of three equal branches of the military. This conviction had brought me into conflict with the leadership staff of the armed forces and led in the final analysis to my early retirement.

Things seemed ready to take another unforeseen twist when on November 5, 1969, I received a summons from the new Defense Minister Helmut Schmidt. He asked me if I would like to join a new and yet-to-be-formed planning team. I then had a long talk with Dr. Sommer of the newspaper *Die Zeit*, who was to head the planning team and whose deputy I was slated to become. Based on the projections we had already done inside the ministry, I could present him with a draft proposal for possible modifications. Sommer and I agreed that our team should come up with alternative plans for the minister so that he would not have to rely exclusively on Fü S. This would enable him to be truly in charge of all planning activities. We also wanted to bring into the process groups of outside experts such as the ZOR (Center for Operations and Research), the operations and research groups of three major private institutes, and the people who analyzed the research and exercises of the armed forces.

I will never know whether my old adversaries in the ministry managed to persuade Schmidt to keep me off the planning team, or if the minister simply could not create an appropriate position for me considering my experience and rank. What weighed on me more heavily, and what Schmidt also stressed, was the possibility that as a member of the planning team I might have to argue in favor of positions that stood in contrast to the concepts I had lobbied for in parliament and before committees over the past three years. Schmidt indicated at the time that he could not guarantee a future for the MRCA (Multi-Role Combat Aircraft) or the frigate project.

The final "no" by the minister came packaged in a friendly retirement ceremony at which we were joined by State Secretary Karl-Wilhelm Berkhan and Lieutenant General Konrad Stangl, the head of the personnel department. This harmonious get-together over a glass of champagne gave me one more opportunity to speak up for the future concept of the Navy and the need for modernization. I gained the impression I had done a last duty for my service branch. On December 31, 1969, I left the West German Navy after eleven years. I was fifty-five years old.

I am grateful to the Navy for many things. Already as a young officer I had the privilege of carrying responsibility and of leading a handful of men during the war to the limits of acceptable risks and sometimes even beyond. We became comrades, and I have stayed in touch with some of them ever since. After my hectic yet fascinating years as a freelance architect I rejoined the Navy in the expectation of becoming a partner in a team of officers where we could work together for the common good beyond all intrigues and personal rivalries. Even if I suffered through many illusions, I would be much poorer in my human experiences without those years in the West German Navy.

During this time I discovered an entirely new political dimension. My connections to the mightiest navy in the world, my contacts with American officers in the Pentagon and at SACLANT in Norfolk, made it clear to me that Germany had undertaken a decisive step between 1949 and 1955. It had become a partner of the great sea powers. Still suffering under the consequences of its greatest defeat, torn in its substance, geographically divided and politically impotent, Germany succeeded in achieving something that Emperor William II had sought in vain, namely, to gain admittance to the "club of world powers" (Michael Salewski) by means of her strong navy. The Kaiser never tired in pointing out to the German people the importance of the sea and the efficacy of sea power. But he failed just as much as Hitler after him to make the maritime factor a strong one in Germany's political pursuits. Hitler's goal of coming to an arrangement with England over matters of naval strength (the Anglo-German Naval Agreement of June 1935) in order to split world hegemony between the Anglo-Saxon sea powers and German domination over the European continent was based on a misconception from the beginning.

Germany's alliance with the naval powers in NATO has in a political sense answered both the question of our economic dependence on access to the sea and the problem of proper defense at sea. Germany, short on raw materials but highly industrialized, depends on the sea more than ever before in her long history. Half of all imports, and virtually all oil and ores, reach Germany by sea. It is a challenge for today and tomorrow to enlighten the German citizens about this dependency. Our ties to the West, to the naval powers, must remain the core of German policy.

Epilogue

We all have a tendency, as we look back, to condense the stations of our life and ascribe certain guiding themes to them.

I can still recite a verse I once read in the magazine *Pflug und Speer* of the youth movement I belonged to, a verse that summarized my feelings very well at the time: *"Den Krämern lasst ihr Gold, den Ruhm den Schläch-tern, bekennt Euch zu den Verächtern, die schwertlos ringen um den Hohen Preis."* (Leave the gold to the merchants, and glory to the warriors; be-come one of the scorners who fight, swordless, for the highest prize.) It was the time of a first rebellion against a world marked by utilitarianism, opportunism, the quest for guaranteed jobs, the pursuit of offices and public acclaim.

Then came the time when one became aware of one's own power and was prepared to lend this power to a cause that promised to change soci-ety and the political scene. A word by the aviator Ernst Udet may express what I mean: "Fate has given each of us the choice to become either a merchant or a soldier, to enjoy life or to forego happiness in favor of the idea that the little vessel of our existence carries out into the eternal stream of history."

After the crash of Icarus we learned to live within the limits of our own resources and to reject empty slogans. What counts is the individual hu-man being and the more or less restricted world that man can and should help shape based on his inclinations, education, and insights for the *bonum commune*, the common good. This is how I understand the term and how I have consciously lived the decades of my life, as a soldier in two navies but also as an architect.

To equate the common good with liberty, equality, and fraternity in order to bring about a society of absolutely free and equal human beings seems simplistic to me. Since the days of the French Revolution, intellectuals no less than the masses have been pushing the demand for greater equality and in the process have clipped our liberties. Grand designs suffocate in the banalities of everyday life, in the prevalent concern to become free of concerns. To be comfortable, to be taken care of from cradle to grave, are hardly incentives to awaken the creative powers that slumber in all of us. To create, deliberately and artificially, unlimited demand for material goods, seems to me a perversion of the common good. The "economic miracle," pride in our technological and scientific achievements, quantitative thinking, and the satisfaction of having amassed prosperity and international acclaim have weakened our appreciation for quality, for what furthers culture and the common good. The majority of our population would like to preserve this state of affairs and perpetuate this pact with the devil: "Stay for a while, you are so nice."

Last, has our state, supposedly based on democracy and justice, been set up to serve the *bonum commune?* Already, de Tocqueville in a grand vision had clamored against the uncontrollable power of political parties, big business, the parliaments, and the bureaucracy. He was fortunate not to be familiar with today's media. I see the dangers of petrified organizational forms of a state based on mere administrative functions. Yes, there are more protests and citizens' initiatives than are good for us. But where are people concerned about the survival of the basic values of our society?

It is essential to keep life in a state of suspense so that free minds can develop, minds that see their main obligation in dedicating themselves to the common good that every state should primarily pursue. We must get away from the empty phrases and ideologies of the day. We must create oases in the desert of hollow rhetoric, watch out critically for mirages that would offer perpetual safety and satisfaction. We need individuals responsible enough to see and mark the danger zones all around us, men who fathom the channel for our ship of life and become navigators to guide the next generation.

One event in my life stands out to me as the ultimate example for this vision of men as pilots and navigators. In 1938, still during the Spanish Civil War, my boat *U 46* undertook a voyage to the ports of Melilla, Ceuta, and Lisbon. In Lisbon I chartered a bus to take those of my men who were not on duty sightseeing in the countryside. It was a hot day. After touring many sites of cultural and artistic interest we decided to cool off by going swimming in a remote bay along the Atlantic coast. We had barely entered the water when we were caught in a current that, no matter what we tried, carried us out to sea. Some of the men became desperate and panicky; others seemed paralyzed in their fear. It was a most unpleasant situation because there was nobody around who might have come to our rescue. I tried to throw off my own fears, gain some distance from the immediate impressions, and think through the situation rationally. In doing so I noticed that light objects floating on the water's surface were not being pulled out to sea but instead were moving toward the shore. This gave me the idea that if we kept our bodies as close to the surface as possible we might be able to swim back, just as the objects I had seen floating on the waves. I communicated my observation to some of the petty officers. Together we persuaded the rest of the men to follow our example of swimming back to the beach by staying close to the surface. Exhausted but safe, we all made it back.

I believe this true story can serve as a model for what I would like to say about becoming engaged and distancing oneself from the concerns of the contemporary world. Our times are marked by apocalyptic visions triggered by the exploitation and destruction of nature, the freeing of Promethean forces. Today we find ourselves in a situation in which the dangers that lurk in the social realm and the insecurity brought on by the information age have become so great that more often than not we react emotionally and irrationally, slaves of wishful thinking and existential fears. Many people are no longer capable of grasping simple factual situations and analyzing them in a critically detached manner free of emotional ballast.

We should learn to distance ourselves from our emotions just like those swimmers. That is how they managed to control the danger that threatened to destroy them. I do realize that appeals to reason are often dismissed as a purely intellectual exercise. They sound great in theory but make little sense when applied to the real world. Man, having conquered some of nature's most awesome threats by superior technology, is today his own worst enemy. As the poet Schiller once put it, "The worst of all horrors is man in his folly." It seems necessary to me to get away from certain creeds dictated by special interests and emotional attachments and to create for the orientation of human society realistic models to counter such folly.

There are many warning signs: riots reminiscent of civil war and bloody "demonstrations" in many German cities and abroad; a return to religious fanaticism in Iran, in Ireland, and in Lebanon; and the racial tensions in the Soviet Union. A clear analysis of existing dangers is vital to prevent future catastrophes. As Colonel General Ludwig Beck once said:

> Nothing is more dangerous than giving in to spontaneous ideas, no matter how clever and genial they may seem, or to engage in wishful thinking, no matter how desirable the envisioned result. We need officers who think

matters through to their logical conclusion, systematically and with solid
mental self-discipline. Their character and their nerves must be strong
enough to carry out what reason tells them to do.

My diaries are in front of me; recollections are rushing through my
mind. What would my life be without these memories? I can still smell
the fragrance of the flowering meadows on the edge of the village where
we used to live. I feel the sand beneath my bare feet. I see myself swimming in the lake toward the rising sun not far from where we pitched our
tents. I stand on the bridge of my boat next to my men. They wear oilskin
clothing and seem permanently attached to their binoculars. I can see
the depth gauge in our submerged boat as we descend to 800 feet. In the
dim glimmer of the emergency lights I see the pale faces of my men as
they look as if mesmerized at the indicator whose movement decides
over life and death. I see the faces of my fellow students at the university,
open to art and culture, and the American officers in front of their moni-
tors at the Strategic Air Command, watching out for the freedom of the
West. Before my eyes appear beggars, thieves, spies, in an onslaught of
events, some of which made me a victim and a loser.

It is a divine gift to remember things that seem insignificant and yet
stick with you thanks to their colorfulness, a weighty expression, a magnificent deed, or because they led to something great and truly meaningful. I remember fear and courage, perfidy and truth, as I pen down these
lines. I never felt the sting of missed opportunities in me. And I have not
hesitated to question my own actions and judgments. Whatever I have
done I did on my own power and kept on going. When my chosen
course led me astray I paid for it.

And one more thing: I was determined to resist any pressure from anyone to write this book. And then I did it anyway. One always finds a reason, even if it is the desire to tell one's grandchildren about a period in
our history that only we can know because we shaped it and suffered
through it. This period will loom like a shadow above us until the end of
our days. But it should and must no longer burden our children and
grandchildren.

There remained the great question of how to speak up clearly for the
truth. How to demonstrate that this life had not only been shaped by
smart and stupid ideas, by acts of commission and omission, by good
and bad consciences, but by the entirety of a human existence. I also had
to guard against the temptation of using big words. Judging from my recollections, I foresee a development that will require tough choices from
us, decisions we cannot run away from through some form of inner or
outward escape.

A different order will emerge, for the old one is obsolete. But as we reconstruct our world we will have to build on the old foundations with men who know their limitations and approach life with inner discipline—without illusions but not as nihilists, courageous but never militant. In Gottfried Benn's words,

> be silent and do your duty;
> defend this only world of ours,
> even if you know it is doomed.

Index of Names, Places, and Ships

About the Author

ERICH TOPP joined the German Navy in 1934 and won distinction as a U-boat commander in World War II. On 17 war patrols he and his men sank 34 enemy vessels and were highly decorated for their accomplishments. Following a brief stint as an ordinary seaman after the war, Topp studied architecture, graduating in 1949 as a certified engineer. For two years he worked as a scientific assistant at the Technical University in Hanover and subsequently embarked on a career as a freelance architect. In 1958, he rejoined the West German Navy, serving three years as the German naval representative to NATO's Military Committee in Washington, D.C. After additional staff commands and promotions, he ended his active service in 1969 as Deputy Commander-in-Chief of the West German Navy with the rank of Rear Admiral. From 1970 to 1984 he worked as an industrial consultant.

ISBN 0-275-93898-0

90000>

9 780275 938987

HARDCOVER BAR CODE

EAN